Dewey Decimal Classification

200

RELIGION

CLASS

D1520587

Dewey Decimal Classification

200

RELIGION

CLASS

Devised by Melvil Dewey

Edited by

Joan S. Mitchell, Editor in Chief
Julianne Beall, Assistant Editor
Giles Martin, Assistant Editor
Winton E. Matthews, Jr., Assistant Editor
Gregory R. New, Assistant Editor
Michael B. Cantlon, Decimal Classification Specialist

OCLC
OCLC Online Computer Library Center, Inc.
Dublin, Ohio
2004

Library of Congress Cataloging-in-Publication Data

Dewey, Melvil, 1851-1931.
    [Dewey decimal classification and relative index. 200 religion class]
    Dewey decimal classification. 200 religion class / devised by Melvil Dewey; edited by Joan S. Mitchell, editor in chief ; Julianne Beall, assistant editor . . . [et al.] ; Michael B. Cantlon, decimal classification specialist.
       p.   cm.
    Includes index.
    ISBN 0-910608-74-1 (alk. paper)
    1. Classification, Dewey decimal. 2. Classification—Books—Religion. I. Title: 200 religion class. II. Mitchell, Joan S. III. Beall, Julianne, 1946- IV. Cantlon, Michael B. V. Title.
Z696.D72R455 2004   2004042230
025.4'62—dc22   CIP

OCLC Online Computer Library Center, Inc.
6565 Frantz Road
Dublin, OH 43017-3395 USA
www.oclc.org/dewey

The paper used in this publication meets the requirements of ANSI/NISO Z39.48-1992 (Permanence of Paper).

ISBN: 0-910608-74-1

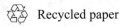

Recycled paper

Contents

Preface   vii

How to Use This Book   ix

Schedule: 200 Religion   1

Manual Notes for 200 Religion   159

Apendixes   177

    Appendix A: Optional Numbers for Books of Bible as Arranged

       in Tanakh (Jewish Bible, Hebrew Bible) (Option A)   179

    Appendix B: 170 Ethics   185

Relative Index   195

Preface

200 Religion Class is an updated reprint from *Dewey Decimal Classification and Relative Index*, Edition 22. It includes the 200 Religion schedule, the Manual notes for 200 Religion, an extended index to 200 Religion, and the 170 Ethics schedule. *200 Religion Class* is intended to be used by libraries with in-depth religious collections and small general collections. The latter may be classified using *Abridged Dewey Decimal Classification and Relative Index*, Edition 14.

In Edition 22, we have completed the two-edition plan that was initiated in Edition 21 to reduce Christian bias in the 200 Religion schedule. In Edition 21, we moved comprehensive works on Christianity from 200 to 230, and relocated the standard subdivisions for Christianity from 201–209 to specific numbers in 230–270. We integrated the standard subdivisions of comparative religion with those for religion in general in 200.1–.9. We also revised and expanded the schedules for two major religions, 296 Judaism and 297 Islam.

Edition 22 contains the rest of the relocations and expansions outlined in the two-edition plan. In the new edition, we have moved specific aspects of religion from 291 to the 201–209 span vacated in Edition 21. These numbers are now used for general topics in religion, and as the source for notation to address specific aspects of religions in 292–299. We have expanded the sources of the Bahai Faith at 297.938. We have also revised and expanded the developments in 299.6 for religions originating among Black Africans and people of Black African descent, and in 299.7–.8 for religions of American native origin. In 299.6–.8, we have reversed the preference order to show ethnic group first, topic second, and have provided a fuller array of topical aspects to be added to the ethnic group numbers.

The members of the Decimal Classification Editorial Policy Committee (EPC) have provided invaluable advice on the development of the 200 Religion schedule. In addition, Stephen Dingler (Hong Kong Baptist University) and Terrance Mann (British Library) tested 200 Religion.

Many colleagues associated with the Dewey Decimal Classification at OCLC and the Library of Congress have made contributions to the publication of *200 Religion Class*. In particular, the assistant editors of the Dewey Decimal Classification, Julianne Beall (Library of Congress), Giles Martin (OCLC), Winton E. Matthews, Jr. (Library of Congress), and Gregory R. New (Library of Congress), developed and edited the 200 Religion schedule in close consultation with Michael Cantlon, Decimal Classification specialist in the Decimal Classification Division at the Library of Congress. Eliza B. Sproat, senior Dewey electronic products manager, participated in the review process. We are also grateful to Judy Kramer Greene for copyediting, and to Libbie Crawford for overseeing production of the book.

Joan S. Mitchell
Editor in Chief
Dewey Decimal Classification
OCLC Online Computer Library Center, Inc.

How to Use This Book

Introduction

200 Religion Class is a convenient source of detailed classification numbers for religion. It includes the following information from Edition 22: the schedule for 200 Religion, the Manual notes that discuss numbers in 200 Religion, and an extended index to religious aspects of topics. Also included are two appendixes: (A) Optional Arrangement for Books of Tanakh, and (B) 170 Ethics.[1]

Since the schedules and Manual notes are reprinted from Edition 22, they include references to tables and schedules in other areas of the Dewey Decimal Classification (DDC) system. For aspects of topics that fall outside of religion, *200 Religion Class* must be used in conjunction with Abridged Edition 14 or Edition 22. For example, the topic "marriage and family" has aspects that fall under several disciplines, including religion. Only the religious aspects of marriage and family appear in *200 Religion Class*; Abridged Edition 14 or Edition 22 must be consulted for aspects of marriage and family in other disciplines, e.g., sociology of marriage and family 306.8.

Structure and Notation of the DDC

In the DDC, basic classes are organized by disciplines or fields of study. At the broadest level, the DDC is divided into ten main classes, which together cover the entire world of knowledge (200 Religion is one of the ten main classes). Each main class is further divided into ten divisions and each division into ten sections (not all the numbers for the divisions and sections have been used). Arabic numerals are used to represent each class in the DDC. A decimal point follows the third digit, after which division by ten continues to the specific degree of classification needed.

Hierarchy in the DDC is expressed through structure and notation. Structural hierarchy means that all topics (aside from the ten main classes) are part of the broader topics above them. Certain notes regarding the nature of a class hold true for all the subordinate classes, including logically subordinate topics classed at coordinate numbers. Notational hierarchy is expressed by length of notation. Numbers at any given level are usually subordinate to (i.e., more specific than) a class whose notation is one digit shorter; coordinate with (i.e., equally specific as) a class whose notation has the same number of significant digits; and superordinate to (i.e., less specific than) a class with numbers one or more digits longer.

Sometimes, other devices must be used to express the hierarchy when it is not possible or desirable to do so through the notation. Special headings, notes, and entries indicate relationships among topics that violate notational hierarchy.

Entries

Entries in the schedules are composed of a DDC number in the number column (the column at the left margin), a heading describing the class that the number represents, and often one or more notes. All entries (numbers, headings, and notes) should be read in the context of the hierarchy.

The first three digits of schedule numbers appear only once in the number column, when first used. They are repeated at the top of each page where their subdivisions continue. Subordinate numbers appear in the number column, beginning with a decimal point, with the initial three digits understood.

---

[1] The Relative Index for *200 Religion Class* does not include information found in the two appendixes.

Numbers and notes in parentheses provide options to standard practice. These options enable the DDC to serve needs beyond those represented in the standard English-language edition. An optional arrangement of books of Tanakh is provided in appendix A.

Numbers in square brackets represent topics that have been relocated or discontinued, or are unassigned. Square brackets are also used for standard subdivision concepts that are represented in another location. Numbers in square brackets are not used.

Number Building

Only a fraction of potential DDC numbers are listed in the schedules. The classifier will often find that to arrive at a precise number for a work it is necessary to build a number that is not specifically listed in the schedules. Many built numbers are included in the Relative Index. Since many of these numbers have been constructed using notation from 172–179 Applied ethics, the 170 Ethics schedule has been included in appendix B.

Relative Index

The Relative Index includes the entries for 200 Religion topics from Edition 22, electronic index terms from WebDewey, and some additional index terms. It also includes index terms for notes in the Manual.

In the Relative Index, topics are listed alphabetically, with terms identifying the disciplines or subdisciplines in which the topics are treated subarranged alphabetically under them. Entries in the Relative Index are arranged alphabetically word by word. For example, "Brahma Samaj" precedes "Brahmanas." Entries with the same word order or phrase but with different marks of punctuation are arranged in the following word order: Term; Term. Subheading; Term (Parenthetical qualifier); Term, inverted term qualifier; Term as part of phrase. For example, "Body (Human)" precedes "Body and soul."

Manual

The Manual contains notes explaining the classification of selected areas in 200 Religion. It is organized by DDC number. There are references to the notes in the Manual from the 200 Religion schedule and from the Relative Index.

More Information

For more information about the use of the Dewey Decimal Classification, consult the introduction to the DDC in Abridged Edition 14, or the introduction to the DDC in volume one of Edition 22. WebDewey, the updated and enhanced electronic version of Edition 22, also includes an introduction to the DDC. More in-depth discussions of the DDC may be found in *Dewey Decimal Classification: Principles and Application*, 3rd ed., by Lois Mai Chan and Joan S. Mitchell (Dublin, Ohio: OCLC, 2003). Up-to-date information about the DDC is posted regularly on the Dewey home page at: www.oclc.org/dewey.

Schedule
200 Religion

200

200 Religion

Beliefs, attitudes, practices of individuals and groups with respect to the ultimate nature of existences and relationships within the context of revelation, deity, worship

Including public relations for religion

Class here comparative religion [*formerly* 291]; religions other than Christianity; works dealing with various religions, with religious topics not applied to specific religions; syncretistic religious writings of individuals expressing personal views and not claiming to establish a new religion or to represent an old one

Class a specific topic in comparative religion, religions other than Christianity in 201–209. Class public relations for a specific religion or aspect of a religion with the religion or aspect, e.g., public relations for a local Christian church 254.4

See also 306.6 for sociology of religion

See Manual at T1—0882 and 200; also at 130 vs. 200; also at 200 vs. 100; also at 201–209 and 292–299

(Option: To give preferred treatment or shorter numbers to a specific religion other than Christianity, use one of the five options described at 290)

SUMMARY

200.1–.9	Standard subdivisions of religion
201	Religious mythology, general classes of religion, interreligious relations and attitudes, social theology
202	Doctrines
203	Public worship and other practices
204	Religious experience, life, practice
205	Religious ethics
206	Leaders and organization
207	Missions and religious education
208	Sources
209	Sects and reform movements
210	Philosophy and theory of religion
.1	Theory of philosophy of religion
211	Concepts of God
212	Existence of God, ways of knowing God, attributes of God
213	Creation
214	Theodicy
215	Science and religion
218	Humankind

220	**Bible**
.01–.09	Standard subdivisions and special topics
.1–.9	Generalities
221	Old Testament (Tanakh)
222	Historical books of Old Testament
223	Poetic books of Old Testament
224	Prophetic books of Old Testament
225	New Testament
226	Gospels and Acts
227	Epistles
228	Revelation (Apocalypse)
229	Apocrypha, pseudepigrapha, intertestamental works
230	**Christianity Christian theology**
.002–.007	Standard subdivisions of Christianity
.01–.09	Standard subdivisions and specific types of Christian theology
.1–.9	Doctrines of specific denominations and sects
231	God
232	Jesus Christ and his family Christology
233	Humankind
234	Salvation and grace
235	Spiritual beings
236	Eschatology
238	Creeds, confessions of faith, covenants, catechisms
239	Apologetics and polemics
240	**Christian moral and devotional theology**
241	Christian ethics
242	Devotional literature
243	Evangelistic writings for individuals and families
246	Use of art in Christianity
247	Church furnishings and related articles
248	Christian experience, practice, life
249	Christian observances in family life
250	**Local Christian church and Christian religious orders**
.1–.9	Standard subdivisions
251	Preaching (Homiletics)
252	Texts of sermons
253	Pastoral office and work (Pastoral theology)
254	Parish administration
255	Religious congregations and orders
259	Pastoral care of families, of specific kinds of persons
260	**Christian social and ecclesiastical theology**
.9	Historical, geographic, persons treatment
261	Social theology and interreligious relations and attitudes
262	Ecclesiology
263	Days, times, places of religious observance
264	Public worship
265	Sacraments, other rites and acts
266	Missions
267	Associations for religious work
268	Religious education
269	Spiritual renewal

270	Historical, geographic, persons treatment of Christianity Church history
.01–.09	Standard subdivisions
.1–.8	Historical periods
271	Religious congregations and orders in church history
272	Persecutions in general church history
273	Doctrinal controversies and heresies in general church history
274–279	Treatment by continent, country, locality
280	Denominations and sects of Christian church
.01–.09	Standard subdivisions and special topics
.2–.4	Branches
281	Early church and Eastern churches
282	Roman Catholic Church
283	Anglican churches
284	Protestant denominations of Continental origin and related bodies
285	Presbyterian churches, Reformed churches centered in America, Congregational churches, Puritanism
286	Baptist, Disciples of Christ, Adventist churches
287	Methodist churches; churches related to Methodism
289	Other denominations and sects
290	Other religions
292	Classical religion (Greek and Roman religion)
293	Germanic religion
294	Religions of Indic origin
295	Zoroastrianism (Mazdaism, Parseeism)
296	Judaism
297	Islam, Babism, Bahai Faith
299	Religions not provided for elsewhere

.1   Systems, value, scientific principles, psychology of religion

Do not use for philosophy and theory; class in 210

.11   Systems

[.12]   Classification

Do not use; class in 201.4

[.13]   Value

Number discontinued; class in 200.1

[.14]   Language and communication

Do not use; class in 210.14

.15   Scientific principles

Class philosophic treatment of the relation of science and religion in 215

.19   Psychological principles

Class here psychology of religion

.2–.5   Standard subdivisions

[.6]   Organizations and management

Do not use; class in 206

.7	**Education, research, related topics**
.71	Education

Class here religion as an academic subject

Class religious education to inculcate religious life and practice, comprehensive works on religious education in 207.5

See also 379.28 for place of religion in public schools

See Manual at 207.5, 268 vs. 200.71, 230.071, 292–299

.8	**History and description with respect to kinds of persons [*formerly also* 306.608]**

Class here attitudes of religions to social groups [*formerly* 291.17834]; discrimination, equality, inequality, prejudice

.9	**Historical, geographic, persons treatment**

See Manual at 200.9 vs. 294, 299.5

.903 4	19th century, 1800–1899

Class here religions of 19th and 20th century origin [*formerly* 291.046]

.92	Persons

See Manual at 200.92 and 201–209, 292–299

> ## 201–209 Specific aspects of religion

Class treatment of religious topics with respect to philosophy of religion, natural theology in 210; class treatment with respect to Christianity in 230–280; class treatment with respect to a specific religion other than Christianity in 292–299; class comprehensive works on comparative religion in 200

See Manual at 200.92 and 201–209, 292–299; also at 201–209 and 292–299

201 Religious mythology, general classes of religion, interreligious relations and attitudes, social theology [*all formerly* 291.1]

SUMMARY

201.3	**Mythology and mythological foundations**
.4	**General classes of religion**
.5	**Interreligious relations**
.6	**Religions and secular disciplines**
.7	**Attitudes of religions toward social issues**

[.012]	Classification

Do not use; class in 201.4

.3   **Mythology and mythological foundations**

Stories of primeval history, beings, origins, and customs archetypally significant in the sacred life, doctrine, and ritual of religions

Class myths on a specific subject with the subject, e.g., creation myths 202.4

See Manual at 398.2 vs. 201.3, 230, 270, 292–299

.4   **General classes of religion**

Including monotheistic, nontheistic, pantheistic, polytheistic religions

Class here classification of religions

Class concepts of God or the gods in world religions in 202.11; class philosophic treatment of concepts of God in 211

.42   Prehistoric religions and religions of nonliterate peoples [*formerly* 291.042]

.43   Goddess religions

See also 202.114 for female goddesses

.44   Shamanism

Class shamanism in a specific religion with the religion, e.g., shamanism in religions of North American native origin 299.71144

.5   **Interreligious relations [*formerly* 291.172]**

Including relations of religions with irreligion

.6   **Religions and secular disciplines [*formerly* 291.175]**

Class guides to religious life and practice on specific topics in secular disciplines in 204.4

For attitudes of religions toward social sciences, see 201.7

.600 1–.619 9   Computer science, information, philosophy, parapsychology and occultism, psychology

Add to base number 201.6 notation 001–199, e.g., religions and psychology 201.615

.64–.69   Language, natural sciences, mathematics, technology, arts, literature, rhetoric, geography, history

Add to base number 201.6 notation 400–900, e.g., religions and science 201.65

.7   Attitudes of religions toward social issues [*formerly* 291.17]

Attitudes of religions toward and influences on secular matters

Including role of organized religions in society [*formerly* 291.171]; communications media [*formerly* 291.175]; sexual relations, marriage, divorce, family [*all formerly* 291.17835]; population [*formerly* 291.178366]

Class here religion and culture, social theology

Class human ecology in 201.77; class guides to religious life and practice on specific topics in the social sciences in 204.4; class sociology of religion in 306.6

> *For attitudes toward social groups, see 200.8; for attitudes toward various religions, see 201.5*

> *See also 205 for religious ethics*

.72   Political affairs [*formerly* 291.177]

Attitudes toward and influences on political activities and ideologies

Including civil war and revolution

Class secular view of religiously oriented political theories and ideologies in 320.55; class secular view of relation of state to religious organizations and groups in 322.1

> *See Manual at 322.1 vs. 201.72, 261.7, 292–299*

.721   Theocracy

Supremacy of organized religion over civil government

.723   Civil rights

Including citizenship, religious freedom

.727   International affairs [*formerly* 291.1787]

.727 3   War and peace

Including conscientious objectors, disarmament, pacifism

> *For nuclear weapons and nuclear war, see 201.7275*

.727 5   Nuclear weapons and nuclear war

.73   Economics [*formerly* 291.1785]

Class socioeconomic problems in 201.76

> *For environment, natural resources, see 201.77*

.76   Social problems and services [*formerly* 291.1783]

Class here socioeconomic problems [*formerly* 291.178]

> *See also 361.75 for welfare work of religious organizations*

.762–.763	Specific social problems

Add to base number 201.76 the numbers following 36 in 362–363, e.g., child abuse and neglect 201.76276 [*formerly* 291.1783271], sexual abuse 201.76276 [*formerly* 291.1783272], adults who were victims of abuse as children 201.762764 [*formerly* 291.1783273], abuse within the family 201.7628292 [*formerly* 291.178327], refugees and victims of political oppression 201.76287 [*formerly* 291.178328], hunger 201.7638 [*formerly* 291.178326], poor people 201.7625; however, for population problems, see 201.7; for environmental problems, see 201.77

.764	Crime and punishment [*formerly* 291.17833]
.77	Environment

Class here human ecology [*formerly* 291.178362], ecology, environmental problems, natural resources, pollution

Class environmental ethics in 205.691

202   Doctrines [*formerly* 291.2]

Class here beliefs, apologetics, polemics; comprehensive works on theology

For social theologies, see 201.7; for religious ethics, see 205

.1	**Objects of worship and veneration**

Class here animism, spiritism

.11	God, gods, goddesses, divinities and deities

Class here supernatural beings

Class concepts of God in philosophy of religion in 211

.112	Attributes of God, of the gods

For attributes of male gods, see 202.113; for attributes of female goddesses, see 202.114

.113	Male gods
.114	Female goddesses

See also 201.43 for goddess religions

.117	Relation to the world

Including miracles, prophecy, providence, revelation, relation to and action in history

For creation and cosmology, see 202.4

.118	Theodicy

Vindication of God's justice and goodness in permitting existence of evil and suffering

.12		Nature

Including fire, sex, sun, trees, water

See also 203.5 for sacred places

.13 Persons

Including ancestors, the dead, heroes, monarchs, saints

.14 Personified abstractions

.15 Good spirits

Class here angels

.16 Evil spirits

Class here demons, devils

.18 Images

.2 Humankind

Including atonement, creation of humankind, repentance, salvation, sin, soul

Class here comprehensive works on karma

Class creation of the world in 202.4

For eschatology, see 202.3. For a specific aspect of karma, see the aspect, e.g., karma as a concept in Buddhist ethics 294.35

.3 Eschatology

Including death, end of the world, heaven, hell, immortality, other worlds, punishments, purgatory, resurrection, rewards

.37 Reincarnation

.4 Creation and cosmology

For creation of humankind, see 202.2

203 Public worship and other practices [*formerly* 291.3]

Practices predominantly public or collective in character

Unless other instructions are given, class a subject with aspects in two or more subdivisions of 203 in the number coming first, e.g., religious healing and ceremonies connected with it 203.1 (*not* 203.8)

Class leaders and organization in 206; class missions and religious education in 207; class comprehensive works on worship in 204.3

.1 Religious healing

See Manual at 615.852 vs. 203.1, 234.131, 292–299

.2   **Divination**

Including omens, oracles, prophecies

Class comprehensive works on divination in 133.3

.3   **Witchcraft**

Class religions based on modern revivals of witchcraft in 299.94; class comprehensive works on witchcraft in 133.43

.4   **Offerings, sacrifices, penances**

.42   Human sacrifice

.5   **Sacred places and pilgrimages**

Standard subdivisions are added for sacred places and pilgrimages together, for sacred places alone

Class here grottoes, holy buildings, pagodas, shrines, temples

Class monasteries in 206.57

.509 3–.509 9   Treatment by specific continents, countries, localities

Class here pilgrimages to specific sacred places

.51   Pilgrimages

[.510 93–.510 99]   Treatment by specific continents, countries, localities

Do not use; class in 203.5093–203.5099

.6   **Sacred times**

Including holy days, religious calendar, religious festivals

See Manual at 203.6, 263.9, 292–299 vs. 394.265–394.267

.7   **Symbolism, symbolic objects, sounds**

Including mandalas, mantras

Class here religious use, significance, purpose of the arts

See also 201.67 for attitudes of religions toward the arts

.8   **Rites and ceremonies**

Conduct and texts

Including liturgy, music, processions, public feasts and fasts, public prayer

Class interdisciplinary works on sacred music in 781.7; class interdisciplinary works on sacred vocal music in 782.22

.81   Birth rites

.82   Initiation rites

.85   Marriage rites

.88   Funeral and mourning rites

               Standard subdivisions are added for either or both topics in heading

204   Religious experience, life, practice [*formerly* 291.4]

               Practices predominantly private or individual in character

               Class here spirituality

               Class religious ethics in 205

.2   Religious experience

               Including conversion, enlightenment

.22   Mysticism

.3   Worship, meditation, yoga

               Class here practical works on prayer, on contemplation; comprehensive works on worship

               For public worship, see 203

.32   Devotional literature

               Including meditations

.33   Prayer books

.35   Meditation

.36   Yoga

               Religious and spiritual discipline

               Including kundalini yoga

               Class interdisciplinary works on yoga in 181.45

                    For Hindu kundalini yoga, see 294.5436

                    See also 613.7046 for hatha yoga, physical yoga

.4   Religious life and practice

               Class here guides to religious life and practice

               For worship, meditation, yoga, see 204.3

[.408 5]   Relatives   Parents

               Do not use; class in 204.41

.408 6   Persons by miscellaneous social characteristics

[.408 655]   Married persons

               Do not use; class in 204.41

.408 7	Gifted persons

Do not use for persons with disabilities and illnesses; class in 204.42

.41   Marriage and family life

Including adoption, divorce, interreligious marriage, religious training of children in the home, single parents

Class here comprehensive works on marriage

For abuse within the family, see 201.7628292; for marriage rites, see 203.85; for ethics of marriage, see 205.63

.42   Persons experiencing illness, trouble, addiction, bereavement

See Manual at 616.86 vs. 158.1, 204.42, 248.8629, 292–299, 362.29

.46   Individual observances

Not provided for elsewhere

Including almsgiving, ceremonial and ritual observances, dietary limitations, observance of restrictions and limitations

.47   Asceticism

Including practice of celibacy, fasting and abstinence, poverty, solitude

205   Religious ethics [*formerly* 291.5]

Including conscience, sin

.6   Specific moral issues, sins, vices, virtues

Add to base number 205.6 the numbers following 17 in 172–179, e.g., sexual relations 205.66, morality of discriminatory practices 205.675

206   Leaders and organization [*formerly* 291.6]

Class here management

.1   Leaders and their work

Variant names: clergy, gurus, messiahs, priests, prophets, shamans

Role, function, duties

Including pastoral counseling and preaching

Class theologians in 202. Class a specific activity of a leader with the activity, e.g., religious healing by shamans 203.1

For founders of religions, see 206.3

See Manual at 200.92 and 201–209, 292–299

[.109 2]   Persons

Do not use; class as instructed in Manual at 200.92 and 292–299

.3   Founders of religions

[.309 2]   Persons

Do not use; class as instructed in Manual at 200.92 and 292–299

.5   **Organizations and organization**

Including associations, congregations, institutions, orders, parties; exercise of religious authority

Class laws and decisions in 208.4

.57   Monasticism and monasteries

Class here religious orders

207   Missions and religious education [*formerly* 291.7]

.2   **Missions**

.5   **Religious education**

Class here comprehensive works on religious education and religion as an academic subject

For education in and teaching of comparative religion, religion as an academic subject, see 200.71; for religious training of children in the home, see 204.41

See Manual at 207.5, 268 vs. 200.71, 230.071, 292–299

208   Sources [*formerly* 291.8]

Class theology based on sacred sources in 202

.2   **Sacred books and scriptures**

For sacred books and scriptures of sects and reform movements, see 208.5

.3   **Oral traditions**

For oral traditions of sects and reform movements, see 208.5

.4   **Laws and decisions**

Class civil law relating to religious matters in 340

For laws and decisions of sects and reform movements, see 208.5

See also 364.188 for offenses against religion as defined and penalized by the state

.5   **Sources of sects and reform movements**

209   Sects and reform movements [*formerly* 291.9]

Class specific aspects of sects and reform movements in 201–208

For specific sects and reform movements, see 280–290

See Manual at 299.93

210   Philosophy and theory of religion

Class here natural theology, philosophical theology; works that use observation and interpretation of evidence in nature, speculation, and reasoning, but not revelation or appeal to authoritative scriptures, to examine religious beliefs

Class a specific topic treated with respect to religions based on revelation or authority with the topic in 201–209, e.g., concepts of God in world religions 202.11; class a specific topic with respect to a specific religion with the religion, e.g., Christian concepts of God 231

(Option: To give local emphasis and a shorter number to a specific religion other than Christianity, class it in this number, and add to base number 21 the numbers following the base number for that religion in 292–299, e.g., Hinduism 210, Mahabharata 219.23; in that case class philosophy and theory of religion in 200, its subdivisions 211–218 in 201–208, specific aspects of comparative religion in 200.1–200.9, standard subdivisions of religion in 200.01–200.09. Other options are described at 290)

.1   **Theory of philosophy of religion**

Including methodology of the philosophy of religion

[.11]   Systems

Do not use; class in 200.11

[.12]   Classification

Do not use; class in 201.4

.14   Language and communication of religion

[.15]   Scientific principles

Do not use; class in 200.15

[.19]   Psychological principles

Do not use; class in 200.19

211   Concepts of God

Including anthropomorphism

Class here comprehensive works on God, on The Holy

Class God, gods and goddesses in comparative religion in 202.11

For existence of God, ways of knowing God, attributes of God, miracles, see 212

.2   **Pantheism**

.3   **Theism**

For pantheism, see 211.2

.32   Polytheism

.33   Dualism

  .34   Monotheism

  .4   **Rationalism (Free thought)**

  .5   **Deism**

  .6   **Humanism and secularism**

        Standard subdivisions are added for either or both topics in heading

  .7   **Agnosticism and skepticism**

        Standard subdivisions are added for either or both topics in heading

  .8   **Atheism**

212   **Existence of God, ways of knowing God, attributes of God**

        Including miracles

  .1   **Existence of God**

        Including proofs

  .6   **Ways of knowing God**

        Former heading: Knowability

        Including role of faith, reason and revelation

        Class proofs in 212.1

  .7   **Attributes of God**

        Including love, omniscience

213   **Creation**

        Including creation of life and human life, evolution versus creation, evolution as method of creation

        See Manual at 231.7652 vs. 213, 500, 576.8

214   **Theodicy**

        Vindication of God's justice and goodness in permitting existence of evil and suffering

        Class here good and evil

  .8   **Providence**

215   **Science and religion**

        Including technology and religion

        Class religion and scientific theories of creation in 213

        See also 201.65 for various religions and science; also 261.55 for Christianity and science

.2 **Astronomy**

Including cosmology

.3 **Physics**

.7 **Life sciences**

Including natural history, paleontology

Anthropology and religion, ethnology and religion relocated to 218

Class evolution versus creation, evolution as method of creation in 213

[216] **[Unassigned]**

Most recently used in Edition 21

[217] **[Unassigned]**

Most recently used in Edition 18

218 **Humankind**

Including anthropology and religion, ethnology and religion [*both formerly* 215.7], immortality

For creation of humankind, human evolution, see 213

[219] **[Unassigned]**

Most recently used in Edition 19

220 **Bible**

Holy Scriptures of Judaism and Christianity

Class Christian Biblical theology in 230.041; class Biblical precepts in Christian codes of conduct in 241.52–241.54; class Jewish Biblical theology in 296.3; class Biblical precepts in Jewish codes of conduct in 296.36

(If option A under 290 is chosen, class here sources of the specified religion; class Bible in 298)

SUMMARY

220.01–.09	**Standard subdivisions and special topics**
.1–.9	**Generalities**
221	**Old Testament (Tanakh)**
222	**Historical books of Old Testament**
223	**Poetic books of Old Testament**
224	**Prophetic books of Old Testament**
225	**New Testament**
226	**Gospels and Acts**
227	**Epistles**
228	**Revelation (Apocalypse)**
229	**Apocrypha, pseudepigrapha, intertestamental works**

.01–.02   Standard subdivisions

[.03]	Dictionaries, encyclopedias, concordances

Do not use for dictionaries and encyclopedias; class in 220.3. Do not use for concordances; class in 220.4–220.5

.04 Special topics of Bible

.046 Apocalyptic passages

Class apocalyptic passages in a book or group of books with the book or group of books, plus notation 0046 from add table under 221–229, e.g., apocalyptic passages in the prophets 224.0046, in Book of Daniel 224.50046

For Revelation (Apocalypse), see 228

.05–.08 Standard subdivisions

.09 Historical, geographic, persons treatment of Bible

Class the canon in 220.12

For geography, history, chronology, persons of Bible lands in Bible times, see 220.9

SUMMARY

220.1	**Origins and authenticity**
.3	**Encyclopedias and topical dictionaries**
.4	**Original texts, early versions, early translations**
.5	**Modern versions and translations**
.6	**Interpretation and criticism (Exegesis)**
.7	**Commentaries**
.8	**Nonreligious subjects treated in Bible**
.9	**Geography, history, chronology, persons of Bible lands in Bible times**

> **220.1–220.9 Generalities**

Class comprehensive works in 220. Class generalities applied to a specific part of the Bible with the part, plus notation 01–09 from add table under 221–229, e.g., a commentary on Job 223.107

.1 Origins and authenticity

.12 Canon

Class here selection of the books accepted as Holy Scripture

.13 Inspiration

The Bible as revelation (word of God)

Including authority of Bible

.132 Inerrancy

.15	Biblical prophecy and prophecies

Class Christian messianic prophecies in 232.12; class Christian eschatological prophecies in 236; class Jewish messianic and eschatological prophecies in 296.33

See also 224 for prophetic books of Old Testament

.3	**Encyclopedias and topical dictionaries**

For dictionaries of specific texts, see 220.4–220.5

>	**220.4–220.5 Texts, versions, translations**

Class here critical appraisal of language and style; concordances, indexes, dictionaries of specific texts; complete texts; selections from more than one part; paraphrases

Class texts accompanied by commentaries in 220.77; class comprehensive works in 220.4. Class selections compiled for a specific purpose with the purpose, e.g., selections for daily meditations 242.2

.4	**Original texts, early versions, early translations**

Class here original texts accompanied by modern translations, comprehensive works on texts and versions

For modern versions and translations, see 220.5

.404	Textual criticism and word studies
.404 6	Textual criticism (Lower criticism)

Use of scientific means to ascertain the actual original texts

.404 7	Theological studies of words or phrases

>	220.42–220.49 Texts in specific languages

Add to each subdivision identified by † the numbers following 220.404 in 220.4046–220.4047, regardless of specific version, e.g., textual criticism of Bible in Latin, of Vulgate 220.476, of Old Testament in Greek, of Septuagint 221.486

Class comprehensive works in 220.4

.42	†Aramaic versions
.43	†Syriac versions
.44	†Hebrew version
.45	†Samaritan versions
.46	Other Semitic language versions

Including Arabic, Ge'ez

†Add as instructed under 220.42–220.49

.47 †Latin versions

.48 †Greek versions

.49 Other early versions

> Including Armenian, Coptic

.5 Modern versions and translations

.51 Polyglot

.52 Versions in English and Anglo-Saxon

> Standard subdivisions are added for versions in English and Anglo-Saxon, for English alone
>
> Class works containing translations in English and one other modern language with the other language, e.g., the Bible in English and German 220.531

.520 01–.520 09 Standard subdivisions

> 220.5201–220.5209 English

> Add to each subdivision identified by * as follows:
> 01–02 Standard subdivisions
> [03] Dictionaries, encyclopedias, concordances
> Do not use; class in 3
> 05–08 Standard subdivisions
> 09 Geographic and persons treatment
> Do not use for historical treatment of the translation; class in 8
> 2 Standard editions
> 3 Concordances, indexes, dictionaries
> 4 Special editions
> Including annotated editions, study editions, editions notable for illustrations
> 6 Selections
> 7 Paraphrases
> 8 History, criticism, explanation of the translation
>
> Class comprehensive works in 220.52

.520 1 English versions before 1582

> Including Coverdale, Tyndale, Wycliffe versions

.520 2 *Douay version

> Class here Rheims-Douay, Rheims-Douay-Challoner versions
>
> *See also 220.5205 for Confraternity-Douay-Challoner version*

.520 3 *Authorized version (King James version)

---

*Add as instructed under 220.5201–220.5209

†Add as instructed under 220.42–220.49

.520 4	Revised version

Including English Revised (1881–1885), American Revised (American Standard) (1901) versions

.520 42	*Revised Standard version (1946–1957)
.520 43	*New Revised Standard version (1990)
.520 5	*Confraternity Bible and New American Bible

Class here Confraternity-Douay-Challoner version

Subdivisions are added for either or both topics in heading

See also 220.5202 for Rheims-Douay, Rheims-Douay-Challoner versions

.520 6	*New English Bible and Revised English Bible

Subdivisions are added for either or both topics in heading

.520 7	*Jerusalem Bible and New Jerusalem Bible

Subdivisions are added for either or both topics in heading

.520 8	Other English translations since 1582

Including New King James, New Century versions

For translations by individuals, see 220.5209

.520 81	*New International Version
.520 82	*Today's English Bible (Good News Bible)
.520 83	*Living Bible and New Living Translation

Subdivisions are added for either or both topics in heading

.520 9	Translations by individuals

Including Goodspeed, Knox, Moffatt, Phillips

.529	Anglo-Saxon
.53–.59	Versions in other languages

Add to base number 220.5 notation 3–9 from Table 6, e.g., the Bible in German 220.531

Works containing translations in two modern languages other than English are classed with the language coming later in Table 6; in more than two modern languages in 220.51

*Add as instructed under 220.5201–220.5209

.6   **Interpretation and criticism (Exegesis)**

Class Christian meditations based on Biblical passages and intended for devotional use in 242.5; class material about the Bible intended for use in preparing Christian sermons in 251; class Christian sermons based on Biblical passages in 252; class material about the Bible for preparation of Jewish sermons and texts of Jewish sermons in 296.47; class Jewish meditations based on Biblical passages and intended for devotional use in 296.72

For textual criticism, see 220.4046; for commentaries, see 220.7

.601   Philosophy and theory

Class here hermeneutics

.61   General introductions to the Bible

Including isagogics (introductory studies prior to actual exegesis)

.64   Symbolism and typology

Standard subdivisions are added for either or both topics in heading

Class here interpretation of specific symbols

.65   Harmonies

.66   Literary criticism

Literary examination of the text in order to reach conclusions about its meaning, structure, authorship, date

Class here higher criticism, internal criticism, redaction criticism

Class language and style of specific texts in 220.4–220.5

See also 809.93522 for the Bible as literature

.663   Form criticism

Analysis of preliterary or oral forms and traditions in Biblical text

.67   Historical criticism

Interpretation of texts in light of the cultural, historical, religious, social milieu in which written

Class form criticism in 220.663

.68   Mythological, allegorical, numerical, astronomical interpretations

Including mythology in the Bible, demythologizing

.7   **Commentaries**

Criticism and interpretation arranged in textual order

.77   Commentaries with text

.8   **Nonreligious subjects treated in Bible**

Class a religious subject treated in Bible with the specific religion and topic, e.g., Christian theology 230, Jewish theology 296.3

.800 01–.800 09	Standard subdivisions
.800 1–.899 9	Specific nonreligious subjects

Add to base number 220.8 notation 001–999, e.g., natural sciences in Bible 220.85; however, for geography, history, chronology, persons of Bible lands in Bible times, see 220.9

.9   Geography, history, chronology, persons of Bible lands in Bible times

Class general history of Bible lands in ancient world in 930

.91   Geography

Class here description and civilization

Class civilization treated separately from geography in 220.95

.92   Collected persons

Class an individual person with the part of the Bible in which the person is chiefly considered, e.g., Abraham 222.11092

See Manual at 220.92; also at 230–280

.93   Archaeology (Material remains)

.95   History

Including civilization treated separately from geography

Class geographic description and civilization treated together in 220.91

.950 01–.950 09   Standard subdivisions

.950 5   Bible stories retold

Including picture books

> **221–229   Specific parts of Bible, Apocrypha, pseudepigrapha, intertestamental works**

Add to each subdivision identified by * as follows (subdivisions from this table may be added for a part of any work that has its own number):
001–08 Standard subdivisions and generalities
        Add to 0 the numbers following 220 in 220.01–220.8, e.g., interpretation of the work or of a part of the work 06
09   Geography, history, chronology, persons
        Add to 09 the numbers following 221.9 in 221.91–221.95, e.g., biography 092

Class comprehensive works in 220

221   **Old Testament (Tanakh)**

Holy Scriptures of Judaism, Old Testament of Christianity

Class Jewish Biblical theology in 296.3; class Biblical precepts in Jewish codes of conduct in 296.36

For historical books, see 222; for Torah, see 222.1; for poetic books, Ketuvim, see 223; for prophetic books, Nevi'im, see 224

See Manual at 221

[.03]   Dictionaries, encyclopedias, concordances

Do not use for dictionaries and encyclopedias; class in 221.3. Do not use for concordances; class in 221.4–221.5

.04   Special topics of Old Testament

.044   Megillot (Five scrolls)

For a specific book of Megillot, see the book, e.g., Ruth 222.35

.046   Apocalyptic passages

Class apocalyptic passages in a book or group of books with the book or group of books, plus notation 0046 from add table under 221–229, e.g., apocalyptic passages in the prophets 224.0046, in Book of Daniel 224.50046

.09   Historical, geographic, persons treatment of Old Testament

Class the canon in 221.12

For geography, history, chronology, persons of Old Testament lands in Old Testament times, see 221.9

.1–.8   **Generalities**

Add to base number 221 the numbers following 220 in 220.1–220.8, e.g., Targums 221.42, commentaries 221.7

.9   **Geography, history, chronology, persons of Old Testament lands in Old Testament times**

Class general history of ancient areas in 930

.91   Geography

Class here description and civilization

Class civilization treated separately from geography in 221.95

.92   Persons

See Manual at 220.92; also at 230–280

.922   Collected treatment

.93   Archaeology (Material remains)

.95   History

              Including civilization treated separately from geography

              Class geographic description and civilization treated together in 221.91

.950 01–.950 09   Standard subdivisions

.950 5   Old Testament stories retold

              Including picture books

> ## 222–224   Books of Old Testament

              Class comprehensive works in 221

              See Manual at 221

              (Option: To arrange the books of the Old Testament (Tanakh) as found in Jewish Bibles, use one of the following:
                  (Option A: Use the optional arrangement of 222–224 given in the Manual at 221
                  (Option B: Class in 296.11

              (A table giving the three numbers for each book is given in the Manual at 221)

222   *Historical books of Old Testament

.1   *Pentateuch (Torah)

              Class here Hexateuch

              For Joshua, see 222.2

.11   *Genesis

.12   *Exodus

              For Ten Commandments, see 222.16

.13   *Leviticus

.14   *Numbers

.15   *Deuteronomy

              For Ten Commandments, see 222.16

.16   *Ten Commandments (Decalogue)

              Class Ten Commandments as code of conduct in Christianity in 241.52; class Ten Commandments as code of conduct in Judaism in 296.36

.2   *Joshua (Josue)

.3   *Judges and Ruth

.32   *Judges

---

*Add as instructed under 221–229

.35	*Ruth

.4 ***Samuel**

.43   *Samuel 1

        Variant name: Kings 1

.44   *Samuel 2

        Variant name: Kings 2

.5 ***Kings**

.53   *Kings 1

        Variant name: Kings 3

.54   *Kings 2

        Variant name: Kings 4

.6 ***Chronicles (Paralipomena)**

.63   *Chronicles 1 (Paralipomenon 1)

.64   *Chronicles 2 (Paralipomenon 2)

.7 ***Ezra (Esdras 1)**

        See also 229.1 for Esdras 1 (also called Esdras 3) of the Apocrypha

.8 ***Nehemiah (Esdras 2, Nehemias)**

        See also 229.1 for Esdras 2 (also called Esdras 4) of the Apocrypha

(.86)   *Tobit (Tobias)

        (Optional number; prefer 229.22)

(.88)   *Judith

        (Optional number; prefer 229.24)

.9 ***Esther**

        (Option: Class here deuterocanonical part of Esther; prefer 229.27)

223   *Poetic books of Old Testament

    Class here Ketuvim (Hagiographa, Writings), wisdom literature

    For Apocryphal wisdom literature, see 229.3. For a specific book of Ketuvim not provided for here, see the book, e.g., Ruth 222.35

.1 ***Job**

.2 ***Psalms**

.7 ***Proverbs**

*Add as instructed under 221–229

.8	***Ecclesiastes (Qohelet)**
.9	***Song of Solomon (Canticle of Canticles, Song of Songs)**
(.96)	*Wisdom of Solomon (Wisdom)

(Optional number; prefer 229.3)

(.98)   *Ecclesiasticus (Sirach)

(Optional number; prefer 229.4)

224   *Prophetic books of Old Testament

Class here Major Prophets, Nevi'im

For a specific book of Nevi'im not provided for here, see the book, e.g., Joshua 222.2

.1	***Isaiah (Isaias)**
.2	***Jeremiah (Jeremias)**
.3	***Lamentations**
(.37)	*Baruch

(Optional number; prefer 229.5)

.4	***Ezekiel (Ezechiel)**
.5	***Daniel**

(Option: Class here Song of the Three Children, Susanna, Bel and the Dragon; prefer 229.6)

.6	***Hosea (Osee)**
.7	***Joel**
.8	***Amos**
.9	***Minor Prophets**

For Hosea, see 224.6; for Joel, see 224.7; for Amos, see 224.8

.91	*Obadiah (Abdias)
.92	*Jonah (Jonas)
.93	*Micah (Micheas)
.94	*Nahum
.95	*Habakkuk (Habacuc)
.96	*Zephaniah (Sophonias)
.97	*Haggai (Aggeus)

*Add as instructed under 221–229

.98   *Zechariah (Zacharias)

.99   *Malachi (Malachias)

(.997)   *Maccabees 1 and 2 (Machabees 1 and 2)

> (Optional number; prefer 229.73)

225   New Testament

> *For Gospels and Acts, see 226; for Epistles, see 227; for Revelation, see 228*

[.03]   Dictionaries, encyclopedias, concordances

> Do not use for dictionaries and encyclopedias; class in 225.3. Do not use for concordances; class in 225.4–225.5

.04   Special topics of New Testament

.046   Apocalyptic passages

> Class apocalyptic passages in a book or group of books with the book or group of books, plus notation 0046 from add table under 221–229, e.g., apocalyptic passages in Gospels 226.0046, in Gospel of Mark 226.30046

> *For Revelation (Apocalypse), see 228*

.09   Historical, geographic, persons treatment of New Testament

> Class the canon in 225.12

> *For geography, history, chronology, persons of New Testament lands in New Testament times, see 225.9*

.1–.8   Generalities

> Add to base number 225 the numbers following 220 in 220.1–220.8, e.g., Authorized Version 225.5203

.9   Geography, history, chronology, persons of New Testament lands in New Testament times

> Add to base number 225.9 the numbers following 221.9 in 221.91–221.95, e.g., individual persons 225.92; however, for Jesus Christ, Mary, Joseph, Joachim, Anne, John the Baptist, see 232

> *See Manual at 220.92; also at 230–280*

226   *Gospels and Acts

> Class here synoptic Gospels

> Subdivisions are added for Gospels and Acts together, for Gospels alone

> *See Manual at 230–280*

---

*Add as instructed under 221–229

.095 05   Gospel stories retold

Number built according to instructions under 221–229

Class Jesus as a historical figure, biography and specific events in life of Jesus in 232.9

.1   **Harmonies of Gospels**

>
226.2–226.5   Specific Gospels

Class comprehensive works in 226

For miracles, see 226.7; for parables, see 226.8

.2   ***Matthew**

Class Golden Rule as code of conduct in 241.54

For Sermon on the Mount, see 226.9

.3   ***Mark**

.4   ***Luke**

Class Golden Rule as code of conduct in 241.54

For Sermon on the Mount, see 226.9

.5   ***John**

Class here comprehensive works on Johannine literature

For Epistles of John, see 227.94; for Revelation (Apocalypse), see 228

.6   ***Acts of the Apostles**

.7   ***Miracles**

Class miracles in context of Jesus' life in 232.955

.8   ***Parables**

Class parables in context of Jesus' life in 232.954

.9   ***Sermon on the Mount**

Class Sermon on the Mount as code of conduct in 241.53

.93   ***Beatitudes**

.96   ***Lord's Prayer**

227   ***Epistles**

Class here Pauline epistles

.1   ***Romans**

*Add as instructed under 221–229

.2   ***Corinthians 1**

Class here comprehensive works on Epistles to Corinthians

For Corinthians 2, see 227.3

.3   ***Corinthians 2**

.4   ***Galatians**

.5   ***Ephesians**

.6   ***Philippians**

.7   ***Colossians**

.8   ***Other Pauline epistles**

.81   *Thessalonians 1

Class here comprehensive works on Epistles to Thessalonians

For Thessalonians 2, see 227.82

.82   *Thessalonians 2

.83   *Timothy 1

Class here comprehensive works on Epistles to Timothy, on Pastoral Epistles

For Timothy 2, see 227.84; for Titus, see 227.85

.84   *Timothy 2

.85   *Titus

.86   *Philemon

.87   *Hebrews

.9   ***Catholic epistles**

.91   *James

.92   *Peter 1

Class here comprehensive works on Epistles of Peter

For Peter 2, see 227.93

.93   *Peter 2

.94   *John 1

Class here comprehensive works on Epistles of John

For John 2, see 227.95; for John 3, see 227.96

.95   *John 2

*Add as instructed under 221–229

.96	*John 3
.97	*Jude

228   *Revelation (Apocalypse)

229   *Apocrypha, pseudepigrapha, intertestamental works

Apocrypha: works accepted as deuterocanonical in some Bibles

Pseudepigrapha, intertestamental works: works from intertestamental times connected with the Bible but not accepted as canonical

Subdivisions are added for Apocrypha, pseudepigrapha, intertestamental works together; for Apocrypha alone

---

> **229.1–229.7   Specific books and works of Apocrypha**

Class comprehensive works in 229

.1   *Esdras 1 and 2

Variant names: Esdras 3 and 4

See also 222.7 for Ezra; also 222.8 for Nehemiah

.2   *Tobit, Judith, deuterocanonical part of Esther

.22   *Tobit (Tobias)

(Option: Class in 222.86)

.24   *Judith

(Option: Class in 222.88)

.27   *Deuterocanonical part of Esther

(Option: Class in 222.9)

.3   *Wisdom of Solomon (Wisdom)

Class here Apocryphal wisdom literature

For Ecclesiasticus, see 229.4

(Option: Class in 223.96)

.4   *Ecclesiasticus (Sirach)

(Option: Class in 223.98)

.5   *Baruch and Epistle of Jeremiah

(Option: Class Baruch in 224.37)

---

*Add as instructed under 221–229

.6   ***Song of the Three Children, Susanna, Bel and the Dragon, Prayer of Manasseh**

(Option: Class Song of the Three Children, Susanna, Bel and the Dragon in 224.5)

.7   ***Maccabees (Machabees)**

.73   *Maccabees 1 and 2 (Machabees 1 and 2)

(Option: Class in 224.997)

.75   *Maccabees 3 and 4 (Machabees 3 and 4)

>   **229.8–229.9   Pseudepigrapha, intertestamental works**

Class comprehensive works in 229.9

For Maccabees 3 and 4, see 229.75

.8   ***Pseudo gospels**

Including agrapha (Jesus' words not appearing in canonical Gospels), Gospel of Thomas

Class comprehensive works on New Testament pseudepigrapha in 229.92

.9   ***Pseudepigrapha**

For pseudo gospels, see 229.8

.91   *Old Testament

For Maccabees 3 and 4, see 229.75

.911   *Historical books

.912   *Poetic books

Including Odes of Solomon

.913   *Prophetic books

Including Apocalypse of Elijah, Ascension of Isaiah, Assumption of Moses, Books of Enoch, Jewish apocalypses

.914   *Testaments

Including Testament of the Twelve Patriarchs

.92   *New Testament

For pseudo gospels, see 229.8; for Epistles, see 229.93; for Apocalypses, see 229.94

.925   *Acts of the Apostles

.93   *Epistles

---

*Add as instructed under 221–229

.94   *Apocalypses

> ## 230–280   Christianity

Unless other instructions are given, observe the following table of preference for the history of Christianity and the Christian church (*except* for biography, explained in Manual at 230–280: Biography), e.g., Jesuit missions in India 266.254 (*not* 271.53054); persecution of Jesuits by Elizabeth I 272.7 (*not* 271.53042, 274.206, or 282.42):

Specific topics	220–260
Persecutions in general church history	272
Doctrinal controversies and heresies in general church history	273
Religious congregations and orders in church history	271
Denominations and sects of Christian church	280
Treatment of Christianity and Christian church by continent, country, locality	274–279
General historical, geographic, persons treatment of Christianity and Christian church (*except* 271–279)	270

Class comprehensive works in 230

For Bible, see 220

See Manual at 230–280

(Option: To give local emphasis and shorter numbers to a specific religion other than Christianity, e.g., Buddhism, class it in these numbers, its sources in 220, comprehensive works in 230; in that case class the Bible and Christianity in 298. Other options are described at 290)

> ## 230–270   Specific elements of Christianity

Class here specific elements of specific denominations and sects
(Option: Class specific elements of specific denominations and sects in 280)

Class comprehensive works in 230

---

*Add as instructed under 221–229

230   Christianity   Christian theology

Including Christian mythology

Class here contextual theology

Class doctrinal controversies in general church history in 273

> *For Christian moral and devotional theology, see 240; for local Christian church and Christian religious orders, see 250; for Christian social and ecclesiastical theology, see 260; for historical, geographic, persons treatment of Christianity and Christian church, see 270; for denominations and sects of Christian church, see 280*

> *See Manual at 398.2 vs. 201.3, 230, 270, 292–299*

SUMMARY

230.002–.007	**Standard subdivisions of Christianity**
.01–.09	**Standard subdivisions and specific types of Christian theology**
.1–.9	**Doctrines of specific denominations and sects**
231	**God**
232	**Jesus Christ and his family Christology**
233	**Humankind**
234	**Salvation and grace**
235	**Spiritual beings**
236	**Eschatology**
238	**Creeds, confessions of faith, covenants, catechisms**
239	**Apologetics and polemics**

[.001]   Philosophy and theory of Christianity

> Do not use; class in 230.01

.002–.003   Standard subdivisions of Christianity

.005   Serial publications of Christianity

[.006]   Organizations and management of Christianity

> Do not use; class in 260

.007   Education, research, related topics of Christianity

[.007 1]   Education

> Do not use; class in 230.071

[.008]   Christianity with respect to kinds of persons

> Do not use; class in 270.08

[.009]   Historical, geographic, persons treatment of Christianity

> Do not use; class in 270

.01   Philosophy and theory of Christianity, of Christian theology

.02–.03   Standard subdivisions of Christian theology

.04　　　　　　Specific types of Christian theology

Class theology of specific denominations and sects in 230.1–230.9

See Manual at 230–280

[.040 1–.040 9]　　Standard subdivisions

Do not use; class in 230.01–230.09

.041　　　　　Biblical theology

Class theology of a specific part of Old or New Testament with the part, e.g., theology of Pauline epistles 227.06; class biblical theology of a specific topic with the topic in 231–260, e.g., New Testament writers' view of war and peace 261.87309015

.041 1　　　　Christian theology of Old Testament

.041 5　　　　Christian theology of New Testament

.042　　　　　Theology of Eastern and Roman Catholic churches

Class specific schools and systems of theology in 230.046

.044　　　　　Protestant theology

Class specific schools of Protestant theology in 230.046

.046　　　　　Specific schools and systems of theology

Including dominion, existentialist, liberal, neo-orthodox, process theologies

[.046 01–.046 09]　　Standard subdivisions

Do not use; class in 230.01–230.09

.046 2　　　　Evangelical and fundamentalist theology

.046 24　　　　Evangelical theology

.046 26　　　　Fundamentalist theology

.046 3　　　　Dispensationalist theology

.046 4　　　　Liberation theology

.05–.06　　Standard subdivisions of Christian theology

.07　　　　Education, research, related topics of Christian theology

.071　　　　Education in Christianity, in Christian theology

Class here Christianity as an academic subject

Class comprehensive works on Christian religious education, religious education to inculcate Christian faith and practice, catechetics in 268

See Manual at 207.5, 268 vs. 200.71, 230.071, 292–299

.071 1   Higher education in Christianity, in Christian theology

> Class here Bible colleges, divinity schools, theological seminaries, graduate and undergraduate faculties of theology; education of ministers, pastors, priests, theologians

> Class training for clergy in a specialized subject with the subject, plus notation 0711 from Table 1, e.g., education in pastoral counseling 253.50711

>> *For higher education for specific denominations and sects, see 230.073*

>> *See Manual at 207.5, 268 vs. 200.71, 230.071, 292–299*

.071 14–.071 19   Higher education in specific continents, countries, localities

> Class here nondenominational and interdenominational schools and courses

.073   Higher education for specific denominations and sects

> Add to base number 230.073 the numbers following 28 in 281–289, e.g., Roman Catholic seminaries 230.0732, a Roman Catholic seminary in Dublin 230.073241835

.08–.09   Standard subdivisions of Christian theology

> *See Manual at 230–280*

.1–.9   Doctrines of specific denominations and sects

> Add to base number 230 the numbers following 28 in 281–289, e.g., Methodist doctrines 230.7

> *See Manual at 230–280; also at 270, 230.11–230.14 vs. 230.15–230.2, 281.5–281.9, 282*

> (Option: Class here specific doctrines of specific denominations and sects; prefer 231–236. If option is chosen, add as above, then add 0* and to the result add the numbers following 23 in 231–236, e.g., Methodist doctrines on salvation 230.704)

>   ## 231–239   Christian doctrinal theology

> Class here antagonism between and reconciliation of a specific Christian doctrine and a secular discipline

> Class specific types of Christian doctrinal theology in 230.042–230.046; class comprehensive works on Christian doctrinal theology in 230; class comprehensive works on doctrines of specific denominations and sects in 230.1–230.9; class comprehensive works on antagonism between and reconciliation of Christian belief and a secular discipline in 261.5

---

*Add 00 for standard subdivisions; see instructions at beginning of Table 1

> ## 231–236   Specific topics in Christian doctrinal theology

Class here specific doctrines of specific denominations and sects
(Option: Class specific doctrines of specific denominations and sects in
230.1–230.9)

Class comprehensive works in 230

231   God

.04   Special topics of God

.042   Ways of knowing God

Including faith, reason, tradition

Class proofs of existence of God based on reason alone in 212.1; class
revelation in 231.74

.044   General concepts of God

Including non-Trinitarian concepts

Class here comprehensive works on Holy Trinity

> ### 231.1–231.3   Holy Trinity

Class comprehensive works in 231.044

.1   **God the Father**

.2   **God the Son**

For Jesus Christ, see 232

.3   **God the Holy Spirit**

For gifts of and baptism in the Holy Spirit, see 234.13

.4   **Attributes**

Including omnipotence, omnipresence, omniscience, transcendence

*For love and wisdom, see 231.6; for sovereignty, see 231.7; for justice and
goodness, see 231.8*

.5   **Providence**

.6   **Love and wisdom**

.7   **Relation to the world**

Including relation to nature, sovereignty

Class here God's relation to individual believers

Class redemption in 234.3; class divine law in 241.2; class believers' experience of God in 248.2; class God's relation to the church in 262.7

For Providence, see 231.5

.72   Kingdom of God

Class Kingdom of God to come in 236

.73   Miracles

Class here miracles associated with saints, comprehensive works on miracles

For miracles associated with Mary, see 232.917; for miracles of Jesus, see 232.955; for stigmata, see 248.29

.74   Revelation

For private visions, see 248.29

.745   Prophecy

For Biblical prophecy and prophecies, see 220.15; for messianic prophecies, see 232.12; for eschatological prophecies, see 236

.76   Relation to and action in history

Including covenant relationship, relationship to the Jewish people

.765   Creation

For creation of humankind, see 233.11

.765 2   Relation of scientific and Christian viewpoints of origin of universe

Class here creationism, creation science, evolution versus creation, reconciliation of evolution and creation

See also 379.28 for teaching creationism in public schools

See Manual at 231.7652 vs. 213, 500, 576.8

.8   **Justice and goodness**

Including good and evil

Class here theodicy (vindication of God's justice and goodness in permitting existence of evil and suffering)

For providence, see 231.5; for Christian ethics, see 241

232   **Jesus Christ and his family   Christology**

> .1–232.8   **Christology**

    Class life of Jesus in 232.9; class comprehensive works in 232

.1   **Incarnation and messiahship of Christ**

            Including typology

.12   Messianic prophecies

.2   **Christ as Logos (Word of God)**

.3   **Christ as Redeemer**

            Including atonement

            Class comprehensive works on the doctrine of redemption in 234.3

            For sacrifice of Christ, see 232.4

.4   **Sacrifice of Christ**

.5   **Resurrection of Christ**

.8   **Divinity and humanity of Christ**

            Including Person; offices as Prophet, Priest, King; intercession

            Class here hypostatic union

            Class non-Trinitarian concepts of Jesus in 232.9

            For incarnation, see 232.1; for Christ as Logos, see 232.2; for Christ as Redeemer, see 232.3

.9   **Family and life of Jesus**

            Class here non-Trinitarian concepts of Jesus, rationalistic interpretations of Jesus

            For Islamic doctrines about Jesus, see 297.2465

            See Manual at 230–280

.900 1–.900 9   Standard subdivisions

.901   Life of Jesus

                  For birth, infancy, childhood of Jesus, see 232.92; for adulthood of Jesus, see 232.95–232.97

.903   Character and personality of Jesus

.904   Jesus as teacher and exemplar

            Including influence

            Class teachings in 232.954

.906	Jewish interpretations of Jesus
.908	Historicity of Jesus
.91	Mary, mother of Jesus

Class here Mariology

Class Mary's husband and parents in 232.93

.911	Immaculate Conception
.912	Annunciation
.913	Virginity
.914	Assumption (Ascent to heaven)
.917	Miracles and apparitions
.92	Birth, infancy, childhood of Jesus

Including Holy Family, circumcision, massacre of innocents, flight into Egypt

Class here Christmas story

For Mary, see 232.91; for Joseph, see 232.932

.921	Virgin birth
.922	Adoration of shepherds
.923	Wise men (Magi)
.927	Childhood of Jesus

For presentation in temple, see 232.928; for Jesus among doctors in temple, see 232.929

.928	Presentation in temple
.929	Jesus among doctors in temple
.93	Mary's husband and parents
.932	Joseph
.933	Joachim and Anne
.94	John the Baptist
.95	Public life of Jesus

Including baptism, temptation, calling of apostles

.954	Teachings

Class texts and interpretations of New Testament passages narrating parables in 226.8

.955	Miracles

Class texts and interpretations of New Testament passages narrating miracles in 226.7

.956	Transfiguration
.957	Last Supper
.958	Last words to disciples
.96	Passion and death of Jesus
.961	Betrayal by Judas

> Class comprehensive works on Judas Iscariot in 226.092

.962	Trial and condemnation
.963	Crucifixion and death
.963 5	Seven last words on cross
.964	Burial
.966	Relics of Passion
.967	Descent into hell
.97	Resurrection, appearances, ascension of Jesus

233 Humankind

Class salvation in 234

.1 Creation and fall

.11 Creation

Including relation of human creation and human evolution

Class comprehensive works on creation in 231.765

.14 Original sin and fall

Class sins in 241.3

.4 Accountability

Including guilt

.5 Nature

Including body, soul, spirit, sexuality; humankind as image and likeness of God, as child of God

Class free will in 233.7

For original sin, see 233.14; for death, see 236.1; for immortality, see 236.22

.7 Freedom of choice between good and evil

Class predestination and free will in relation to salvation in 234.9

For accountability, see 233.4

234   **Salvation and grace**

> Variant name for salvation: soteriology

> Including election, innate virtues, merit, universal priesthood

.1   **Kinds and means of grace**

> Including actual and sanctifying grace

.13   Spiritual gifts

> Including interpretation of tongues, prophecy, working of miracles, helps, governments, apostleship, teaching, exhortation, speaking words of wisdom and knowledge

> Class here gifts of and baptism in the Holy Spirit

> *For faith, see 234.23*

.131   Healing

> Spiritual, emotional, or physical

> *For discussion of whether cures are miracles, see 231.73*

> *See Manual at 615.852 vs. 203.1, 234.131, 292–299*

.132   Speaking in tongues (Glossolalia)

.16   Sacraments

> Class liturgy and ritual of sacraments in 265

.161   Baptism

.161 2   Infant baptism

.161 3   Adult baptism

.162   Confirmation

.163   Eucharist (Holy Communion, Lord's Supper)

.164   Holy Orders

.165   Matrimony

.166   Penance

> Including confession

.167   Anointing of the sick

.2   **Faith and hope**

> *See also 236 for eschatology; also 241.4 for virtues*

.23   Faith

.25   Hope

.3   **Redemption**

.4	**Regeneration**
.5	**Repentance and forgiveness**

Including atonement, reconciliation

.6	**Obedience**
.7	**Justification**
.8	**Sanctification and holiness**
.9	**Predestination and free will**

235   Spiritual beings

For Mariology, see 232.91

.2   **Saints**

Class miracles associated with saints in 231.73

For Joseph, see 232.932; for Joachim and Anne, see 232.933; for John the Baptist, see 232.94

See Manual at 230–280

.24   Beatification and canonization

>   **235.3–235.4   Pure spirits**

Class comprehensive works in 235

For God, see 231

.3   **Angels**

Including archangels, celestial hierarchy, cherubim, seraphim

.4   **Devils (Demons)**

Class here spiritual warfare

.47   Satan (Lucifer)

236   Eschatology

Including Antichrist

Class here Kingdom of God to come

.1   **Death**

.2   **Future state (Life after death)**

Class resurrection of the dead in 236.8

For intermediate state, see 236.4

.21   Eternity

.22	Immortality

> *For conditional immortality, see 236.23*

.23	Conditional immortality (Annihilationism)
.24	Heaven
.25	Hell
.4	**Intermediate state**

Probation after death

Including limbo of fathers (limbus patrum), limbo of infants (limbus infantium)

> *For purgatory, see 236.5*

.5	**Purgatory**
.8	**Resurrection of the dead**
.9	**Last Judgment and related events**

Including Armageddon, Day of the Lord, end of the world, Judgment of Christ, millennium, rapture, Second Coming of Christ, tribulation

Class interdisciplinary works on end of the world in 001.9

[237]   **[Unassigned]**

Most recently used in Edition 16

238   **Creeds, confessions of faith, covenants, catechisms**

Class catechetics in 268. Class creeds and catechisms on a specific doctrine with the doctrine, e.g., attributes of God 231.4

.1	**Early and Eastern creeds**
.11	Apostles' Creed
.14	Nicene and post-Nicene creeds of Western Church

Including Constantinopolitan Creed

.142	Nicene Creed
.144	Athanasian Creed
.19	Eastern Church
.2–.9	**Other denominations**

Add to base number 238 the numbers following 28 in 282–289, e.g., Lutheran catechisms 238.41

239   Apologetics and polemics

> Apologetics: systematic argumentation in defense of the divine origin and authority of Christianity

> Standard subdivisions are added for either or both topics in heading

> Class apologetics of specific denominations in 230.1–230.9. Class apologetics and polemics on a specific doctrine with the doctrine, e.g., on doctrine of Holy Trinity 231.044

> *See also 273 for doctrinal controversies and heresies in general church history*

.1   **Apologetics and polemics in apostolic times**

> *For polemics against doctrines of specific groups in apostolic times, see 239.2–239.4*

> ――――――――――

>   **239.2–239.4   Polemics against doctrines of specific groups in apostolic times**

> Class comprehensive works in 239.1

.2   **Polemics against Jews in apostolic times**

.3   **Polemics against pagans and heathens in apostolic times**

.4   **Polemics against Neoplatonists in apostolic times**

.7   **Polemics against rationalists, agnostics, apostates, atheists in postapostolic times**

> Including polemics against deists, materialists, scientists, secular humanists

.9   **Polemics against other groups in postapostolic times**

> Class comprehensive postapostolic defenses of and attacks on doctrines of specific denominations or sects in 230.1–230.9. Class attacks on doctrines of a specific religion with the religion, e.g., doctrines of Judaism 296.3

.93   Polemics against new age groups and doctrines

240   Christian moral and devotional theology

SUMMARY

241	**Christian ethics**
242	**Devotional literature**
243	**Evangelistic writings for individuals and families**
246	**Use of art in Christianity**
247	**Church furnishings and related articles**
248	**Christian experience, practice, life**
249	**Christian observances in family life**

241   Christian ethics

Variant name: Moral theology

See Manual at 241 vs. 261.8

.04   Specific branches, denominations, sects

Add to base number 241.04 the numbers following 28 in 280.2–289, e.g., Protestant ethics 241.0404

.1   **Conscience**

.2   **Laws and bases of morality**

Including divine law, natural law

Class here relation of law and gospel

For codes of conduct, see 241.5

.3   **Sin and vices**

Standard subdivisions are added for either or both topics in heading

Including specific vices

Class original sin in 233.14

For specific moral issues, see 241.6

.31   Mortal and venial sin

.4   **Virtues**

Including specific virtues

Class faith and hope as means of salvation in 234.2

For specific moral issues, see 241.6

.5   **Codes of conduct**

For specific moral issues, see 241.6

.52   Ten Commandments

.53   Sermon on the Mount

.54   Golden Rule

.6   **Specific moral issues**

Add to base number 241.6 the numbers following 17 in 172–179, e.g., morality of warfare 241.6242, of abortion 241.6976; however, for specific vices, see 241.3; for specific virtues, see 241.4

242   Devotional literature

Class here texts of meditations, contemplations, prayers for individuals and families, religious poetry intended for devotional use

Unless other instructions are given, observe the following table of preference, e.g., prayers and meditations for daily use based on passages from the Bible 242.2 (*not* 242.5):

Prayers and meditations for use in times of illness, trouble, bereavement	242.4
Prayers and meditations for specific classes of persons	242.6
Prayers and meditations for daily use	242.2
Prayers and meditations for church year, other Christian feast and fast days	242.3
Prayers and meditations based on passages from the Bible	242.5
Specific prayers and groups of prayers	242.7
Collections of prayers	242.8

Class devotional literature on a specific subject with the subject, e.g., meditations on passion and death of Jesus 232.96

For evangelistic writings, see 243; for hymns, see 264.23

.08   History and description with respect to kinds of persons

Do not use for devotional literature for specific classes of persons; class in 242.6

.2   **Prayers and meditations for daily use**

Not limited to saints' days or specific parts of the church year

Including meditations and prayers for Sunday, Sabbath

Class prayers and meditations for daily use for specific classes of persons in 242.6

.3   **Prayers and meditations for church year, other Christian feast and fast days**

Class orayers and meditations for church year, other Christian feast and fast days for specific classes of persons in 242.6

\>   242.33–242.36   Church year

Class comprehensive works in 242.3

For Pentecost and time after Pentecost (Ordinary time), see 242.38

.33   Advent and Christmas

.332   Advent

.335   Christmas season

Class here Christmas day

.34	Lent

For Holy Week, see 242.35

.35	Holy Week
.36	Easter season

Including Ascension Day

Class here Easter Sunday

.37	Other Christian feast and fast days

Including saints' days

.38	Pentecost and time after Pentecost (Ordinary time)
.4	**Prayers and meditations for use in times of illness, trouble, bereavement**
.5	**Prayers and meditations based on passages from the Bible**

Class interpretation and criticism of Bible passages for other than devotional use in 220.6; class Bible prayers in 242.722

.6	**Prayers and meditations for specific classes of persons**

Class here prayers and meditations for daily use, church year, other Christian feast and fast days for specific classes of persons

Add to base number 242.6 the numbers following 248.8 in 248.82–248.89, e.g., prayers and meditations for college students 242.634; however, for prayers and meditations for use in times of illness, trouble, bereavement, see 242.4

Class collections of prayers for specific classes of persons in 242.82–242.89

.7	**Specific prayers and groups of prayers**
.72	Specific types of prayers

Including doxologies

Class here prayers to Father, Son, Holy Spirit

.722	Bible prayers

>	242.74–242.76 Prayers addressed to spiritual beings other than God

Class comprehensive works in 242.7

.74	Prayers to Mary

Including Ave Maria (Hail Mary), Rosary

.75	Prayers to Joseph, Joachim, Anne
.76	Prayers to saints and angels

For Joseph, Joachim, Anne, see 242.75

.8   **Collections of prayers**

Class here prayer books

For specific prayers and groups of prayers, see 242.7

.800 1–.800 7   Standard subdivisions

.800 8   History and description with respect to kinds of persons

Do not use for collections of prayers for specific classes of persons; class in 242.82–242.89

.800 9   Historical, geographic, persons treatment

.801–.809   Collections of prayers by adherents of specific denominations and sects

Add to base number 242.80 the numbers following 28 in 281–289, e.g., collections of private prayers by Methodists 242.807

.82–.89   Collections of prayers for specific classes of persons

Add to base number 242.8 the numbers following 248.8 in 248.82–248.89, e.g., collections of private prayers for college students 242.834

For collections of prayers by adherents of specific denominations and sects, see 242.801–242.809

243   **Evangelistic writings for individuals and families**

Works designed to convert readers, promote repentance

Class evangelistic sermons in 252.3

[244]   **[Unassigned]**

Most recently used in Edition 15

[245]   **[Unassigned]**

Most recently used in Edition 21

246   **Use of art in Christianity**

Religious meaning, significance, purpose

Class attitude of Christianity and Christian church toward secular art, the arts in 261.57; class creation, description, critical appraisal as art in 700

For church furnishings and related articles, see 247

\>   **246.1–246.4**   **Schools and styles**

Class specific elements by school and style in 246.5–246.9; class comprehensive works in 246; class interdisciplinary works on schools and styles of Christian art in 709.015–709.05

.1   **Byzantine and Gothic art**

.2   **Early Christian and Romanesque art**

.4 **Renaissance and modern art**

Including Protestant art

> **246.5–246.9 Specific elements**

Class comprehensive works in 246

.5 **Icons, symbols, insignia**

.53 Icons

.55 Symbols

Including banners, emblems, incense, votive offerings

Class here Christian symbolism

For colors and lights, see 246.6

.558 Crosses and crucifixes

Standard subdivisions are added for either or both topics in heading

.56 Insignia

Including insignia of rank

.6 **Colors and lights**

.7 **Dramatic, musical, rhythmic arts**

Including dance, liturgical dance

.72 Dramatic arts

.723 Passion plays

.725 Puppetry

.75 Music

Class here comprehensive works on music in Christianity

Class attitude of Christianity and Christian church toward secular music in 261.578; class interdisciplinary works on Christian sacred music in 781.71

For music in public worship, see 264.2

.9 **Architecture**

Add to base number 246.9 the numbers following 726 in 726.4–726.9, e.g., cathedral church buildings 246.96; however, for church furnishings, see 247

247 **Church furnishings and related articles**

Including paintings, plastic arts, sculpture, structural decoration, textiles

.1 **Furniture**

248   Christian experience, practice, life

Class here spirituality

See Manual at 230–280

SUMMARY

248.06	**Organizations and management**
.2	**Religious experience**
.3	**Worship**
.4	**Christian life and practice**
.5	**Witness bearing**
.6	**Stewardship**
.8	**Guides to Christian life for specific classes of persons**

.06   Organizations and management

Class pious societies, sodalities, confraternities in 267

.2   **Religious experience**

.22   Mysticism

.24   Conversion

For moral renewal and commitment, see 248.25

>   248.242–248.246   Conversion from one system of belief to another

Class comprehensive works in 248.24

For conversion of Christians to another religion, see the religion, e.g., conversion of Christians to Judaism 296.714

.242   Conversion from Protestantism to Roman Catholicism

.244   Conversion from Roman Catholicism to Protestantism

.246   Conversion from non-Christianity to Christianity

.25   Moral renewal and commitment

.29   Other religious experiences

Including stigmata, private visions

Class spiritual gifts in 234.13; class speaking in tongues (glossolalia) in 234.132

.3   **Worship**

Class here comprehensive works on worship

Class texts of prayers and devotions in 242

For observances in family life, see 249; for public worship, see 264

.32   Prayer

.34	Meditation and contemplation

Standard subdivisions are added for either or both topics in heading

.4 Christian life and practice

Class here Christian marriage and family

For Christian ethics, see 241; for worship, see 248.3; for witness bearing, see 248.5; for stewardship, see 248.6; for Christian observances in family life, see 249

.408 History and description with respect to kinds of persons

Do not use for guides to Christian life for specific classes of persons; class in 248.8

.46 Individual observances

Including ceremonial and ritual observances, observance of restrictions and limitations

For asceticism, see 248.47; for pilgrimages, see 263.041

.47 Asceticism

Attitudes and practices aside from and beyond normal moral duties adopted as aids to moral and spiritual development

Including practice of celibacy, fasting and abstinence, poverty, solitude, other physical austerities, e.g., flagellation

For clerical celibacy, see 253.25; for practices of religious congregations and orders, see 255

.48 Guides to Christian life by or for adherents of specific branches, denominations, sects

Add to base number 248.48 the numbers following 28 in 280.2–289, e.g., guides for Roman Catholics 248.482

Class guides to Christian life for specific classes of persons who are adherents of specific denominations and sects in 248.8

.5 Witness bearing

.6 Stewardship

.8 Guides to Christian life for specific classes of persons

Class here guides to Christian life for specific classes of persons who are adherents of specific denominations and sects

Class guides to a specific aspect of Christian life with the aspect, e.g., prayer 248.32

.808 History and description with respect to kinds of persons

[.808 1] Men

Do not use; class in 248.842

[.808 2]	Women

Do not use; class in 248.843

| [.808 3] | Young people |

Do not use for children; class in 248.82. Do not use for adolescents; class in 248.83

| [.808 4] | Persons in specific stages of adulthood |

Do not use; class in 248.84

| .808 5 | Relatives |

Do not use for parents; class in 248.845

| .808 6 | Persons by miscellaneous social characteristics |

| .808 65 | Persons by marriage status |

Do not use for men by marital status; class in 248.8422–248.8429. Do not use for women by marital status; class in 248.8432–248.8439

| [.808 653] | Separated and divorced persons |

Do not use; class in 248.846

| [.808 655] | Married persons |

Do not use; class in 248.844

| .808 7 | Gifted persons |

Do not use for persons with disabilities or illnesses; class in 248.86

| [.808 8] | Occupational and religious groups |

Do not use for adherents of specific denominations or sects; class in 248.48. Do not use for occupational groups; class in 248.88. Do not use for clergy or persons in religious orders; class in 248.89

> 248.82–248.85   Guides to Christian life for specific age groups

Class persons of specific ages in specific occupational groups or experiencing illness, trouble, bereavement in 248.86–248.89; class comprehensive works in 248.8

| .82 | Children |

Through age eleven

| .83 | Adolescents and college students |

Standard subdivisions are added for adolescents and college students together, for adolescents alone

| .832 | Male adolescents |

| .833 | Female adolescents |

.834   College students

Male and female

.84   Adults

For persons in late adulthood, see 248.85

.842   Men

.842 1   Fathers

Regardless of marital status

.842 2–.842 9   Men by marital status

Add to base number 248.842 the numbers following —0865 in notation 08652–08659 from Table 1, e.g., guides for husbands 248.8425

Class fathers in 248.8421

.843   Women

.843 1   Mothers

Regardless of marital status

.843 2–.843 9   Women by marital status

Add to base number 248.843 the numbers following —0865 in notation 08652–08659 from Table 1, e.g., guides for wives 248.8435

Class mothers in 248.8431

.844   Married couples

Class husbands in 248.8425; class wives in 248.8435

.845   Parents

Class here Christian child rearing, Christian religious training of children in the home

For fathers, see 248.8421; for mothers, see 248.8431

.846   Separated and divorced persons

For separated and divorced men, see 248.8423; for separated and divorced women, see 248.8433

.85   Persons in late adulthood

> 248.86–248.89   Guides to Christian life for occupational classes; persons experiencing illness, trouble, bereavement

Class comprehensive works in 248.8

.86   Persons experiencing illness, trouble, bereavement

.861–.864   Persons experiencing specific illnesses and disabilities

> Add to base number 248.86 the numbers following 362 in 362.1–362.4, e.g., persons experiencing addiction 248.8629
>
> *See Manual at 616.86 vs. 158.1, 204.42, 248.8629, 292–299, 362.29*

.866   Persons experiencing bereavement

.88   Occupational classes

> *For religious groups, see 248.89*

.89   Religious groups

.892   Clergy

> *For persons in religious orders, see 248.894*

.894   Persons in religious orders

.894 2   Men

.894 22   Vocation

.894 25   Selection and novitiate

.894 3   Women

.894 32   Vocation

.894 35   Selection and novitiate

249   Christian observances in family life

> Class here family prayer; family observance of religious restrictions, rites, ceremonies

---

> ## 250–280   Christian church

> Class comprehensive works in 260

250   Local Christian church and Christian religious orders

> Standard subdivisions are added for local Christian church and Christian religious orders together, for local Christian church alone
>
> Class public worship in 264; class missions in 266; class religious education in 268

SUMMARY

250.1–.9	**Standard subdivisions**
251	**Preaching (Homiletics)**
252	**Texts of sermons**
253	**Pastoral office and work (Pastoral theology)**
254	**Parish administration**
255	**Religious congregations and orders**
259	**Pastoral care of families, of specific kinds of persons**

[.68]   Management

> Do not use for management of local Christian church and Christian religious orders together; class in 250. Do not use for management of local Christian church; class in 254

.9   **Historical, geographic, persons treatment**

> Class general historical treatment of local church in specific continents, countries, localities in 274–279; class historical, geographic, persons treatment of specific denominations in 280

>   **251–254 Local church**

Class here basic Christian communities

Class the local church in overall church organization in 262.2; class comprehensive works in 250

For pastoral care of families, of specific kinds of persons, see 259

See Manual at 260 vs. 251–254, 259

251   **Preaching (Homiletics)**

Class texts of sermons in 252; class pastoral methods in 253.7

.001–.009   Standard subdivisions

.01   Preparation

.02   Sermon outlines

.03   Delivery

> Class here voice, expression, gesture

.07   Radio and television preaching

> Class specific aspects of radio and television preaching in 251.01–251.03

.08   Homiletic illustrations

.1–.9   **Material for preparation of sermons for specific occasions, for specific classes of persons**

> Add to base number 251 the numbers following 252 in 252.1–252.9, e.g., material for preparation of sermons arranged for the church year 251.6

252   Texts of sermons

Class sermons on a specific subject with the subject, e.g., God's Providence 231.5

.001–.009   Standard subdivisions

.01–.09   Texts of sermons by specific denominations and sects

Add to base number 252.0 the numbers following 28 in 281–289, e.g., Anglican sermons 252.03

.1   Texts of sermons for baptisms, confirmations, funerals, weddings

Class sermons for memorial occasions in 252.9

.3   Texts of sermons for evangelistic meetings

.5   Texts of sermons for specific classes of persons

.53   Children

Through age eleven

.55   Adolescents and young adults

Junior-high-school, high-school, college students

Including academic, chapel, convocation, commencement sermons

.56   Persons in late adulthood, and persons experiencing illness, trouble, bereavement

.58   Occupational classes

For religious groups, see 252.59

.59   Religious groups

.592   Clergy

For persons in religious orders, see 252.594

.594   Persons in religious orders

.6   Texts of sermons for church year and public occasions

Standard subdivisions are added for texts of sermons for church year and public occasions together, for church year alone

---

\>   252.61–252.64   Church year

Class comprehensive works in 252.6

.61   Advent and Christmas

.612   Advent

.615   Christmas season

Class here Christmas day

.62   Lent

	.625	Holy Week
	.63	Easter season

Including Ascension Day

Class here Easter Sunday

	.64	Pentecost and time after Pentecost (Ordinary time)
	.67	Other feast and fast days

Including saints' days

	.68	Secular occasions

Including elections, holidays, thanksgivings

.7 Texts of sermons for consecrations, ordinations, installations

.9 Texts of sermons for memorial occasions

253 Pastoral office and work (Pastoral theology)

Class here the work of priests, ministers, pastors, rectors, vicars, curates, chaplains, elders, deacons, assistants, laity in relation to the work of the church at the local level

Class local clergy and laity in relation to the government, organization and nature of the church as a whole in 262.1; class the ordination of women in 262.14; class the role of clergy in religious education in 268

.08 History and description with respect to kinds of persons

Do not use for pastoral care of specific kinds of persons; class in 259

Class here pastoral care performed by kinds of persons

.09 Historical, geographic, persons treatment

.092 Persons treatment

Do not use for biography of clergy in the period prior to 1054; class in 270.1–270.3. Do not use for biography of clergy in the period subsequent to 1054; class in 280

See Manual at 230–280

.2 Life and person

Including professional and personal qualifications

Class education of clergy in 230.0711; class guides to Christian life for clergy in 248.892

.22 Families of clergy

.25 Clerical celibacy

Add to base number 253.25 the numbers following 28 in 281–289, e.g., clerical celibacy in Roman Catholic church 253.252, in Roman Catholic church in United States 253.25273

> **253.5–253.7 Pastoral duties and responsibilities**

> Class methods for services to families, to specific kinds of persons in 259; class comprehensive works in 253
>
> *For preaching, see 251; for parish administration, see 254*

.5 **Counseling and spiritual direction**

> Class pastoral counseling, spiritual direction of specific kinds of persons in 259; class premarital, marriage, family counseling in 259.12–259.14

.52 Pastoral psychology

.53 Spiritual direction

.7 **Pastoral methods**

> Including group work, telephone work

.76 Pastoral methods in homes

.78 Use of radio and television

254 Parish administration

.001–.009 Standard subdivisions

.01–.09 Parish administration by specific denominations and sects

> Add to base number 254.0 the numbers following 28 in 281–289, e.g., administration of Roman Catholic parishes 254.02

.1 **Initiation of new churches**

.2 **Parish administration in specific kinds of communities**

> Class a specific activity in a specific kind of community with the activity, e.g., membership promotion 254.5

.22 Urban communities

.23 Suburban communities

.24 Rural communities

.3 **Use of communications media**

> Including use of audiovisual materials

.4 **Public relations and publicity**

> *For use of communications media, see 254.3*

.5 **Membership**

> Promotion and growth

.6 **Programs**

> Planning and execution

.7 **Buildings, equipment, grounds**

.8   **Finance**

> Including budget, expenditures, income, methods of raising money

255   Religious congregations and orders

> Class here monasticism, comprehensive works on Christian religious congregations and orders
>
> When adding from 271 to indicate kinds of orders or specific orders, add only the notation for the kind or order. Do not use the footnote instruction to add as instructed under 271, but add notation from the table under 255.1–255.7 if it applies, or add notation 01–09 from Table 1. For example, the correct number for contemplative orders in the United Kingdom is 255.010941 (*not* 255.01041); for Benedictines in the United Kingdom 255.100941 (*not* 255.1041)
>
>> *For guides to Christian life for persons in religious orders, see 248.894; for religious congregations and orders in church organization, see 262.24; for religious congregations and orders, monasticism in church history, see 271. For specific types of activity of religious congregations and orders, see the activity, e.g., pastoral counseling 253.5, missionary work 266*

.001–.009   Standard subdivisions

.01–.09   Specific kinds of congregations and orders

> Add to base number 255.0 the numbers following 271.0 in 271.01–271.09 for the kind only, e.g., contemplative orders 255.01; then, for each kind having its own number, add notation 01–09 from Table 1 (*not* as instructed under 271), e.g., contemplative orders in the United Kingdom 255.010941

.1–.7   **Roman Catholic orders of men**

> Add to base number 255 the numbers following 271 in 271.1–271.7 for the order only, e.g., Benedictines 255.1; then, for each order having its own number, add further as follows (*not* as instructed at 271), e.g., Benedictines in the United Kingdom 255.100941, the rule of St. Benedict 255.106:
>
> | | |
> |---|---|
> | 001–009 | Standard subdivisions |
> | 02 | Constitutions |
> | 04 | Statutes, ordinances, customs |
> | 06 | Rule |

.8   **Non-Roman Catholic orders of men**

.81   Monasticism of Eastern churches

> Add to base number 255.81 the numbers following 281 in 281.5–281.9, e.g., Eastern Orthodox monasticism 255.819

.83   Anglican orders of men

.9   **Congregations and orders of women**

.900 1–.900 9   Standard subdivisions

.901–.909   Specific kinds of congregations and orders

> Add to base number 255.90 the numbers following 271.0 in 271.01–271.09 for the kind only, e.g., contemplative orders 255.901; then, for each kind having its own number, add notation 01–09 from Table 1 (*not* as instructed under 271), e.g., contemplative orders in the United Kingdom 255.9010941

.91–.97   Roman Catholic orders of women

Add to base number 255.9 the numbers following 271.9 in 271.91–271.97 for the order only, e.g., Dominican sisters 255.972 ; then, for each order having its own number, add further as instructed under 255.1–255.7 (*not* as instructed at 271), e.g., Dominicans in the United Kingdom 255.97200941, the rule of the Dominicans 255.97206

.98   Non-Roman Catholic orders of women

.981   Monasticism of women of Eastern churches

Add to base number 255.981 the numbers following 281 in 281.5–281.9, e.g., Eastern Orthodox monasticism of women 255.9819

.983   Anglican orders of women

[256]   [Unassigned]

Most recently used in Edition 14

[257]   [Unassigned]

Most recently used in Edition 14

[258]   [Unassigned]

Most recently used in Edition 17

259   Pastoral care of families, of specific kinds of persons

Former heading: Activities of the local church

Performed by clergy or laity

Class here pastoral counseling of specific kinds of persons

Unless other instructions are given, observe the following table of preference, e.g., pastoral care of bereaved young people 259.6 (*not* 259.2):

Pastoral care of the bereaved	259.6
Pastoral care of delinquents and criminals	259.5
Pastoral care of persons with disabilities, with physical or mental illnesses	259.4
Pastoral care of families	259.1
Pastoral care of young people	259.2
Pastoral care of persons in late adulthood	259.3

Class comprehensive works on pastoral care of more than one kind of person in 253

See also 253.08 for pastoral care performed by kinds of persons; also 361.75 for works limited to social welfare work by religious organizations

See Manual at 260 vs. 251–254, 259

[.01–.07]   Standard subdivisions

Do not use; class in 253.01–253.07

.08	History and description with respect to kinds of persons

Do not use for bereaved persons; class in 259.6

[.083]	Young people

Do not use; class in 259.2

.084	Persons in specific stages of adulthood
[.084 2]	Young adults

Do not use; class in 259.25

[.084 6]	Persons in late adulthood

Do not use; class in 259.3

.086	Persons by miscellaneous social characteristics
[.086 92]	Antisocial and asocial persons

Do not use; class in 259.5

.087	Gifted persons

Do not use for persons with disabilities and illnesses; class in 259.4

.088	Occupational and religious groups
[.088 371 8]	Students

Do not use; class in 259.2

[.09]	Historical, geographic, persons treatment

Do not use; class in 253.09

.1	**Pastoral care of families**
.12	Family counseling

For premarital counseling, see 259.13; for marriage counseling, see 259.14

.13	Premarital counseling
.14	Marriage counseling
.2	**Pastoral care of young people**
.22	Pastoral care of children

Through age eleven

.23	Pastoral care of adolescents

Ages twelve through seventeen; junior-high-school and high-school students

Class here comprehensive works on pastoral care of adolescents and young adults

For pastoral care of young adults eighteen and older, see 259.25

.24	Pastoral care of college students

Class here campus ministry

.25 Pastoral care of young adults

> Aged eighteen and above

> *For pastoral care of college students, see 259.24*

.3 Pastoral care of persons in late adulthood

.4 Pastoral care of persons with disabilities, with physical or mental illnesses

> Class here programs for visiting the sick

> Add to base number 259.4 the numbers following 362 in 362.1–362.4, e.g., pastoral care of those who have attempted suicide 259.428

.5 Pastoral care of delinquents and criminals

> Class here prison chaplaincy, pastoral care of antisocial and asocial persons

.6 Pastoral care of the bereaved

260 Christian social and ecclesiastical theology

> Institutions, services, observances, disciplines, work of Christianity and Christian church

> Class here comprehensive works on Christian church

> *For local church and religious orders, see 250; for denominations and sects, see 280*

> *See Manual at 260 vs. 251–254, 259*

SUMMARY

260.9	**Historical, geographic, persons treatment**
261	**Social theology and interreligious relations and attitudes**
262	**Ecclesiology**
263	**Days, times, places of religious observance**
264	**Public worship**
265	**Sacraments, other rites and acts**
266	**Missions**
267	**Associations for religious work**
268	**Religious education**
269	**Spiritual renewal**

.9 Historical, geographic, persons treatment

> Do not use for historical, geographic, persons treatment of Christian church; class in 270

261 Social theology and interreligious relations and attitudes

> Attitude of Christianity and Christian church toward and influence on secular matters, attitude toward other religions, interreligious relations

> Class here Christianity and culture

> Class sociology of religion in 306.6

.1   **Role of Christian church in society**

Class specific socioeconomic problems in 261.8

.2   **Christianity and other systems of belief**

.21   Christianity and irreligion

Including Christianity and communism, Christianity and the apostate and indifferent

.22–.29   Christianity and other religions

Add to base number 261.2 the numbers following 29 in 292–299, e.g., Christianity and Islam 261.27

.5   **Christianity and secular disciplines**

Class here antagonism between and reconciliation of Christian belief and a secular discipline

For antagonism between and reconciliation of a specific Christian doctrine and a secular discipline, see the doctrine in 231–239, e.g., relation between Christian doctrine on the soul and modern biology 233.5

See Manual at 261.5

.51   Philosophy, logic, related disciplines

.513   Parapsychology and occultism

.515   Psychology

.52   Communications media

Class here comprehensive works on attitude toward and use of communications media

For a specific use of communications media by the church, see the use, e.g., use in parish administration 254.3

.55   Science

Class the relation of scientific and Christian views on creation in 231.765

.56   Technology

.561   Medicine

.57   The arts

.578   Music

.58   Literature

.7   Christianity and political affairs

Including civil war and revolution

Class here Christianity and civil rights

For Christianity and international affairs, see 261.87

See Manual at 322.1 vs. 201.72, 261.7, 292–299

.72   Religious freedom

.73   Theocracy

Supremacy of church over civil government

.8   Christianity and socioeconomic problems

Class here comprehensive works on the Christian view of socioeconomic and political affairs

For Christianity and political affairs, see 261.7

See also 361.75 for welfare services of religious organizations

See Manual at 241 vs. 261.8

.83   Social problems and services

.832   Social welfare problems and services

.832 1–.832 5   Problems of and services to persons with illnesses and disabilities, the poor

Add to base number 261.832 the numbers following 362 in 362.1–362.5, e.g., Christian attitude toward alcoholism 261.832292, toward the poor 261.8325

.832 6   Hunger

.832 7   Abuse within the family

.832 71   Child abuse and neglect

For sexual abuse, see 261.83272

.832 72   Sexual abuse

.832 73   Adults who were victims of abuse as children

.832 8   Refugees and victims of political oppression

.833   Crime

Add to base number 261.833 the numbers following 364 in 364.1–364.8, e.g., Christian attitude toward treason 261.833131, toward capital punishment 261.83366

[.834]   Christian attitudes toward social groups

Relocated to 270.08

.835	Sexual relations, marriage, divorce, family

Add to base number 261.835 the numbers following 306 in 306.7–306.8, e.g., Christian attitude toward divorce 261.83589

Class abuse within the family in 261.8327

.836   Population

Including abortion, family planning

Ecology relocated to 261.88

.85   Economics

Including management of business enterprises

For environment, natural resources, see 261.88

.87   International affairs

.873   War and peace

For civil war and revolution, see 261.7

.873 2   Nuclear weapons and nuclear war

.88   Environment

Class here ecology [*formerly* 261.836], environmental problems, natural resources, pollution

Class environmental ethics in 241.691

262   Ecclesiology

Church government, organization, nature

See Manual at 260 vs. 251–254, 259

SUMMARY

262.001–.009	**Standard subdivisions**
.01–.09	**Government and organization, ecclesiology of specific denominations and sects**
.1	**Governing leaders of churches**
.2	**Local church and religious congregations and orders in church organization**
.3	**Government and organization of systems governed by papacy and episcopacy**
.4	**Government and organization of systems governed by election**
.5	**General councils**
.7	**Nature of the church**
.8	**Church and ministerial authority and its denial**
.9	**Church law and discipline**

.001   Philosophy and theory

.001 1   Ecumenism

Do not use for systems; class in 262.001

See Manual at 280.042 vs. 262.0011

.001 109   Historical, geographic, persons treatment

> Do not use for history of the ecumenical movement; class in 280.042

.001 7   Church renewal

.002–.005   Standard subdivisions

.006   Organizations and particular aspects of administration

.006 8   Particular aspects of administration

> Notation 068 from Table 1 is not used by itself in 262; however, add notation 0681–0688 as appropriate for particular aspects of administration, e.g., financial administration of United Methodist Church 262.0760681

.007–.009   Standard subdivisions

.01–.09   Government and organization, ecclesiology of specific denominations and sects

> Add to base number 262.0 the numbers following 28 in 281–289, e.g., government and organization of the United Methodist Church 262.076

.1   **Governing leaders of churches**

> Authority, function, role

[.109 2]   Persons treatment

> Do not use for biography of church leaders; class in 270. Do not use for biography of leaders of specific denominations; class in 280

> *See Manual at 230–280*

.11   Apostolic succession

>   262.12–262.15   Governing leaders by rank

Class comprehensive works in 262.1

.12   Episcopacy

> Class here bishops, archbishops, national conferences of bishops

> Add to base number 262.12 the numbers following 28 in 281–289, e.g., episcopacy of Anglican churches 262.123, of Church of England 262.12342

> *For papacy and patriarchate, see 262.13*

.13   Papacy and patriarchate

> Standard subdivisions are added for papacy and patriarchate together, for Roman Catholic papacy alone

---

>   262.131–262.136   Specific aspects of Roman Catholic papacy

Class comprehensive works in 262.13

.131	Papal infallibility
.132	Temporal power of the pope
.135	College of Cardinals
.136	Administration

> Including congregations, offices of Curia Romana, Synod of Bishops, tribunals
>
> *For national conferences of bishops, see 262.12; for College of Cardinals, see 262.135*

.14   Local clergy

> Class here ordination of women
>
> Add to base number 262.14 the numbers following 28 in 281–289, e.g., local Methodist clergy 262.147
>
> Class works that treat the ordination of women only in relation to its effect on the local church in 253

.15   Laity

> Body of church members
>
> Add to base number 262.15 the numbers following 28 in 281–289, e.g., laity of Lutheran church 262.1541, in United States 262.154173

>   262.17–262.19   Governing leaders by system of government

> Class leaders by rank in a specific system of government in 262.12–262.15; class comprehensive works in 262.1

.17   Governing leaders in papal and episcopal systems

.18   Governing leaders in presbyterian systems

.19   Governing leaders in congregational systems

.2   **Local church and religious congregations and orders in church organization**

> *For administration of parishes, see 254; for government and administration of religious congregations and orders, see 255*
>
> *See Manual at 260 vs. 251–254, 259*

.22   Parishes

.24   Religious congregations and orders

.26   Small groups

> Including basic Christian communities

> **262.3–262.4   Specific forms of church organization**

Class comprehensive works on government and organization of specific denominations and sects regardless of form of organization in 262.01–262.09; class comprehensive works in 262. Class a specific aspect of government and organization with the aspect, e.g., role of bishops in a system governed by episcopacy 262.12 (*not* 262.3)

.3   **Government and organization of systems governed by papacy and episcopacy**

Including sees, dioceses, cathedral systems

.4   **Government and organization of systems governed by election**

Including congregational systems, presbyteries, synods

.5   **General councils**

Add to base number 262.5 the numbers following 28 in 281–289, e.g., ecumenical councils of Roman Catholic Church 262.52

Class legal acts of general councils in 262.9. Class nonlegal decrees on a specific subject with the subject, e.g., statements on original sin 233.14

.7   **Nature of the church**

Including God's relation to the church

.72   Attributes, marks, notes

Including apostolicity, catholicity, credibility, holiness, infallibility, necessity, unity, visibility and invisibility

.73   Communion of saints

.77   Mystical body of Christ

.8   **Church and ministerial authority and its denial**

Including heresy, schism

.9   **Church law and discipline**

Class here canon (ecclesiastical) law

Class civil law relating to church or religious matters in 340

See also 364.188 for offenses against religion as defined and penalized by the state

> **262.91–262.94   Roman Catholic law**

Class comprehensive works in 262.9

.91   Acts of the Holy See

> Including apostolic letters, briefs, encyclicals, papal bulls and decrees

> Class acts on a specific subject with the subject, e.g., on the nature of the church 262.7

.92   Early Roman Catholic codes

.922   Early codes to Gratian, ca. 1140

.923   Corpus iuris canonici

.924   Quinque compilationes antiquae

.93   Codex iuris canonici (1917)

.931   General principles (Canons 1–86)

.932   Persons (Canons 87–725)

> Clergy, religious, laity

.933   Things (Canons 726–1551)

> Including benefices, sacraments, sacred times and places, teaching office, temporal goods, worship

.934   Procedure (Canons 1552–2194)

> Including trials, cases of beatification and canonization

.935   Crimes and penalties (Canons 2195–2414)

.94   Codex iuris canonici (1983)

.98   Branches and other denominations and sects

> Add to base number 262.98 the numbers following 28 in 280.2–289, e.g., Anglican ecclesiastical law 262.983

263   Days, times, places of religious observance

.04   Special topics of days, times, places of religious observance

.041   Pilgrimages

[.041 093–.041 099]   Specific continents, countries, localities

> Do not use; class in 263.0423–263.0429

.042   Holy places

> Class here pilgrimages to holy places in specific continents, countries, localities

> *For works treating miracles and shrines associated with them, see 231.73; for miracles associated with Mary and shrines associated with them, see 232.917; for miracles of Jesus and shrines associated with them, see 232.955*

[.042 093–.042 099]   Specific continents, countries, localities

Do not use; class in 263.0423–263.0429

.042 3–.042 9   Specific continents, countries, localities

Add to base number 263.042 notation 3–9 from Table 2, e.g., Santiago de Compostela 263.0424611

> **263.1–263.3   Sabbath and Sunday**

Class comprehensive works in 263.3

.1   **Biblical Sabbath**

.2   **Observance of the seventh day**

.3   **Sunday**

Class here Sunday observance, comprehensive works on Sabbath and Sunday

For Biblical Sabbath, see 263.1; for observance of the seventh day, see 263.2

.9   **Church year and other days and times**

Standard subdivisions are added for church year and other days and times together, for church year alone

See Manual at 203.6, 263.9, 292–299 vs. 394.265–394.267

> 263.91–263.94   Church year

Class comprehensive works in 263.9

.91   Advent and Christmas

.912   Advent

.915   Christmas season

Class here Christmas day

.92   Lent

.925   Holy Week

.93   Easter season

Including Ascension Day

Class here Easter Sunday

.94   Pentecost and time after Pentecost (Ordinary time)

.97   Other feast and fast days

For saints' days, see 263.98

.98 Saints' days

Standard subdivisions are added for individual saint's days

264 Public worship

Ceremonies, rites, services (liturgy and ritual)

Class works not limited by denomination or sect about sacraments, other rites and acts in 265; class Sunday school services in 268.7; class comprehensive works on worship in 248.3

SUMMARY

264.001–.009	**Standard subdivisions**
.01–.09	**Public worship by denominations and sects**
.1	**Prayer**
.2	**Music**
.3	**Scripture readings and communion sacrament**
.4	**Responsive readings**
.7	**Prayer meetings, Holy Hours, novenas**
.9	**Sacramentals**

.001 Philosophy and theory

Class here liturgical renewal

.002–.009 Standard subdivisions

> 264.01–264.09 Public worship by denominations and sects

Class here works limited by denomination or sect about sacraments, other rites and acts

Class comprehensive works in 264; class comprehensive works on sacraments, other rites and acts in 265

.01 Early and Eastern churches

Add to base number 264.01 the numbers following 281 in 281.1–281.9, e.g., liturgy and ritual of Eastern Orthodox churches 264.019; then add further as instructed under 264.04–264.09, e.g., Eastern Orthodox Mass 264.019036

.02 Roman Catholic Church

.020 01–.020 09 Standard subdivisions

.020 1–.020 9 History, meaning, place of liturgy, ritual, prayers in public worship

Add to base number 264.02 notation 01–09 from the table under 264.04–264.09, e.g., the Mass 264.02036; however, for texts, see 264.021–264.029

> 264.021–264.029 Texts of liturgy, ritual, prayers

Class comprehensive works in 264.02

.021	Texts of calendars and ordos
.022	Texts of ceremonials

> Ceremonials: canonization of saints, election and coronation of popes, creation of cardinals, other papal functions and services; instructions for bishops

.023	Texts of missals

> Class here sacramentaries
>
> *For lectionary, see 264.029*

.024	Texts of breviaries

> *For psalters, see 264.028*

.025	Texts of ritual

> Class here Pontificale Romanum, Rituale Romanum
>
> Add to base number 264.025 the numbers following 265 in 265.1–265.7, e.g., texts of baptism 264.0251

.027	Texts of special books
.027 2	Texts for special times of year

> Including Holy Week

.027 4	Texts for special liturgical services

> Including funeral services outside the Mass, litanies, novenas, stations of the cross

.028	Texts of psalters
.029	Texts of lectionary
.03	Anglican churches

> Including rubrics
>
> Class here Book of Common Prayer; Common Worship

.030 01–.030 09	Standard subdivisions
.030 1–.030 9	History, meaning, place of liturgy, ritual, prayers in public worship

> Add to base number 264.03 notation 01–09 from the table under 264.04–264.09, e.g., prayer 264.0301; however, for texts, see 264.031–264.038

> 264.031–264.038   Texts of liturgy, ritual, prayers

Class comprehensive works in 264.03

.031	Texts of calendars, festivals, fasts
.032	Texts of lectionary

> Including texts of epistles, Gospels

.033	Texts of morning prayer and litany
.034	Texts of evening prayer and vespers
.035	Texts of sacraments, ordinances, services

> Add to base number 264.035 the numbers following 265 in 265.1–265.9, e.g., texts of baptism 264.0351
>
> Class texts of morning prayer and litany in 264.033; class texts of evening prayer and vespers in 264.034

.036	Texts of collects
.038	Texts of psalters
.04–.09	Other specific denominations and sects

> Add to base number 264.0 the numbers following 28 in 284–289, e.g., United Methodist services 264.076; then add further as follows:
> 001–009 Standard subdivisions
> 01–07 Specific elements
>   History, meaning, place in public worship, texts
>   Add to 0 the numbers following 264 in 264.1–264.7, e.g., the Lord's Supper 036, the Lord's Supper in the United Methodist Church 264.076036
> 08   Sacraments
>   History, meaning, place in public worship, texts
>   Add to 08 the numbers following 265 in 265.1–265.7, e.g., the ceremony of baptism 081, the ceremony of baptism in the United Methodist Church 264.076081; however, for Holy Communion (Eucharist, Lord's Supper, Mass), see 036
> 09   Sacramentals, other rites and acts
>   History, meaning, place in public worship, texts
> 091   Sacramentals
> 098–099 Other rites and acts
>   Add to 09 the numbers following 265 in 265.8–265.9, e.g., funeral services 0985, United Methodist funerals 264.0760985

> **264.1–264.9   Specific elements**
>
> History, meaning, place in public worship, texts
>
> Class specific elements in public worship of specific denominations and sects in 264.01–264.09; class use of the arts (*except* music), of color in public worship in 246; class liturgical year in 263.9; class comprehensive works in 264
>
> Specific elements as part of the Mass are classed in 264.36, e.g., Eucharistic prayers (*not* 264.1)

.1	**Prayer**

> Class prayers for a specific ceremony with the ceremony, e.g., prayers for funerals 265.85

.13 Texts of prayers

> Including litanies

> Class comprehensive collections of public and private prayers in 242.8

.15 Liturgy of the hours (Divine office)

> Including psalters

> Class here breviaries

.2 Music

> Class comprehensive works on music in Christianity in 246.75; class interdisciplinary works on Christian sacred music in 781.71; class interdisciplinary works on sacred vocal music in 782.22

.23 Hymns

> Class here texts of hymns for devotional use of individuals and families

> Class hymnals containing both text and music, interdisciplinary works on hymns in 782.27

.3 Scripture readings and communion sacrament

.34 Scripture readings

> Class here common lectionary

.36 Holy Communion (Eucharist, Lord's Supper, Mass)

> Including specific elements when part of the Mass

> *For viaticum, see 265.7*

.4 Responsive readings

.7 Prayer meetings, Holy Hours, novenas

.9 Sacramentals

> *For consecrations and dedications, see 265.92*

265 Sacraments, other rites and acts

> Standard subdivisions are added for sacraments and other rites and acts together, for sacraments alone

> Not limited by denomination or sect

> Class works limited by denomination or sect about sacraments, other rites and acts in 264.01–264.09

> **265.1–265.7 Sacraments**

> Class comprehensive works in 265

> *For Holy Communion (Eucharist, Lord's Supper, Mass), see 264.36*

.1	**Baptism**
.12	Infant baptism
.13	Adult baptism

Class here Christian initiation (baptism and confirmation) of adults, catechumenate

For confirmation, see 265.2; for religious education for catechumens, see 268.434

.2	**Confirmation**
.4	**Holy Orders**
.5	**Matrimony**
.6	**Penance**
.61	Contrition

Examination of conscience, prayers preparatory to confession

.62	Confession
.63	Satisfaction

Penitential prayers and acts for the remission of sin

.64	Absolution
.66	Indulgences
.7	**Viaticum and anointing of the sick**
.8	**Rites in illness and death**
.82	Religious ceremonies for the afflicted

For viaticum and anointing of the sick, see 265.7

.85	Religious ceremonies for the dead

Class here funeral services

For requiem Mass, see 264.36

.9	**Other acts**

Including ceremonies of joining a church, foot washing, laying on of hands, love feasts (agapes)

.92	Consecrations and dedications
.94	Exorcism

266   Missions

Class here missionary societies, religious aspects of medical missions

Class medical services of medical missions in 362.1

For mission schools, see 371.071

.001–.008   Standard subdivisions

.009   Historical, geographic, persons treatment

Do not use for foreign missions originating in specific continents, countries, localities; class in 266.023. Do not use for historical, geographic, persons treatment of missions of specific denominations and sects; class in 266.1–266.9

Class here joint and interdenominational missions; foreign missions by continent, country, locality served

.02   Kinds of missions

.022   Home missions

.023   Foreign missions

[.023 091–.023 099]   Geographic and persons treatment

Do not use for foreign missions characterized only by place served; class in 266.009. Do not use for foreign missions originating in specific areas; class in 266.0231–266.0239

.023 1–.023 9   Persons treatment and foreign missions originating in specific areas

Add to base number 266.023 notation 1–9 from Table 2, e.g., missions originating in France 266.02344; then add 0* and again add notation 1–9 from Table 2 for place served, e.g., French missions to Africa 266.0234406

.1–.9   Missions of specific denominations and sects

Add to base number 266 the numbers following 28 in 281–289, e.g., Anglican missions 266.3; Anglican missions serving Africa 266.36

267   Associations for religious work

Class here pious societies, sodalities, confraternities

For religious congregations and orders, see 255; for missionary societies, see 266

See Manual at 230–280

.1   Associations for religious work for both men and women

.13   Interdenominational and nondenominational associations

For Moral Rearmament, see 267.16

.16   Moral Rearmament

*Add 00 for standard subdivisions; see instructions at beginning of Table 1

.18	Specific branches, denominations, sects

Add to base number 267.18 the numbers following 28 in 280.2–289, e.g., Baptist Adult Union 267.186132

.2 Men's associations

.23 Interdenominational and nondenominational associations

For Young Men's Christian Associations, see 267.3

.24 Specific branches, denominations, sects

Add to base number 267.24 the numbers following 28 in 280.2–289, e.g., Baptist societies 267.246

.3 Young Men's Christian Associations

[.309] Historical, geographic, persons treatment

Do not use; class in 267.39

.39 Historical, geographic, persons treatment

Add to base number 267.39 notation 01–9 from Table 2, e.g., Young Men's Christian Association in New York City 267.397471

.4 Women's associations

.43 Interdenominational and nondenominational associations

For Young Women's Christian Associations, see 267.5

.44 Specific branches, denominations, sects

Add to base number 267.44 the numbers following 28 in 280.2–289, e.g., Baptist societies 267.446

.5 Young Women's Christian Associations

[.509] Historical, geographic, persons treatment

Do not use; class in 267.59

.59 Historical, geographic, persons treatment

Add to base number 267.59 notation 01–9 from Table 2, e.g., Young Women's Christian Association in New York City 267.597471

.6 Young adults' associations

.61 Interdenominational and nondenominational associations

For Young Men's Christian Associations, see 267.3; for Young Women's Christian Associations, see 267.5

.62 Specific branches, denominations, sects

Add to base number 267.62 the numbers following 28 in 280.2–289, e.g., Baptist Young People's Union 267.626132

.7 **Boys' associations**

> *For Young Men's Christian Associations, see 267.3*

.8 **Girls' associations**

> *For Young Women's Christian Associations, see 267.5*

268 Religious education

Class here catechetics (the science or art devoted to organizing the principles of religious teaching), curricula, comprehensive works on Christian religious education

Class Christian religious schools providing general education in 371.071; class place of religion in public schools in 379.28. Class textbooks on a specific subject with the subject, e.g., textbooks on missions 266

> *For religious education at the university level, see 230.0711; for study of Christianity in secular secondary schools, see 230.0712*

> *See Manual at 207.5, 268 vs. 200.71, 230.071, 292–299*

[.068] Management

> Do not use; class in 268.1

.08 History and description with respect to kinds of persons

> Do not use for education of specific kinds of persons; class in 268.4

> Class here education, teaching performed by kinds of persons

[.088 2] History and descriptions with respect to religious groups

> Do not use; class in 268.8

.1 **Administration**

> *For plant management, see 268.2; for personnel management, see 268.3*

.2 **Buildings and equipment**

.3 **Personnel**

> Class here preparation, role, training, personnel management

> *See Manual at 230–280*

.4 **Religious education of specific groups**

> Class here curricula, records and rules, teaching methods, services for specific groups

[.408 3–.408 4] Age groups

> Do not use; class in 268.43

.43 Specific age groups

.432	Children

Through age eleven

See also 372.84 for religion courses in secular elementary schools

(.432 04) Special topics of children

(.432 045) Textbooks

(Option: Class here religious education textbooks; prefer the specific subject, e.g., textbooks on Christianity 230, textbooks on missions 266)

.433 Adolescents

(.433 04) Special topics of adolescents

(.433 045) Textbooks

(Option: Class here religious education textbooks; prefer the specific subject, e.g., textbooks on Christianity 230, textbooks on missions 266)

.434 Adults

(.434 04) Special topics of adults

(.434 045) Textbooks

(Option: Class here religious education textbooks; prefer the specific subject, e.g., textbooks on Christianity 230, textbooks on missions 266)

.5 Records and rules

Including attendance, decorations, honor rolls, prizes, promotion

Class records and rules for specific groups in 268.4

.6 Methods of instruction and study

Class methods for a specific group with the group, e.g., methods for instruction of children 268.432071

.63 Lecture and audiovisual methods

.632 Lecture method

.635 Audiovisual methods

.67 Dramatic method

Class use of dramatic arts for religious purposes not limited to religious education in 246.72

.7 Services

Including anniversaries, festivals, music, rallies, special days

Class services for specific groups in 268.4

.8   Specific branches, denominations, sects

> Add to base number 268.8 the numbers following 28 in 280.2–289, e.g.,
> Presbyterian religious education 268.85

> Class a specific element in religious education by specific denominations and
> sects with the element in 268.1–268.7, e.g., religious education of children in
> Baptist churches 268.432088286

269   Spiritual renewal

> Class history of the pentecostal movement in 270.82

.2   Evangelism

> *See also 243 for evangelistic writings for individuals and families; also
> 248.5 for witness bearing by individual lay Christians; also 252.3 for texts
> of evangelistic sermons; also 266 for missionary evangelization*

.24   Revival and camp meetings

.26   Evangelism by radio and television

.6   Retreats

> Add to base number 269.6 the numbers following 248.8 in 248.82–248.89, e.g.,
> retreats for men 269.642

> **270–280   Historical, geographic, persons treatment of Christianity; Church history; Christian denominations and sects**

> Unless other instructions are given, observe the following table of preference
> for the history of Christianity and the Christian church (*except* for biography,
> explained in Manual at 230–280), e.g., persecution of Jesuits by Elizabeth I
> 272.7 (*not* 271.53042, 274.206, or 282.42):

Persecutions in general church history	272
Doctrinal controversies and heresies in general church history	273
Religious congregations and orders in church history	271
Denominations and sects of Christian church	280
Treatment of Christianity and Christian church by continent, country, locality	274–279
General historical, geographic, persons treatment of Christianity and Christian church (*except* 271–279)	270

> Class comprehensive works in 270

> *See Manual at 230–280*

270   Historical, geographic, persons treatment of Christianity   Church history

Class here collected writings of apostolic and church fathers (patristics)

Observe table of preference under 230–280

> *For historical, geographic, persons treatment of specific denominations and sects, see 280*
>
> *See Manual at 230–280; also at 270, 230.11–230.14 vs. 230.15–230.2, 281.5–281.9, 282; also at 398.2 vs. 201.3, 230, 270, 292–299*

SUMMARY

270.01–.09	**Standard subdivisions**
.1–.8	**Historical periods**
271	**Religious congregations and orders in church history**
272	**Persecutions in general church history**
273	**Doctrinal controversies and heresies in general church history**
274–279	**Treatment by continent, country, locality**

.01–.07   Standard subdivisions

.08   Christianity with respect to kinds of persons, church history with respect to kinds of persons

> Class here Christian attitudes toward social groups [*formerly* 261.834]; discrimination, equality, inequality, prejudice

.09   Areas, regions, places in general, persons

[.093–.099]   Treatment by continent, country, locality

> Do not use; class in 274–279

> >   **270.1–270.8   Historical periods**
>
> Class historical periods in specific continents, countries, localities in 274–279; class comprehensive works in 270

.1   **Apostolic period to 325**

.2   **Period of ecumenical councils, 325–787**

.3   **787–1054**

> Class here comprehensive works on Middle Ages
>
> *For a specific part of Middle Ages, see the part, e.g., late Middle Ages 270.5*

.38   Great schism, 1054

.4   **1054–1200**

.5   **Late Middle Ages through Renaissance, 1200–1517**

.6   **Period of Reformation and Counter-Reformation, 1517–1648**

Including 17th century

For 1648–1699, see 270.7

.7   **Period from Peace of Westphalia to French Revolution, 1648–1789**

.8   **Modern period, 1789–**

.81   1789–1900

.82   1900–1999

Class here comprehensive works on evangelicalism, fundamentalism, pentecostalism, charismatic movement

Add to base number 270.82 the numbers following —0904 in notation 09041–09049 from Table 1, e.g., 1960–1969 in church history 270.826

Class ecumenical movement in 280.042; class pentecostal churches that are independent denominations in 289.94; class evangelical churches, fundamentalist churches that are independent denominations in 289.95

For evangelicalism, fundamentalism, pentecostalism, charismatic movement in the period 2000 to present, see 270.83. For evangelicalism, fundamentalism, pentecostalism, charismatic movement in a specific branch or denomination, see the branch or denomination, e.g., Protestant fundamentalism 280.4

.83   2000–

> **271–273   Special topics of church history**

Class comprehensive works in 270

271   **Religious congregations and orders in church history**

Class here history of monasticism, history of specific monasteries and convents even if not connected with a specific order

Add to each subdivision identified by * as follows:
001–008   Standard subdivisions
[009]   Historical treatment
  Do not use; class in base number without further addition
[0091–0099]   Geographic and persons treatment
  Do not use; class in 01–09
01–09   Geographic and persons treatment
  Add to base number 0 notation 1–9 from Table 2, e.g., collected biography 022, collected biography of Benedictines 271.1022, Benedictines in the United Kingdom 271.1041

Class persecutions involving religious congregations and orders in 272; class doctrinal controversies and heresies involving congregations and orders in 273

SUMMARY

271.001–.009	**Standard subdivisions**
.01–.09	**Specific kinds**
.1	**Benedictines**
.2	**Dominicans (Friars Preachers, Black Friars)**
.3	**Franciscans (Gray Friars)**
.4	**Augustinians**
.5	**Regular clerics**
.6	**Passionists and Redemptorists**
.7	**Roman Catholic orders of men not otherwise provided for**
.8	**Non-Roman Catholic orders of men**
.9	**Congregations and orders of women**

.001–.009   Standard subdivisions

>   271.01–271.09   Specific kinds of congregations and orders

Class comprehensive works in 271

.01   *Contemplative religious orders

.02   *Eremitical religious orders

.03   *Teaching orders

.04   *Preaching orders

.06   *Mendicant religious orders

.07   *Nursing orders

.08   *Canons regular

.09   Other specific kinds

.092   *Brothers

See also 271.093 for lay brothers

.093   *Lay brothers

.094   *Third orders

Secular and regular

.095   *Secular institutes

>   **271.1–271.8   Specific orders of men**

Class comprehensive works in 271

*Add as instructed under 271

> **271.1–271.7   Roman Catholic orders of men**

Class comprehensive works in 271

.1   ***Benedictines**

.11   *Confederated Benedictines

For Olivetans, see 271.13

.12   *Cistercians (Bernardines)

.125   *Trappists

.13   *Olivetans

.14   *Cluniacs

Including Camaldolese, Silvestrians, Monks of Saint Paul the Hermit

For Carthusians, see 271.71

.16   *Celestines

.17   Mechitarists and Basilians

.18   Antonines (Antonians), Maronites, Chaldeans, Syrians

.19   *Canons

Including Crosier Fathers, Crosiers of the Red Star, Premonstratensians

Class Augustinians in 271.4

.2   ***Dominicans (Friars Preachers, Black Friars)**

.3   ***Franciscans (Gray Friars)**

Including Alcantarines, Observants, Recollects

See also 271.4 for Augustinian Recollects

.36   *Capuchins

.37   *Conventuals

.38   *Third Order Regular

.4   ***Augustinians**

Including Augustinian Recollects

.42   *Trinitarians

.45   *Mercedarians

.47   *Servites

---

*Add as instructed under 271

.49		Other Augustinians

Including Brothers Hospitallers of St. John of God, Minims

.5		***Regular clerics**
.51		*Theatines
.52		*Barnabites
.53		*Jesuits (Society of Jesus)
.54		*Somaschi
.55		*Camillians
.56		*Minor Clerks Regular (Caracciolini)
.57		*Clerks Regular of the Mother of God
.58		*Piarists
.6		***Passionists and Redemptorists**
.62		*Passionists
.64		*Redemptorists
.7		**Roman Catholic orders of men not otherwise provided for**
.71		*Carthusians
.73		*Carmelites (White Friars)
.75		*Sulpicians
.76		*Oblates
.77		*Lazarists (Vincentians)
.78		*Christian Brothers (Brothers of the Christian Schools)
.79		Other Roman Catholic orders of men
.791		*Orders of knighthood

Class here military orders

.791 2		*Knights of Malta (Knights Hospitalers of St. John of Jerusalem)
.791 3		*Knights Templars
.791 4		*Teutonic Knights
.8		**Non-Roman Catholic orders of men**
.81		Monasteries of Eastern churches

Add to base number 271.81 the numbers following 281 in 281.5–281.9, e.g., Eastern Orthodox monasteries 271.819, on Mount Athos 271.81949565

*Add as instructed under 271

.83   Anglican orders of men

.9   Congregations and orders of women

.900 01–.900 08   Standard subdivisions

.900 09   Historical treatment

[.900 091–.900 099]   Geographic and persons treatment

> Do not use; class in 271.9001–271.9009

.900 1–.900 9   Geographic and persons treatment

> Add to base number 271.900 notation 1–9 from Table 2, e.g., collected biography of women religious 271.90022, congregations and orders of women in France 271.90044

.901–.909   Specific kinds of congregations and orders

> Add to base number 271.90 the numbers following 271.0 in 271.01–271.09, e.g., contemplative orders 271.901

> 271.91–271.98   Specific orders of women

Class comprehensive works in 271.9

> 271.91–271.97   Roman Catholic orders of women

Class comprehensive works in 271.9

.91   *Sisters of Charity orders

.92   *Sisters of Mercy orders

.93   *Sacred Heart orders

.94   *Sisters of Bon Secours

.95   *Little Sisters of the Poor

.97   Other Roman Catholic orders of women

.971   *Carmelites

.972   *Dominicans

.973   *Franciscan orders

> Class here Poor Clares

.974   *Ursulines

.975   *Visitation orders

.976   *Saint Joseph orders

.977   *Presentation orders

*Add as instructed under 271

.98	Non-Roman Catholic orders of women
.981	Women's convents of Eastern churches

> Add to base number 271.981 the numbers following 281 in 281.5–281.9, e.g., Eastern Orthodox convents of women 271.9819

.983	Anglican orders of women

272 Persecutions in general church history

Regardless of denomination

Class here martyrs

Class relation of state to church in 322.1

> *See also 364.188 for offenses against religion as defined and penalized by the state*

.1 Persecutions of Apostolic Church by imperial Rome

.2 Persecutions by Inquisition

.3 Persecutions of Waldenses and Albigenses

.4 Persecutions of Huguenots

.5 Persecutions of Molinists and Quietists

.6 Persecutions of Anglican reformers by Mary I

.7 Persecutions of Roman Church by Elizabeth I and Anglicans

.8 Persecutions of Quakers, Baptists, witches by Puritans and others of Puritan times

.9 Modern persecutions and martyrs

273 Doctrinal controversies and heresies in general church history

Class persecutions resulting from controversies and heresies in 272; class churches founded on specific doctrines in 280

> *See also 239 for apologetics and polemics*

.1 1st–2nd centuries

Class here Christian gnosticism

Class comprehensive works and non-Christian Gnosticism in 299.932

> *For gnosticism of 3rd century, see 273.2*

.2   **3rd century**

Including Christian Manicheism

Class comprehensive works and non-Christian Manicheism in 299.932

For Sabellianism, see 273.3

.3   **Sabellianism**

.4   **4th century**

Including Arianism, Donatism

.5   **5th century**

Including Pelagianism

.6   **6th–16th centuries**

Including Albigensianism, Catharism, Waldensianism

Class here antinomianism

For later antinomianism, see 273.7–273.9; for Albigensian, Catharist, Waldensian churches, see 284.4

.7   **17th century**

Including Molinism, Pietism; comprehensive works on Jansenism

For Jansenist churches, see 284.84

.8   **18th century**

.9   **19th century and later centuries**

Including modernism

274–279   Treatment by continent, country, locality

Add to base number 27 notation 4–9 from Table 2, e.g., Christianity, Christian church in Europe 274, in France 274.4; then to the result add the numbers following 27 in 270.01–270.8, e.g., Christian church in France during the Reformation 274.406

Class geographic treatment of a specific subject with the subject, plus notation 09 from Table 1, e.g., persecutions in France 272.0944

274   Christianity in Europe   Christian church in Europe

Number built according to instructions under 274–279

275   Christianity in Asia   Christian church in Asia

Number built according to instructions under 274–279

276   Christianity in Africa   Christian church in Africa

Number built according to instructions under 274–279

277   **Christianity in North America   Christian church in North America**

Number built according to instructions under 274–279

278   **Christianity in South America   Christian church in South America**

Number built according to instructions under 274–279

279   **Christianity in other parts of the world   Christian church in other parts of the world**

Number built according to instructions under 274–279

280   Denominations and sects of Christian church

Including nondenominational and interdenominational churches

Class here general historical and geographic treatment of, comprehensive works on specific denominations and sects and their individual local churches

Class persecution of or by specific churches in 272

> *For a specific element of specific denominations and sects, see the element, e.g., doctrines 230*
>
> *See also 273 for doctrines of specific churches considered as heresies*
>
> *See Manual at 201–209 and 292–299; also at 230–280*

(Option: Class here specific elements of specific denominations and sects; prefer 230–270. If option is chosen, add to the number for each specific denomination, sect, group as follows:

001–008	Standard subdivisions
[009]	Historical, geographic, persons treatment
	Do not use; class in 07
02	Basic textual sources
	Class Bible in 220
03–06	Doctrinal, moral, devotional, social, ecclesiastical theology
	Add to 0 the numbers following 2 in 230–260, e.g., the
	denomination and international affairs 06187
07	Historical, geographic, persons treatment
	Add to 07 the numbers following 27 in 270.1–279, e.g., 20th
	century 07082)

SUMMARY

280.01–.09	Standard subdivisions and special topics of denominations and sects of Christian church
.2–.4	Branches
281	Early church and Eastern churches
282	Roman Catholic Church
283	Anglican churches
284	Protestant denominations of Continental origin and related bodies
285	Presbyterian churches, Reformed churches centered in America, Congregational churches, Puritanism
286	Baptist, Disciples of Christ, Adventist churches
287	Methodist churches; churches related to Methodism
289	Other denominations and sects

.01–.03	Standard subdivisions
.04	Special topics of denominations and sects of Christian church
.042	Relations between denominations

> Class here ecumenical movement
>
> *See Manual at 280.042 vs. 262.0011*

| .05–.09 | Standard subdivisions |

> ### 280.2–280.4   Branches
>
> Class specific denominations and sects in 281–289; class comprehensive works in 280

.2   Eastern and Roman Catholic churches

Class comprehensive works on Roman Catholic Church and Eastern churches in communion with Rome in 282

For specific denominations and sects, see 281–282

.4   Protestant churches and Protestantism

Standard subdivisions are added for either or both topics in heading

Class here dissenters, free churches, nonconformists (British context); works on Protestant evangelicalism, fundamentalism, pentecostalism, charismatic movement

Class comprehensive works on evangelicalism, fundamentalism, pentecostalism, charismatic movement in general church history in 270.82

For specific Protestant denominations, see 283–289

> ## 281–289   Specific denomination or sect
>
> Class comprehensive works in 280
>
> (Option: Class a specific denomination or sect requiring local emphasis in 289.2)

281   Early church and Eastern churches

> ### 281.1–281.4   Early church
>
> Use these subdivisions only for building other numbers in 230–260, e.g., theology in the Ante-Nicene church 230.13; never use these subdivisions by themselves. When building numbers in 230–260 using these subdivisions, use 281.1 for comprehensive works
>
> Class collected writings of apostolic and church fathers (patristics) in 270; class all works on early church in 270.1–270.3. Class a specific work of an apostolic or church father on a specific subject with the subject, e.g., philosophy 189.2
>
> *See Manual at 270, 230.11–230.14 vs. 230.15–230.2, 281.5–281.9, 282*

.1   **Apostolic Church to the time of the great schism, 1054**

> *For Apostolic Church to 100, see 281.2; for Ante-Nicene church, see 281.3;*
> *for Post-Nicene church, see 281.4*

.2   **Apostolic Church to 100**

.3   **Ante-Nicene church, 100–325**

.4   **Post-Nicene church, 325–1054**

.5   **Eastern churches**

> Including Catholics of Eastern rites (Eastern rite churches in communion with
> Rome), St. Thomas (Mar Thoma, Syro-Malabar) Christians

> *For Monophysite churches, see 281.6; for Coptic and Ethiopian churches,*
> *see 281.7; for Nestorian churches, see 281.8; for Eastern Orthodox*
> *churches, see 281.9*

> *See Manual at 270, 230.11–230.14 vs. 230.15–230.2, 281.5–281.9, 282*

.6   **Monophysite churches**

> Including Eutychian Church

> *For Coptic and Ethiopian churches, see 281.7*

> *See Manual at 270, 230.11–230.14 vs. 230.15–230.2, 281.5–281.9, 282*

.62   Armenian Church

.63   Jacobite Church

> Class here Syrian Orthodox Church, Jacobite Patriarchate of Antioch

> *See also 281.95691 for Eastern Orthodox Church in Syria*

.7   **Coptic and Ethiopian churches**

> *See Manual at 270, 230.11–230.14 vs. 230.15–230.2, 281.5–281.9, 282*

.72   Coptic Church (Coptic Orthodox Church)

.75   Ethiopian Church (Ethiopian Orthodox Church)

.8   **Nestorian churches**

> *See Manual at 270, 230.11–230.14 vs. 230.15–230.2, 281.5–281.9, 282*

.9   **Eastern Orthodox churches**

> *See Manual at 270, 230.11–230.14 vs. 230.15–230.2, 281.5–281.9, 282*

.909   Historical, geographic, persons treatment

[.909 3]   Geographic treatment in ancient world

> Do not use for early church; class in 270

[.909 4–.909 9]   Treatment by specific continents, countries, localities in modern world

> Do not use; class in 281.94–281.99

.94–.99   Treatment by continent, country, locality

> Add to base number 281.9 notation 4–9 from Table 2, e.g., Russian
> Orthodox Church 281.947, Orthodox Church in America 281.97

282   Roman Catholic Church

Class here the Catholic traditionalist movement, comprehensive works on Roman
Catholic Church and Eastern rite churches in communion with Rome

Class modern schisms in Roman Catholic Church in 284.8

For Eastern rite churches in communion with Rome, see 281.5–281.8

See Manual at 270, 230.11–230.14 vs. 230.15–230.2, 281.5–281.9, 282

.09   Historical, geographic, persons treatment

> *See Manual at 270, 230.11–230.14 vs. 230.15–230.2, 281.5–281.9, 282*

[.093]   Geographic treatment in ancient world

> Do not use for early church; class in 270

[.094–.099]   Treatment by specific continents, countries, localities in modern
world

> Do not use; class in 282.4–282.9

.4–.9   Treatment by continent, country, locality

> Add to base number 282 notation 4–9 from Table 2, e.g., Roman Catholic
> Church in Latin America 282.8

>   **283–289   Protestant and other denominations**

Class comprehensive works on Protestant churches in 280.4; class
comprehensive works on Protestant and other denominations in 280

See Manual at 283–289

283   Anglican churches

[.094–.099]   Treatment by specific continents, countries, localities in modern
world

> Do not use; class in 283.4–283.9

.3   Branches not in communion with the See of Canterbury

Including Reformed Episcopal Church and its affiliates

See Manual at 230–280; also at 283–289

.4–.9   Treatment by continent, country, locality

Class here national churches in communion with the See of Canterbury

Add to base number 283 notation 4–9 from Table 2, e.g., Church of England
283.42, Episcopal Diocese of Long Island 283.74721

284 Protestant denominations of Continental origin and related bodies

For Protestant denominations of Continental origin not provided for here, see the denomination, e.g., Baptists 286

.094 3   Central Europe   Germany

Class here Evangelische Kirche in Deutschland [*formerly* 284.143]

.1   Lutheran churches

[.109 4–.109 9]   Treatment by specific continents, countries, localities in modern world

Do not use; class in 284.14–284.19

(.12)   (Permanently unassigned)

(Optional number used to provide local emphasis or a shorter number for Lutheran church in a specific country other than the United States; prefer 284.14–284.19)

.13   Specific denominations, branches, synods centered in the United States

See Manual at 230–280; also at 283–289

[.130 1–.130 9]   Standard subdivisions

Do not use; class in 284.101–284.109

.131   *The American Lutheran Church

.131 2   *The Evangelical Lutheran Church

.131 3   *United Evangelical Lutheran Church

.131 4   *The Lutheran Free Church

.132   *The Evangelical Lutheran Synodical Conference of North America

For Wisconsin Evangelical Lutheran Synod, see 284.134

.132 2   *The Lutheran Church—Missouri Synod

For Synod of Evangelical Lutheran Churches, see 284.1323

.132 3   *Synod of Evangelical Lutheran Churches (Slovak)

.133   *The Lutheran Church in America

.133 2   *American Evangelical Lutheran Church

.133 3   *Augustana Evangelical Lutheran Church

.133 4   *Finnish Evangelical Lutheran Church

.133 5   *The United Lutheran Church in America

.134   *Wisconsin Evangelical Lutheran Synod

---

*Do not use notation 094–099 from Table 1; class in 284.14–284.19

.135   *Evangelical Lutheran Church in America

.14–.19   Treatment by continent, country, locality

> Add to base number 284.1 notation 4–9 from Table 2, e.g., Lutheran Church of Sweden 284.1485, Memorial Evangelical Lutheran Church of Washington, D.C. 284.1753; however, Evangelische Kirche in Deutschland relocated from 284.143 to 284.0943

> (Option: Class Lutheran churches in a specific country other than the United States in 284.12)

.2   Calvinistic and Reformed churches of European origin

> Standard subdivisions are added for either or both topics in heading

> Class here comprehensive works on Calvinistic churches, on Reformed churches

>> *For Huguenot churches, see 284.5; for Presbyterian churches, see 285; for Reformed churches centered in America, see 285.7*

>> *See also 285.9 for Puritanism*

[.209 4–.209 9]   Treatment by specific continents, countries, localities in modern world

> Do not use; class in 284.24–284.29

.24–.29   Treatment by continent, country, locality

> Add to base number 284.2 notation 4–9 from Table 2, e.g., Reformed churches in Holland 284.2492, in South Africa 284.268

.3   Hussite and Anabaptist churches

> Including Lollards, Wycliffites

>> *See also 289.7 for Mennonite churches*

.4   Albigensian, Catharist, Waldensian churches

.5   Huguenot churches

.6   Moravian churches

>> *For Hussite churches, see 284.3*

[.609 4–.609 9]   Treatment by specific continents, countries, localities in modern world

> Do not use; class in 284.64–284.69

.64–.69   Treatment by continent, country, locality

> Add to base number 284.6 notation 4–9 from Table 2, e.g., Moravian churches in Germany 284.643

---

*Do not use notation 094–099 from Table 1; class in 284.14–284.19

.8   **Modern schisms in Roman Catholic Church**

> Including Constitutional Church, Gallican schismatic churches, Liberal Catholic Church, Little Church of France, Old Catholic churches, Philippine Independent Church

.84   Jansenist churches

.9   **Arminian and Remonstrant churches**

285   Presbyterian churches, Reformed churches centered in America, Congregational churches, Puritanism

> Standard subdivisions are added for Presbyterian churches, Reformed churches centered in America, Congregational churches together; for Presbyterian churches alone

>   **285.1–285.2   Presbyterian churches of United States, of British Commonwealth origin**

> Class comprehensive works on Presbyterian churches, Presbyterian churches of other origin in 285

> (If option under 280 is followed, use 285.001–285.008 for standard subdivisions, 285.02–285.07 for specific elements of Presbyterian churches)

.1   **Presbyterian churches of United States origin**

[.109 4–.109 9]   Treatment by specific continents, countries, localities in modern world

> Do not use; class in 285.14–285.19

.13   Specific denominations

> *See Manual at 230–280; also at 283–289*

[.130 1–.130 9]   Standard subdivisions

> Do not use; class in 285.101–285.109

.131   *United Presbyterian Church in the U.S.A.

.132   *Presbyterian Church in the United States of America

.133   *Presbyterian Church in the United States

.134   *United Presbyterian Church of North America

.135   *Cumberland Presbyterian Church

.136   *Reformed Presbyterian churches

.137   *Presbyterian Church (U.S.A.)

.14–.19   Treatment by continent, country, locality

> Add to base number 285.1 notation 4–9 from Table 2, e.g., the Hudson River Presbytery 285.17473

---

*Do not use notation 094–099 from Table 1; class in 285.14–285.19

.2   **Presbyterian churches of British Commonwealth origin**

[.209 4–.209 9]   Treatment by specific continents, countries, localities in modern world

Do not use; class in 285.24–285.29

.23   Specific denominations

Including Countess of Huntingdon's Connexion

See Manual at 230–280; also at 283–289

[.230 1–.230 9]   Standard subdivisions

Do not use; class in 285.201–285.209

.232   †United Reformed Church in the United Kingdom

Class Congregational Church of England and Wales in 285.842

.233   †Church of Scotland

.234   †Free Church of Scotland

.235   †Presbyterian Church of Wales (Welsh Calvinistic Methodist Church)

.24–.29   Treatment by continent, country, locality

Add to base number 285.2 notation 4–9 from Table 2, e.g., Presbyterianism in Ireland 285.2415, a Church of Scotland parish in Edinburgh 285.24134

Class United Church of Canada in 287.92; class Uniting Church in Australia in 287.93

.7   **Reformed churches centered in America**

[.709 4–.709 9]   Treatment by specific continents, countries, localities in modern world

Do not use; class in 285.74–285.79

.73   Specific denominations

See Manual at 230–280; also at 283–289

[.730 1–.730 9]   Standard subdivisions

Do not use; class in 285.701–285.709

.731   *Christian Reformed Church

.732   *Reformed Church in America (Dutch)

.733   *Reformed Church in the United States (German)

.734   *Evangelical and Reformed Church

*Do not use notation 094–099 from Table 1; class in 285.74–285.79

†Do not use notation 094–099 from Table 1; class in 285.24–285.29

.74–.79   Treatment by continent, country, locality

> Add to base number 285.7 notation 4–9 from Table 2, e.g., First Reformed Church of Schenectady, N.Y. 285.774744

.8   Congregationalism

[.809 4–.809 9]   Treatment by specific continents, countries, localities in modern world

> Do not use; class in 285.84–285.89

(.82)   (Permanently unassigned)

> (Optional number used to provide local emphasis or a shorter number for Congregational churches in a specific country other than the United States; prefer 285.84–285.89)

.83   Specific denominations centered in the United States

> *See Manual at 230–280; also at 283–289*

[.830 1–.830 9]   Standard subdivisions

> Do not use; class in 285.801–285.809

.832   †Congregational Churches of the United States

.833   †Congregational Christian Churches

.834   †United Church of Christ

> *For Evangelical and Reformed Church, see 285.734*

.84–.89   Treatment by continent, country, locality

> Class here specific denominations centered outside the United States

> Add to base number 285.8 notation 4–9 from Table 2, e.g., Congregational Church of England and Wales 285.842, Congregational churches in New England 285.874

> Class United Church of Canada in 287.92; class Uniting Church in Australia in 287.93

> (Option: Class Congregational churches in a specific country other than the United States in 285.82)

.9   Puritanism

†Do not use notation 094–099 from Table 1; class in 285.84–285.89

286   Baptist, Disciples of Christ, Adventist churches

Standard subdivisions are added for Baptist, Disciples of Christ, Adventist churches together; for Baptist churches alone

---

> ### 286.1–286.5   Baptist churches

Class comprehensive works in 286

(If option under 280 is followed, use 286.001–286.008 for standard subdivisions, 286.02–286.07 for specific elements of Baptist churches)

.1   Regular Baptists (Calvinistic Baptists)

[.109 4–.109 9]   Treatment by specific continents, countries, localities in modern world

Do not use; class in 286.14–286.19

(.12)   (Permanently unassigned)

(Optional number used to provide local emphasis or a shorter number for Regular Baptist churches in a specific country other than the United States; prefer 286.14–286.19)

.13   Specific denominations centered in the United States

See Manual at 230–280; also at 283–289

[.130 1–.130 9]   Standard subdivisions

Do not use; class in 286.101–286.109

.131   *American Baptist Churches in the U.S.A.

Former name: American (Northern) Baptist Convention

.132   *Southern Baptist Convention

.133   *National Baptist Convention of the United States of America

.134   *National Baptist Convention of America

.135   *Progressive National Baptist Convention

.136   *American Baptist Association

.14–.19   Treatment by continent, country, locality

Class here specific denominations centered outside the United States

Add to base number 286.1 notation 4–9 from Table 2, e.g., Association of Regular Baptist Churches of Canada 286.171, a Southern Baptist association in Tennessee 286.1768

(Option: Class Regular Baptist churches in a specific country other than the United States in 286.12)

.2   Freewill Baptists

---

*Do not use notation 094–099 from Table 1; class in 286.14–286.19

.3 **Seventh-Day Baptists**

.4 **Old School Baptists**

Including Antimission, Primitive Baptists

.5 **Other Baptist churches and denominations**

Including Baptist General Conference, Church of the Brethren, Dunkers

.6 **Disciples of Christ (Campbellites)**

[.609 4–.609 9] Treatment by specific continents, countries, localities in modern world

Do not use; class in 286.64–286.69

.63 Specific denominations

Including Christian Church (Disciples of Christ), Churches of Christ

See Manual at 230–280; also at 283–289

[.630 1–.630 9] Standard subdivisions

Do not use; class in 286.601–286.609

.64–.69 Treatment by continent, country, locality

Add to base number 286.6 notation 4–9 from Table 2, e.g., the Christian Church (Disciples of Christ) in Florida 286.6759

.7 **Adventist churches**

[.709 4–.709 9] Treatment by specific continents, countries, localities in modern world

Do not use; class in 286.74–286.79

.73 Specific denominations

Including Advent Christian Church, Church of God General Conference

See Manual at 230–280; also at 283–289

[.730 1–.730 9] Standard subdivisions

Do not use; class in 286.701–286.709

.732 Seventh-Day Adventist Church

[.732 094–.732 099] Treatment by specific continents, countries, localities in modern world

Do not use; class in 286.74–286.79

.74–.79 Treatment by continent, country, locality

Add to base number 286.7 notation 4–9 from Table 2, e.g., Seventh-Day Adventists in South America 286.78

287   Methodist churches; churches related to Methodism

Standard subdivisions are added for Methodist churches and churches related to Methodism together; for Methodist churches alone

.1   Wesleyan Methodist Church

[.109 4–.109 9]   Treatment by specific continents, countries, localities in modern world

Do not use; class in 287.14–287.19

.14–.19   Treatment by continent, country, locality

Add to base number 287.1 notation 4–9 from Table 2, e.g., Wesleyan Methodist Church in British Isles 287.141, Wesleyan Methodist Church in New South Wales 287.1944

.2   Miscellaneous Methodist churches

Including Congregational Methodist Church, Free Methodist Church of North America

.4   Primitive Methodist Church

[.409 4–.409 9]   Treatment by specific continents, countries, localities in modern world

Do not use; class in 287.44–287.49

.44–.49   Treatment by continent, country, locality

Add to base number 287.4 notation 4–9 from Table 2, e.g., Primitive Methodist Church in British Isles 287.441

.5   Methodist churches in British Isles

[.509 41–.509 42]   British Isles

Do not use; class in 287.54

.53   Specific denominations

Including Bible Christians, Methodist New Connexion, Protestant Methodists, United Methodist Church (Great Britain), United Methodist Free Churches, Wesleyan Conference, Wesleyan Reformers, Yearly Conference of People Called Methodists

For Wesleyan Methodist Church in British Isles, see 287.141; for Primitive Methodist Church in British Isles, see 287.441

See also 285.23 for Countess of Huntingdon's Connexion; also 285.235 for Welsh Calvinistic Methodist Church

See Manual at 230–280; also at 283–289

[.530 1–.530 9]   Standard subdivisions

Do not use; class in 287.501–287.509

.532   *United Conference of Methodist Churches

---

*Do not use notation 0941–0942 from Table 1; class in 287.54

.533	*Independent Methodists
.534	*Wesleyan Reform Union
.536	*Methodist Church of Great Britain
.54	Treatment by country and locality

> Add to base number 287.54 the numbers following —4 in notation 41–42 from Table 2, e.g., Methodist Church of Great Britain in Wales 287.5429

.6   United Methodist Church

> *See also 287.53 for United Methodist Church (Great Britain)*

[.609 4–.609 9]	Treatment by specific continents, countries, localities in modern world

> Do not use; class in 287.64–287.69

.63	Specific antecedent denominations

> *For Methodist Protestant Church, see 287.7; for Evangelical United Brethren Church, see 289.9*
>
> *See Manual at 230–280; also at 283–289*

[.630 1–.630 9]	Standard subdivisions

> Do not use; class in 287.601–287.609

.631	†The Methodist Church (1939–1968)
.632	†Methodist Episcopal Church
.633	†Methodist Episcopal Church, South
.64–.69	Treatment by continent, country, locality

> Add to base number 287.6 notation 4–9 from Table 2, e.g., United Methodist churches in Ohio 287.6771

.7   Methodist Protestant Church

.8   Black Methodist churches of United States origin

[.809 4–.809 9]	Treatment by specific continents, countries, localities in modern world

> Do not use; class in 287.84–287.89

.83	Specific denominations

> Including African Methodist Episcopal Church, African Methodist Episcopal Zion Church, Christian Methodist Episcopal Church
>
> *See Manual at 230–280; also at 283–289*

[.830 1–.830 9]	Standard subdivisions

> Do not use; class in 287.801–287.809

---

*Do not use notation 0941–0942 from Table 1; class in 287.54

†Do not use notation 094–099 from Table 1; class in 287.64–287.69

| .84–.89 | Treatment by continent, country, locality |

Add to base number 287.8 notation 4–9 from Table 2, e.g., Black Methodist churches in Georgia 287.8758, in Liberia 287.86662

.9   Churches related to Methodism

Limited to those listed below

.92   United Church of Canada

.93   Uniting Church in Australia

.94   Church of South India

.95   Church of North India

.96   Salvation Army

.99   Church of the Nazarene

[288]   [Unassigned]

Most recently used in Edition 19

289   Other denominations and sects

SUMMARY

289.1	**Unitarian and Universalist churches**
.3	**Latter-Day Saints (Mormons)**
.4	**Church of the New Jerusalem (Swedenborgianism)**
.5	**Church of Christ, Scientist (Christian Science)**
.6	**Society of Friends (Quakers)**
.7	**Mennonite churches**
.8	**Shakers (United Society of Believers in Christ's Second Appearing)**
.9	**Denominations and sects not provided for elsewhere**

.1   Unitarian and Universalist churches

Class here Anti-Trinitarianism, Socinianism, Unitarianism

[.109 4–.109 9]   Treatment by specific continents, countries, localities in modern world

Do not use; class in 289.14–289.19

.13   Specific denominations

See Manual at 230–280; also at 283–289

[.130 1–.130 9]   Standard subdivisions

Do not use; class in 289.101–289.109

.132   *Unitarian Universalist Association

.133   *Unitarian churches

.134   *Universalist churches

*Do not use notation 094–099 from Table 1; class in 289.14–289.19

.14–.19   Treatment by continent, country, locality

> Add to base number 289.1 notation 4–9 from Table 2, e.g., Unitarianism in Boston 289.174461

(.2)   (Permanently unassigned)

> (Optional number used to provide local emphasis or a shorter number for a specific denomination or sect; prefer the number for the specific denomination or sect in 281–289)

.3   Latter-Day Saints (Mormons)

[.309 4–.309 9]   Treatment by specific continents, countries, localities in modern world

> Do not use; class in 289.34–289.39

.32   Sources (Sacred books)

.322   Book of Mormon

.33   Specific branches

> *See Manual at 230–280; also at 283–289*

[.330 1–.330 9]   Standard subdivisions

> Do not use; class in 289.301–289.309

.332   Church of Jesus Christ of Latter-Day Saints

[.332 094–.332 099]   Treatment by specific continents, countries, localities in modern world

> Do not use; class in 289.34–289.39

.333   Community of Christ

> Former name: Reorganized Church of Jesus Christ of Latter-Day Saints

[.333 094–.333 099]   Treatment by specific continents, countries, localities in modern world

> Do not use; class in 289.34–289.39

.34–.39   Treatment by continent, country, locality

> Add to base number 289.3 notation 4–9 from Table 2, e.g., Mormons in Utah 289.3792

.4   Church of the New Jerusalem (Swedenborgianism)

[.409 4–.409 9]   Treatment by specific continents, countries, localities in modern world

> Do not use; class in 289.44–289.49

.44–.49   Treatment by continent, country, locality

> Add to base number 289.4 notation 4–9 from Table 2, e.g., Swedenborgianism in Europe 289.44

.5   Church of Christ, Scientist (Christian Science)

[.509 4–.509 9]   Treatment by specific continents, countries, localities in modern world

>> Do not use; class in 289.54–289.59

.52   Sources

> Writings by Mary Baker Eddy

.54–.59   Treatment by continent, country, locality

> Add to base number 289.5 notation 4–9 from Table 2, e.g., First Church of Christ, Scientist, Boston 289.574461

.6   Society of Friends (Quakers)

[.609 4–.609 9]   Treatment by specific continents, countries, localities in modern world

>> Do not use; class in 289.64–289.69

.63   Specific denominations

> *See Manual at 230–280; also at 283–289*

[.630 1–.630 9]   Standard subdivisions

>> Do not use; class in 289.601–289.609

.64–.69   Treatment by continent, country, locality

> Add to base number 289.6 notation 4–9 from Table 2, e.g., Quakers in England 289.642

.7   Mennonite churches

[.709 4–.709 9]   Treatment by specific continents, countries, localities in modern world

>> Do not use; class in 289.74–289.79

.73   Specific branches

> Including Amish, Church of God in Christ, Defenseless Mennonites, General Conference Mennonites, Hutterian Brethren

> *See Manual at 230–280; also at 283–289*

[.730 1–.730 9]   Standard subdivisions

>> Do not use; class in 289.701–289.709

.74–.79   Treatment by continent, country, locality

> Add to base number 289.7 notation 4–9 from Table 2, e.g., Amish churches in Lancaster County, Pennsylvania 289.774815

.8   Shakers (United Society of Believers in Christ's Second Appearing)

.9   Denominations and sects not provided for elsewhere

Including Christian and Missionary Alliance, Churches of God, Dukhobors, Evangelical Congregational Church, Evangelical United Brethren Church, Messianic Judaism (Jewish Christians), Plymouth Brethren, United Brethren in Christ

Class nondenominational and interdenominational churches in 280; class Protestant nondenominational and interdenominational churches in 280.4

See Manual at 201–209 and 292–299

(Option: Class a specific denomination or sect requiring local emphasis in 289.2)

.92   Jehovah's Witnesses

.93   African independent churches

Independent denominations originating in Africa and not connected to another denomination

Including Celestial Church of Christ, Cherubim and Seraphim Church, Eglise de Jésus-Christ sur la terre par le prophète Simon Kimbangu

.94   Pentecostal churches

Including Assemblies of God, United Pentecostal Church

Class comprehensive works on the pentecostal movement in general church history in 270.82

.95   Independent fundamentalist and evangelical churches

Including Evangelical Free Church of America, Independent Fundamental Churches of America

Class comprehensive works on fundamentalist, evangelical movements in general church history in 270.82

.96   Unification Church

.97   Unity School of Christianity

.98   New Thought

Class eclectic New Thought, comprehensive works in 299.93

290 Other religions

Limited to specific religions other than Christianity

Except for modifications shown under specific entries, add to each subdivision identified by † as follows:

01–05 Standard subdivisions
[06] Organizations and management
Do not use; class in 6
07 Education, research, related topics
071 Education
Class here the religion as an academic subject
Class comprehensive works on religious education, religious education to inculcate religious faith and practice in 75
See Manual at 207.5, 268 vs. 200.71, 230.071, 292–299
08–09 Standard subdivisions
1–9 Specific elements
Add the numbers following 20 in 201–209, e.g., organizations 65

Class religion in general, comprehensive works on religions other than Christianity in 200; class specific aspects of religion in 201–209

(Options: To give preferred treatment or shorter numbers to a specific religion, use one of the following:

(Option A: Class the religion in 230–280, its sources in 220, comprehensive works in 200; in that case class the Bible and Christianity in 298

(Option B: Class in 210, and add to base number 21 the numbers following the base number for the religion in 292–299, e.g., Hinduism 210, Mahabharata 219.23; in that case class philosophy and theory of religion in 200, its subdivisions 211–218 in 201–208, specific aspects of comparative religion in 200.1–200.9, standard subdivisions of religion in 200.01–200.09

(Option C: Class in 291, and add to base number 291 the numbers following the base number for that religion in 292–299, e.g., Hinduism 291, Mahabharata 291.923

(Option D: Class in 298, which is permanently unassigned

(Option E: Place first by use of a letter or other symbol, e.g., Hinduism 2H0 (preceding 220), or 29H (preceding 291 or 292); add to the base number thus derived, e.g., to 2H or to 29H, the numbers following the base number for the religion in 292–299, e.g., Shivaism 2H5.13 or 29H.513)

[291] Comparative religion

Relocated to 200

(Option: To give preferred treatment or shorter numbers to a specific religion other than Christianity, class it in this number, and add to base number 291 the numbers following the base number for that religion in 292–299, e.g., Hinduism 291, Mahabharata 291.923. Other options are described at 290)

[.04] Special topics

Provision discontinued because without meaning in context

[.042]	Prehistoric religions and religions of nonliterate peoples
	Relocated to 201.42

[.046]	Religions of 19th and 20th century origin
	Relocated to 200.9034

[.1]   **Religious mythology, general classes of religion, interreligious relations and attitudes, social theology**

> Relocated to 201

[.17]	Social theologies and interreligious relations and attitudes
	Attitudes of religions toward social issues relocated to 201.7

[.171]	Role of organized religions in society
	Relocated to 201.7

[.172]	Interreligious relations
	Relocated to 201.5

[.175]	Religions and secular disciplines
	Attitudes of religions toward secular disciplines relocated to 201.6; communications media relocated to 201.7

[.177]	Political affairs
	Relocated to 201.72

[.178]	Socioeconomic problems
	Relocated to 201.76

[.178 3]	Social problems and services
	Relocated to 201.76

[.178 326]	Hunger
	Relocated to 201.7638

[.178 327]	Abuse within the family
	Relocated to 201.7628292

[.178 327 1]	Child abuse and neglect
	Relocated to 201.76276

[.178 327 2]	Sexual abuse
	Relocated to 201.76276

[.178 327 3]	Adults who were victims of abuse as children
	Relocated to 201.762764

[.178 328]	Refugees and victims of political oppression
	Relocated to 201.76287

[.178 33]   Crime and punishment

                          Relocated to 201.764

[.178 34]   Social groups

                          Relocated to 200.8

[.178 35]   Sexual relations, marriage, divorce, family

                          Relocated to 201.7

[.178 36]   Ecology and population

[.178 362]   Human ecology

                          Relocated to 201.77

[.178 366]   Population

                          Relocated to 201.7

[.178 5]   Economics

                          Relocated to 201.73

[.178 7]   International affairs

                          Relocated to 201.727

[.2]   Doctrines

                  Relocated to 202

[.3]   Public worship and other practices

                  Relocated to 203

[.4]   Religious experience, life, practice

                  Relocated to 204

[.5]   Religious ethics

                  Relocated to 205

[.6]   Leaders and organization

                  Relocated to 206

[.7]   Missions and religious education

                  Relocated to 207

[.8]   Sources

                  Relocated to 208

[.9]   Sects and reform movements

                  Relocated to 209

292   Classical religion (Greek and Roman religion)

See also 299 for modern revivals of classical religions

See Manual at 200.92 and 201–209, 292–299; also at 201–209 and 292–299; also at 203.6, 263.9, 292–299 vs. 394.265–394.267; also at 322.1 vs. 201.72, 261.7, 292–299; also at 398.2 vs. 201.3, 230, 270, 292–299; also at 615.852 vs. 203.1, 234.131, 292–299; also at 616.86 vs. 158.1, 204.42, 248.8629, 292–299, 362.29

.001–.005	Standard subdivisions
[.006]	Organizations and management

          Do not use; class in 292.6

.007	Education, research, related topics
.007 1	Education

          Class here classical religion as an academic subject

          Class comprehensive works on religious education, religious education to inculcate religious faith and practice in 292.75

          See Manual at 207.5, 268 vs. 200.71, 230.071, 292–299

.008–.009	Standard subdivisions

>	292.07–292.08	Classical religion by specific culture

          Class specific elements regardless of culture in 292.1–292.9; class comprehensive works in 292

.07	Roman religion
.08	Greek religion
.1–.9	**Specific elements**

          Add to base number 292 the numbers following 20 in 201–209, e.g., mythology 292.13, organizations 292.65

          Class classical religion as an academic subject in 292.0071

293   †Germanic religion

          Class here Scandinavian religion, Norse religion

See also 299 for modern revivals of Germanic religion

See Manual at 200.92 and 201–209, 292–299; also at 201–209 and 292–299; also at 203.6, 263.9, 292–299 vs. 394.265–394.267; also at 207.5, 268 vs. 200.71, 230.071, 292–299; also at 322.1 vs. 201.72, 261.7, 292–299; also at 398.2 vs. 201.3, 230, 270, 292–299; also at 615.852 vs. 203.1, 234.131, 292–299; also at 616.86 vs. 158.1, 204.42, 248.8629, 292–299, 362.29

†Add as instructed under 290

294   Religions of Indic origin

Including Divine Light Mission, Radha Soami Satsang

See Manual at 200.92 and 201–209, 292–299; also at 201–209 and 292–299; also at 203.6, 263.9, 292–299 vs. 394.265–394.267; also at 207.5, 268 vs. 200.71, 230.071, 292–299; also at 322.1 vs. 201.72, 261.7, 292–299; also at 398.2 vs. 201.3, 230, 270, 292–299; also at 615.852 vs. 203.1, 234.131, 292–299; also at 616.86 vs. 158.1, 204.42, 248.8629, 292–299, 362.29

SUMMARY

294.3	**Buddhism**
.4	**Jainism**
.5	**Hinduism**
.6	**Sikhism**

.3   Buddhism

[.306]   Organizations and management

Do not use; class in 294.36

.307   Education, research, related topics

.307 1   Education

Class here Buddhism as an academic subject

Class comprehensive works on religious education, religious education to inculcate religious faith and practice in 294.375

See Manual at 207.5, 268 vs. 200.71, 230.071, 292–299

.33   Religious mythology, interreligious relations and attitudes, and social theology

Add to base number 294.33 the numbers following 201 in 201.3–201.7, e.g., social theology 294.337

.34   Doctrines and practices

.342   Doctrines

For social theology, see 294.337; for Buddhist ethics, see 294.35

.342 04   Doctrines of specific branches, sects, reform movements

Add to base number 294.34204 the numbers following 294.39 in 294.391–294.392, e.g., Zen doctrines 294.3420427

.342 1–.342 4   Specific doctrines

Add to base number 294.342 the numbers following 202 in 202.1–202.4, e.g., reincarnation 294.34237

.343–.344   Public worship and other practices; religious experience, life, practice

Add to base number 294.34 the numbers following 20 in 203–204, e.g., religious experience 294.3442

.35–.37	Religious ethics, leaders and organization, missions, religious education

Add to base number 294.3 the numbers following 20 in 205–207, e.g., the Buddha 294.363, organizations 294.365

See Manual at 207.5, 268 vs. 200.71, 230.071, 292–299

.38	Sources
.382	Sacred books and scriptures (Tripiṭaka, Tipiṭaka)

Works sacred to both Theravadins and Mahayanists

Class here comprehensive treatment of Theravadin and Mahayanist sacred texts

For works sacred only to Mahayanists, see 294.385

.382 2	Vinayapiṭaka
.382 3	Sūtrapiṭaka (Suttapiṭaka)
.382 32	Khuddakanikāya
.382 322	Dhammapada
.382 325	Jatakas
.382 4	Abhidharmapiṭaka (Abhidhammapiṭaka)
.383	Oral traditions
.384	Laws and decisions
.385	Sources of branches, sects, reform movements

Including Buddhist Tantras, Mahayanist sacred works

.39	Branches, sects, reform movements

Class specific aspects of branches, sects, reform movements in 294.33–294.38

.391	Theravada Buddhism

Variant names: Southern, Hinayana Buddhism

Including Mahasanghika, Saravastivada, Sautrantika schools

.392	Mahayana Buddhism (Northern Buddhism)

Including Madhyamika, Yogacara (Vijnana) schools

.392 3	Tibetan Buddhism (Lamaism)

See also 299.54 for Bon

.392 5	Tantric Buddhism
.392 6	Pure Land sects

.392 7	Zen (Ch'an)
	Including Rinzai, Soto
.392 8	Nichiren Shoshu and Sōka Gakkai

.4 †Jainism

.49   Sects and reform movements

         Number built according to instructions under 290

         Class specific aspects of sects and reform movements in 294.41–294.48

.492   Svetambara

.493   Digambara

.5   Hinduism

         Class here Brahmanism

SUMMARY

294.501–.509	**Standard subdivisions**
.51–.53	**Mythology, relations, doctrines, public worship and other practices**
.54	**Religious experience, life, practice, religious ethics**
.55	**Sects and reform movements**
.56–.57	**Leaders, organization, missions, religious education**
.59	**Sources**

[.506]   Organizations and management

         Do not use; class in 294.56

.507   Education, research, related topics

.507 1   Education

         Class here Hinduism as an academic subject

         Class comprehensive works on religious education, religious education to inculcate religious faith and practice in 294.575

         See Manual at 207.5, 268 vs. 200.71, 230.071, 292–299

.509   Historical, geographic, persons treatment

.509 013   3999–1000 B.C.

         Class here religion of Vedic period

.51–.53   Mythology, relations, doctrines, public worship and other practices

         Add to base number 294.5 the numbers following 20 in 201–203, e.g., gods and goddesses 294.5211

†Add as instructed under 290

.54	Religious experience, life, practice, religious ethics

Practices predominantly private or individual in character

Class here spirituality

.542	Religious experience

Including conversion, enlightenment

.542 2	Mysticism

.543	Worship, meditation, yoga

Class here description, interpretation, criticism, history, practical works on prayer, on contemplation; comprehensive works on worship

For public worship, see 294.538

.543 2	Devotional literature

Including meditations

.543 3	Prayer books

.543 5	Meditation

.543 6	Yoga

Religious and spiritual discipline

Including bhakti yoga, jnana yoga, karma yoga, kundalini yoga, raja yoga

Class yoga philosophy, raja yoga philosophy, interdisciplinary works on yoga in 181.45

See also 613.7046 for hatha yoga, physical yoga

.544	Religious life and practice

Add to base number 294.544 the numbers following 204.4 in 204.41–204.47, e.g., asceticism 294.5447

.548	Religious ethics

Including conscience, dharma, sin, vice

.548 6	Specific moral issues, sins, vices, virtues

Add to base number 294.5486 the numbers following 17 in 172–179, e.g., morality of family relationships 294.54863

.55	Sects and reform movements

Class Buddhism in 294.3; class Jainism in 294.4; class Sikhism in 294.6. Class a specific aspect of a Hindu sect or reform movement with the subject, e.g., doctrines of Vishnuism 294.52

.551	Early Hindu sects

.551 2	Vishnuism

Including International Society for Krishna Consciousness

.551 3	Shivaism
	Including Lingayats
.551 4	Shaktaism
	Class here Tantric Hinduism
.551 5	Ganapataism
.551 6	Shanmukaism
.551 7	Sauraism
.555	Ramakrishna movement
.556	Reformed Hinduism
.556 2	Brahma Samaj
.556 3	Arya-Samaj
.56–.57	Leaders, organization, missions, religious education

Add to base number 294.5 the numbers following 20 in 206–207, e.g., the role of the guru 294.561

Class Hinduism as an academic subject in 294.5071

See Manual at 207.5, 268 vs. 200.71, 230.071, 292–299

.59	Sources
.592	Sacred books and scriptures

Add to each subdivision identified by * as follows:
04   Special topics
041   Sanskrit texts
          Including textual criticism
          Class Sanskrit texts accompanied by translations in
          045; class Sanskrit texts accompanied by
          commentaries in 047
045   Translations
          Class here Sanskrit texts accompanied by translations
          Add to 045 notation 1–9 from Table 6, e.g.,
          translations into English 04521
          Class texts accompanied by commentaries in 047
046   Interpretation and criticism
          *For textual criticism, see 041; for commentaries,
          see 047*
047   Commentaries
          Criticism and interpretation arranged in textual order
          Including texts accompanied by commentaries
048   Nonreligious subjects treated in sacred books and
          scriptures
          Class a religious subject treated in sacred books and
          scriptures with the subject, e.g., rites and ceremonies
          294.538

.592 1	*Vedic literature

>   294.59212–294.59215   The Vedas

Class here Samhitas, Brahmanas, Aranyakas

Class Upanishads in 294.59218; class Vedic religion in 294.509013; class comprehensive works on the Vedas in 294.5921

.592 12	*Rigveda
.592 13	*Samaveda
.592 14	*Yajurveda
.592 15	*Atharvaveda
.592 18	Upanishads
.592 2	*Ramayana
.592 3	*Mahabharata

For Bhagavad Gita, see 294.5924

.592 4	*Bhagavad Gita
.592 5	Puranas
.592 6	Dharmasastras

Including Code of Manu

.593	Oral traditions
.594	Laws and decisions
.595	Sources of sects and reform movements

Including Hindu tantras

.6	**†Sikhism**
.663	Founders of Sikhism

Number built according to instructions under 290

Class here role and function of the ten Sikh gurus

295   †Zoroastrianism (Mazdaism, Parseeism)

Class Mithraism in 299.15

See Manual at 200.92 and 201–209, 292–299; also at 201–209 and 292–299; also at 203.6, 263.9, 292–299 vs. 394.265–394.267; also at 207.5, 268 vs. 200.71, 230.071, 292–299; also at 322.1 vs. 201.72, 261.7, 292–299; also at 398.2 vs. 201.3, 230, 270, 292–299; also at 615.852 vs. 203.1, 234.131, 292–299; also at 616.86 vs. 158.1, 204.42, 248.8629, 292–299, 362.29

*Add as instructed under 294.592

†Add as instructed under 290

296   Judaism

*See Manual at 200.92 and 201–209, 292–299; also at 201–209 and 292–299;
also at 203.6, 263.9, 292–299 vs. 394.265–394.267; also at 322.1 vs. 201.72,
261.7, 292–299; also at 398.2 vs. 201.3, 230, 270, 292–299; also at 615.852
vs. 203.1, 234.131, 292–299; also at 616.86 vs. 158.1, 204.42, 248.8629,
292–299, 362.29*

SUMMARY

296.01–.09	**Standard subdivisions**	
.1	**Sources**	
.3	**Theology, ethics, views of social issues**	
.4	**Traditions, rites, public services**	
.6	**Leaders, organization, religious education, outreach activity**	
.7	**Religious experience, life, practice**	
.8	**Denominations and movements**	

[.06]   Organizations and management

Do not use; class in 296.6

.07   Education, research, related topics

.071   Education

Class here Judaism as an academic subject

Class comprehensive works on Jewish religious education, religious
education to inculcate religious faith and practice in 296.68

See Manual at 207.5, 268 vs. 200.71, 230.071, 292–299

.071 1   Higher education

Class here Jewish theological faculties, rabbinical seminaries,
yeshivot, education of rabbis

.08   History and description with respect to kinds of persons

Class here Jewish attitudes toward social groups; discrimination, equality,
inequality, prejudice

.09   Historical, geographic, persons treatment

Class here history of specific synagogues

*See also 320.54095694 for Zionism; also 909.04924 for world history
of Jews*

\>   296.0901–296.0905   Historical periods

Add to each subdivision identified by * as instructed under —0901–0905 in
Table 1, e.g., museums of ancient Judaism 296.0901074

Class comprehensive works in 296.09

.090 1   *To 499 A.D.

---

*Add as instructed under 296.0901–296.0905

.090 13	*Earliest Judaism to 586 B.C.
.090 14	*Second Temple period, 586 B.C.–70 A.D.
.090 15	*Early rabbinic period, 70–499
.090 2–.090 5	6th–21st centuries

Add to base number 296.090 the numbers following —090 in notation 0902–0905 from Table 1, e.g., Judaism in the Middle Ages 296.0902

.092 Persons

Class here persons not associated with one activity or denomination

Class a person associated with one activity or denomination with the activity or denomination with which the person is associated, e.g., a theologian 296.3092, a Reform rabbi 296.8341092

.1 Sources

Class Jewish theology based on these sources in 296.3

For Torah and sacred scripture (Tanakh, Old Testament), see 221

See Manual at 221

SUMMARY

296.12	**Talmudic literature**
.14	**Midrash**
.15	**Sources of specific sects and movements**
.16	**Cabalistic literature**
.18	**Halakhah (Legal literature)**
.19	**Aggadah (Nonlegal literature)**

(.11) Tanakh

(Optional number; prefer 221)

Arranged as found in Jewish Bibles

See Manual at 221: Optional numbers for books of Bible

[.110 3] Dictionaries, encyclopedias, concordances

Do not use for dictionaries and encyclopedias; class in 296.1113.

Do not use for concordances; class in 296.1114–296.1115

(.111) Generalities

(Optional number; prefer 221)

Add to base number 296.111 the numbers following 221 in 221.04–221.9, e.g., criticism and interpretation 296.1116

*Add as instructed under 221–229

(.112)	*‡Torah (Pentateuch)
(.112 1)	*‡Genesis
(.112 2)	*‡Exodus

                    For Ten Commandments, see 296.1126

(.112 3)	*‡Leviticus
(.112 4)	*‡Numbers
(.112 5)	*‡Deuteronomy

                    For Ten Commandments, see 296.1126

(.112 6)	*‡Ten Commandments (Decalogue)
(.113)	*‡Prophetic books (Nevi'im)
(.113 1)	*Former Prophets (Nevi'im rishonim)

                    (Optional number; prefer 222)

                        For individual books of Former Prophets, see 296.1132–296.1135

(.113 2)	*‡Joshua
(.113 3)	*‡Judges
(.113 4)	*‡Samuel
(.113 41)	*‡Samuel 1
(.113 42)	*‡Samuel 2
(.113 5)	*‡Kings
(.113 51)	*‡Kings 1
(.113 52)	*‡Kings 2
(.113 6)	*Later Prophets (Nevi'im aharonim)

                    (Optional number; prefer 224)

                        For Isaiah, see 296.1137; for Jeremiah, see 296.1138; for Ezekiel, see 296.1139; for Minor Prophets, see 296.114

(.113 7)	*‡Isaiah
(.113 8)	*‡Jeremiah
(.113 9)	*‡Ezekiel
(.114)	*‡Minor Prophets

                    For Zephaniah, Haggai, Zechariah, Malachi, see 296.115

---

*Add as instructed under 221–229

‡(Optional number; prefer 222–224)

(.114 1)	*‡Hosea
(.114 2)	*‡Joel
(.114 3)	*‡Amos
(.114 4)	*‡Obadiah
(.114 5)	*‡Jonah
(.114 6)	*‡Micah
(.114 7)	*‡Nahum
(.114 8)	*‡Habakkuk
(.115)	*‡Zephaniah, Haggai, Zechariah, Malachi
(.115 1)	*‡Zephaniah
(.115 2)	*‡Haggai
(.115 3)	*‡Zechariah
(.115 4)	*‡Malachi
(.116)	*‡Writings (Ketuvim)
(.116 1)	*‡Psalms
(.116 2)	*‡Proverbs
(.116 3)	*‡Job
(.116 4)	*Megillot (Five scrolls)
	(Optional number; prefer 221.044)
(.116 41)	*‡Song of Solomon (Canticle of Canticles, Song of Songs)
(.116 42)	*‡Ruth
(.116 43)	*‡Lamentations
(.116 44)	*‡Ecclesiastes (Kohelet, Qohelet)
(.116 45)	*‡Esther
(.116 5)	*‡Daniel
(.116 6)	*‡Ezra
(.116 7)	*‡Nehemiah
(.116 8)	*‡Chronicles
(.116 81)	*‡Chronicles 1
(.116 82)	*‡Chronicles 2

*Add as instructed under 221–229

‡(Optional number; prefer 222–224)

(.118)	*Apocrypha

(Optional number; prefer 229)

For pseudepigrapha, see 229.9

(.118 1)   *Esdras 1 and 2

(Optional number; prefer 229.1)

Variant names: Esdras 3 and 4

See also 296.1166 for Ezra; also 296.1167 for Nehemiah

(.118 2)   *Tobit, Judith, Additions to Esther

(Optional number; prefer 229.2)

(.118 22)   *Tobit

(Optional number; prefer 229.22)

(.118 24)   *Judith

(Optional number; prefer 229.24)

(.118 27)   *Additions to Esther

(Optional number; prefer 229.27)

(.118 3)   *Wisdom of Solomon (Wisdom)

(Optional number; prefer 229.3)

Class here Apocryphal wisdom literature

For Ecclesiasticus, see 296.1184

(.118 4)   *Ecclesiasticus (Sirach)

(Optional number; prefer 229.4)

(.118 5)   *Baruch and Epistle of Jeremiah

(Optional number; prefer 229.5)

(.118 6)   *Song of the Three Children, Susanna, Bel and the Dragon

(Optional number; prefer 229.6)

(.118 7)   *Maccabees (Machabees)

(Optional number; prefer 229.7)

(.118 73)   *Maccabees 1 and 2 (Machabees 1 and 2)

(Optional number; prefer 229.73)

(.118 75)   *Maccabees 3 and 4 (Machabees 3 and 4)

(Optional number; prefer 229.75)

*Add as instructed under 221–229

(.118 8)   *Prayer of Manasseh

(Optional number; prefer 229.6)

> 296.12–296.14   Talmudic literature and Midrash

Add to each subdivision identified by ‡ as follows:
001–009   Standard subdivisions
04   Hebrew and Aramaic texts
Including textual criticism
Class texts accompanied by modern commentaries since 1500 in 07
05   Translations
Add to 05 notation 1–9 from Table 6, e.g., literature in English 0521
Class texts accompanied by modern commentaries since 1500 in 07
06   Interpretation and criticism (Exegesis)
Add to 06 the numbers following 220.6 in 220.601–220.68, e.g., historical criticism 067
For textual criticism, see 04; for modern commentaries since 1500, see 07
07   Modern commentaries since 1500
Criticism and interpretation arranged in textual order
Including texts accompanied by modern commentaries
Commentaries written before 1500 are classed with the text without addition of 07
08   Nonreligious subjects treated in Talmudic literature and Midrash
Add to base number 08 notation 001–999, e.g., natural sciences in Talmudic literature and Midrash 085
Class a religious subject treated in Talmudic literature and Midrash with the subject, e.g., Jewish ethics 296.36

Class comprehensive works in 296.1

.12   ‡Talmudic literature

.120 092   Persons

Number built according to instructions under 296.12–296.14

Class here Soferim, Tannaim, Amoraim, Geonim

.123   ‡Mishnah

.123 1   ‡Order Zera'im

Including tractates Berakhot, Bikkurim, Demai, Ḥallah, Kilayim, Ma'aser Sheni, Ma'aserot, Orlah, Pe'ah, Shevi'it, Terumot

---

*Add as instructed under 221–229
‡Add as instructed under 296.12–296.14

.123 2	‡Order Moʻed
	Including tractates Beẓah, Eruvin, Ḥagigah, Megillah, Moʻed Katan, Pesaḥim, Rosh Hashanah, Shabbat, Shekalim, Sukkah, Taʻanit, Yoma
.123 3	‡Order Nashim
	Including tractates Gittin, Ketubbot, Kiddushin, Nazir, Nedarim, Sotah, Yevamot
.123 4	‡Order Nezikin
	Including tractates Avodah Zarah, Bava Batra, Bava Kamma, Bava Meẓia, Eduyyot, Horayot, Makkot, Sanhedrin, Shevuʻot
.123 47	‡Tractate Avot (Pirke Avot)
.123 5	‡Order Kodashim
	Including tractates Arakhin, Bekhorot, Ḥullin, Keritot, Kinnim, Meʻilah, Menaḥot, Middot, Tamid, Temurah, Zevaḥim
.123 6	‡Order Tohorot
	Including tractates Kelim, Makhshirin, Mikvaʼot, Negaʻim, Niddah, Oholot (Ahilot), Parah, Tevul Yom, Tohorot, Ukẓin, Yadayim, Zavim
.123 7	Minor tractates
.124	‡Palestinian Talmud (Jerusalem Talmud, Talmud Yerushalmi)
.124 1–.124 7	Individual orders and tractates
	Add to base number 296.124 the numbers following 296.123 in 296.1231–296.1237, e.g., Order Zeraʻim in Palestinian Talmud 296.1241
.125	‡Babylonian Talmud
	Often called simply the Talmud
.125 1–.125 7	Individual orders and tractates
	Add to base number 296.125 the numbers following 296.123 in 296.1231–296.1237, e.g., tractate Shabbat in Babylonian Talmud 296.1252
.126	Tosefta and Baraita
.126 2	‡Tosefta
.126 21–.126 27	Individual orders and tractates
	Add to base number 296.1262 the numbers following 296.123 in 296.1231–296.1237, e.g., order Nezikin in Tosefta 296.12624
.126 3	‡Baraita

‡Add as instructed under 296.12–296.14

.127	Specific types of Talmudic literature
.127 4	‡Halakhah
.127 6	‡Aggadah
.14	‡Midrash
.141	‡Midrashic Halakhah
.142	‡Midrashic Aggadah
.15	Sources of specific sects and movements
.155	Writings of Qumran community

Class here comprehensive works on Dead Sea Scrolls

For Old Testament texts in Dead Sea Scrolls, see 221.44; for pseudepigrapha in Dead Sea Scrolls, see 229.91

See also 296.815 for comprehensive works on Qumran community

.16	Cabalistic literature

Class here interdisciplinary works on cabala

The texts of religious cabalistic works are classed here even if the editor introduces and annotates them from an occult or Christian point of view

Class Jewish mystical experience in 296.712; class Jewish mystical movements in 296.8

For cabalistic traditions in occultism, see 135.47

.162	Zohar
.18	Halakhah (Legal literature)

Including early rabbinical legal writings, comprehensive works on rabbinical writings to 1400

Class here commandments (mitzvot) treated as laws, the 613 commandments, comprehensive works on Jewish law

Class commandments (mitzvot) treated as ethical values in 296.36; class Jewish law relating to secular matters in 340.58

For Torah, see 222.1; for Talmudic Halakhah, see 296.1274; for Midrashic Halakhah, see 296.141. For early rabbinical writings to 1400 on a specific subject, see the subject, e.g., creation 296.34; for laws on a specific religious topic, see the topic, e.g., laws concerning marriage rites 296.444

.180 92	Persons

Class here Rishonim, Aharonim

‡Add as instructed under 296.12–296.14

.181   Legal writings of Maimonides

> Class here comprehensive works on writings of Maimonides

> *For philosophical writings of Maimonides, see 181.06. For writings on a specific religious topic, see the topic, e.g., the Thirteen Articles of Faith 296.3*

.181 2   Mishneh Torah

.182   Work of Joseph Caro

> Class here Shulḥan 'arukh

.185   Responsa

> Class responsa on a specific religious topic with the topic, e.g., responsa concerning marriage rites 296.444

.185 4   Responsa of reform movements

> Add to base number 296.1854 the numbers following 296.834 in 296.8341–296.8344, e.g., Reform responsa 296.18541

.188   Nonreligious subjects treated in halakhah

.188 000 1–.188 000 9   Standard subdivisions

.188 001–.188 999   Specific nonreligious subjects treated in halakhah

> Add to base number 296.188 notation 001–999, e.g., agriculture in halakhah 296.18863

.19   Aggadah (Nonlegal literature)

> Stories, legends, parables, proverbs, anecdotes, ancient or modern, told for religious edification

> Class here comprehensive works on Aggadah

> Class Jewish folklore in 398.2089924

> *For Talmudic Aggadah, see 296.1276; for Midrashic Aggadah, see 296.142*

> *See also 296.45371 for Passover Haggadah*

.3   **Theology, ethics, views of social issues**

> Standard subdivisions are added for theology, ethics, social issues together; for theology alone

> Class here Biblical theology, the Thirteen Articles of Faith

> *See also 181.06 for Jewish philosophy*

> *See Manual at 200 vs. 100*

.31   God and spiritual beings

.311   God

.311 2   Attributes and names of God

.311 4	Relation to the world

For revelation, see 296.3115; for miracles, see 296.3116; for relation to and action in history, see 296.3117; for creation, see 296.34

.311 5   Revelation

.311 55   Prophecy

Class Biblical prophecy and prophecies in 221.15; class the prophetic books of the Bible in 224; class messianic prophecies in 296.336

.311 6   Miracles

.311 7   Relation to and action in history

.311 72   Relationship to the Jewish people (Covenant relationship)

.311 73   Land of Israel

.311 74   Specific historical events

Including the Holocaust

.311 8   Theodicy

Vindication of God's justice and goodness in permitting existence of evil and suffering

.315   Angels

.316   Devils (Demons)

.32   Humankind

Including atonement, creation of humankind, free will, repentance, salvation, sin, soul

For eschatology, see 296.33

.33   Eschatology

Including death, resurrection, immortality

.336   Messianism

See also 232.906 for Jewish interpretations of Jesus

.34   Creation

For creation of humankind, see 296.32

.35   Apologetics and polemics

.36   Ethics

Including Biblical precepts, conscience, ethical wills, sin

Class here general works on commandments (mitzvot) treated as ethical values

Add to base number 296.36 the numbers following 17 in 172–179, e.g., morality of family relationships 296.363

Class works on commandments (mitzvot) treated as laws in 296.18; class guides to conduct of life in 296.7

See also 296.12347 for talmudic tractate Avot (Pirke Avot)

.37   Judaism and secular disciplines

Class here attitudes of Judaism toward and influence on secular issues, religious views and teachings about secular disciplines, works treating relation between Jewish belief and a secular discipline

Class Jewish philosophy of a secular discipline and Jewish theories within a secular discipline with the discipline, e.g., Jewish philosophy 181.06

For Judaism and social issues, see 296.38

See also 296.12–296.14 for nonreligious subjects treated in Talmudic literature and Midrash; also 296.188 for nonreligious subjects treated in halakhah

.371   Judaism and philosophy, parapsychology and occultism, psychology

.375   Judaism and natural sciences, mathematics

.376   Judaism and technology

Including Judaism and medicine

.377   Judaism and the arts

.38   Judaism and social sciences

Attitudes of Judaism toward and influence on social issues

Including Judaism and environment

Class here Judaism and socioeconomic problems, Jewish social theology

Class Jewish view of marriage and family in 296.74

.382   Judaism and politics

Attitude toward and influence on political activities and ideologies

Class here Judaism and civil rights

See Manual at 322.1 vs. 201.72, 261.7, 292–299

.382 7   International affairs, war and peace

Including attitude of Judaism toward civil and revolutionary wars, conscientious objectors, pacifism

.383   Judaism and economics

Class Judaism and environment in 296.38

.39   Judaism and other systems of belief

Including Judaism and atheism, Judaism and irreligion

.396   Judaism and Christianity

.397   Judaism and Islam

.4   Traditions, rites, public services

Class individual observances not provided for here in 296.7

SUMMARY

296.41	**Sabbath**
.43	**Festivals, holy days, fasts**
.44	**Rites and customs for occasions that occur generally once in a lifetime**
.45	**Liturgy and prayers**
.46	**Use of the arts and symbolism**
.47	**Sermons and preaching (Homiletics)**
.48	**Pilgrimages and sacred places**
.49	**Traditions, rites, public services of ancient Judaism to 70 A.D.**

.41   Sabbath

Class liturgy and prayers for Sabbath in 296.45

.412   Prohibited activity

> 296.43–296.44   Festivals, holy days, fasts; rites and customs for occasions that occur generally once in a lifetime

Class here personal ritual observances to be performed at specific times or in conjunction with specific rites

Class comprehensive works in 296.43

For specific rites of ancient Judaism to 70 A.D. not provided for elsewhere, see 296.49

.43   Festivals, holy days, fasts

For liturgy and prayers for festivals, holy days, fasts, see 296.453; for Sabbath, see 296.41

See Manual at 203.6, 263.9, 292–299 vs. 394.265–394.267

.431   High Holy Days

For Yom Kippur (Day of Atonement), see 296.432

.431 5   Rosh Hashanah (New Year)

.432   Yom Kippur (Day of Atonement)

.433   Sukkot (Feast of Tabernacles)

.433 9	Simḥat Torah
.435	Hanukkah (Feast of the Dedication)
.436	Purim (Feast of Lots)
.437	Pesach (Passover)
.438	Shavuot (Feast of Weeks, Pentecost)
.439	Other festivals, holy days, fasts

Including Lag b'Omer, Tishah b'Av

.439 1	Festivals, holy days, fasts associated with the land of Israel

Including Sabbatical Year (shemittah)

.44	Rites and customs for occasions that occur generally once in a lifetime

See also 296.7 for rites and customs which continue throughout life

For liturgy and prayers for occasions that occur generally once in a lifetime, see 296.454

.442	Special rites for male Jews
.442 2	Berit milah (Circumcision)
.442 3	Pidyon haben (Redemption of first-born male)
.442 4	Bar mitzvah
.443	Special rites for female Jews

Including naming ceremonies

For observance of laws of family purity, see 296.742

.443 4	Bat mitzvah
.444	Marriage and divorce rites and traditions

Standard subdivisions are added for marriage and divorce rites and traditions together, for marriage rites alone, for marriage traditions alone

Including issues concerning who may be married, descent of Jewish identity

For guides to marriage and family life, see 296.74

.444 3	Interreligious marriage
.444 4	Divorce rites and traditions

Standard subdivisions are added for either or both topics in heading

.445	Burial and mourning rites and traditions

Standard subdivisions are added for any or all topics in heading

Including memorial services

| .446 | Synagogue dedication |
| .45 | Liturgy and prayers |

Description, interpretation, conduct, texts of rites and public services; private and public prayers, blessings, benedictions

Including prayer at meals

Class here Ashkenazic liturgy; worship; liturgy and prayers for Sabbath; prayer books, e.g., siddurim

Class devotional reading for the individual in 296.72

| .450 4 | Liturgy of specific groups |

Including Ari liturgy

Class Ashkenazic liturgy or liturgy of unspecified group in 296.45

| [.450 401–.450 409] | Standard subdivisions |

Do not use; class in 296.4501–296.4509

.450 42	Sephardic liturgy
.450 44	Hasidic liturgy
.450 46	Reform liturgy
.450 47	Conservative liturgy
.450 48	Reconstructionist liturgy
.452	Piyyutim

> 296.453–296.454   Liturgy and prayers for festivals, holy days, fasts; for occasions that occur generally once in a lifetime

Add to each subdivision identified by * the numbers following 296.45 in 296.45042–296.45048, e.g., Passover Haggadah of the Sephardic rite 296.45371042

Class comprehensive works in 296.45

| .453 | *Liturgy and prayers for festivals, holy days, fasts |

Class here Mahzorim

| .453 1–.453 6 | Liturgy and prayers for High Holy Days, Sukkot, Hanukkah, Purim |

Add to base number 296.453 the numbers following 296.43 in 296.431–296.436, e.g., liturgy and prayers for High Holy Days 296.4531; then add further as instructed under 296.453–296.454, e.g., Reform prayer books for High Holy Days 296.4531046

| .453 7 | *Liturgy and prayers for Pesach (Passover) |

*Add as instructed under 296.453–296.454

.453 71	*Passover Haggadah (Seder service)

.453 8–.453 9	Liturgy and prayers for Shavuot, other festivals, holy days, fasts

Add to base number 296.453 the numbers following 296.43 in 296.438–296.439, e.g., prayers for Shavuot 296.4538; then add further as instructed under 296.453–296.454, e.g., prayers for Shavuot of the Sephardic rite 296.4538042

.454	Liturgy and prayers for occasions that occur generally once in a lifetime

Add to base number 296.454 the numbers following 296.44 in 296.442–296.446, e.g., liturgy and prayers for weddings 296.4544; then add further as instructed under 296.453–296.454, e.g., Reform prayer books for weddings 296.4544046

.46	Use of the arts and symbolism

Including synagogue buildings

.461	Liturgical articles

Including mezuzot, prayer shawls

.461 2	Phylacteries (Tefillin)

.461 5	Torah scrolls

Class here scribes (soferim)

.462	Music

Class here cantors

Class works containing both text and music, interdisciplinary works on Jewish liturgical music in 782.36

.47	Sermons and preaching (Homiletics)

Add to base number 296.47 the numbers following 296.4 in 296.41–296.44, e.g., High Holy Day sermons 296.4731

Class sermons on a specific subject with the subject, e.g., sermons on social issues 296.38

.48	Pilgrimages and sacred places

[.480 93–.480 99]	Specific continents, countries, localities

Do not use; class in 296.482–296.489

.481	Pilgrimages

Class pilgrimages to specific sacred places in 296.482–296.489

.482	Jerusalem

*Add as instructed under 296.453–296.454

.483–.489 Geographic treatment of sacred places in specific continents, countries, localities

> Add to base number 296.48 notation 3–9 from Table 2, e.g., sacred places in Iraq 296.48567; however, for Jerusalem, see 296.482

> Class the Land of Israel as a theme in Jewish theology in 296.31173

.49 Traditions, rites, public services of ancient Judaism to 70 A.D.

> Not provided for elsewhere

.491 The Temple

.492 Sacrifices and offerings

.493 Ark of the Covenant

.495 Ancient priesthood

.6 Leaders, organization, religious education, outreach activity

.61 Leaders and their work

> Role, function, duties

> Class here ordination, work of rabbis; activities of leaders and other congregational workers designed to promote religious and social welfare of social groups in community, pastoral care; chaplaincy

> *For ancient priesthood, see 296.495*

> *See also 296.4615 for scribes; also 296.462 for cantors*

[.610 92] Persons

> Do not use for persons treatment of religious leaders primarily associated with a specific religious activity; class in 296.1–296.7, e.g., a theologian 296.3092. Do not use for persons treatment of religious leaders primarily associated with a specific denomination or movement; class in 296.8, e.g., a Reform rabbi 296.8341092. Do not use for persons treatment of other religious leaders; class in 296.092

.65 Synagogues and congregations

> Role and function

> *See also 296.46 for synagogue buildings*

.650 9 Historical, geographic, persons treatment

> Class history of specific synagogues in 296.09

.67 Organizations and organization

Theory and history of organizations other than synagogues and congregations

Including religious authority, excommunication, schism; sanhedrin

Class laws and decisions in 296.18. Class organizations sponsored by one denomination with the denomination in 296.8, e.g., Union of Orthodox Congregations of America 296.83206073

For synagogues and congregations, see 296.65

See also 369.3924 for Jewish service and fraternal associations, e.g., B'nai B'rith

.68 Religious education

Class Judaism as an academic subject in 296.071

For religious education at the level of higher education, see 296.0711

See Manual at 207.5, 268 vs. 200.71, 230.071, 292–299

.680 83 History and description with respect to young people

Class here afternoon weekday schools, Hebrew schools, Jewish religious schools, Sunday schools; religious education in Jewish day schools

Class comprehensive works on Jewish day schools in 371.076

.69 Outreach activity for the benefit of converts and nonobservant Jews

.7 Religious experience, life, practice

Standard subdivisions are added for religious experience, life, practice together; for religious life and practice together

Practices which continue throughout life

Including asceticism

Class here guides to religious life, spirituality

For ethics, see 296.36; for traditions, rites, public services, see 296.4

[.708 5] Relatives   Parents

Do not use; class in 296.74

.708 6 Persons by miscellaneous social characteristics

[.708 655] Married persons

Do not use; class in 296.74

.71 Religious experience

.712 Mysticism

Class cabalistic literature in 296.16; class Jewish mystical movements in 296.8

.714   Conversion

> Class here conversion of non-Jews to Judaism

> Class outreach activity for the benefit of converts and nonobservant Jews in 296.69. Class conversion of Jews to another religion with the religion, e.g., conversion of Jews to Christianity 248.246

.715   Return of Jews from non-observance to religious observance

.72   Devotional reading for the individual

> Including meditation and meditations

> Class devotional literature in the form of Aggadah in 296.19

.73   Kosher observance (Kashrut observance)

> Observance of dietary laws

> Including ritual slaughter (shehitah)

.74   Marriage and family life

> Including Jewish child rearing

> Class here social theology of marriage and family, comprehensive works on marriage

> > *For ethics of marriage, see 296.363; for marriage and divorce rites and traditions, see 296.444*

.742   Observance of laws of family purity

> > *For ritual bath (mikveh), see 296.75*

.75   Ritual bath (Mikveh)

.8   Denominations and movements

> Class specific aspects of denominations and movements in 296.1–296.7

.81   Denominations and movements of ancient origin

> Including Hellenistic movement, Karaites, Zealots

.812   Pharisees

.813   Sadducees

.814   Essenes

> > *For Qumran community, see 296.815*

.815   Qumran community

> > *See also 296.155 for writings of Qumran community*

.817   Samaritans

.82   Medieval and early modern denominations and movements to ca. 1750

> Including Sabbatianism

.83	Modern denominations and movements after ca. 1750
.832	Orthodox Judaism
.833	Mystical Judaism
.833 2	Hasidism
.833 22	Habad Lubavitch Hasidism
.834	Reform movements
	Including Humanistic Judaism
.834 1	Reform Judaism
.834 2	Conservative Judaism
.834 4	Reconstructionist Judaism

297   Islam, Babism, Bahai Faith

Standard subdivisions are added for Islam, Babism, Bahai Faith together; for Islam alone

See Manual at 200.92 and 201–209, 292–299; also at 201–209 and 292–299; also at 203.6, 263.9, 292–299 vs. 394.265–394.267; also at 322.1 vs. 201.72, 261.7, 292–299; also at 398.2 vs. 201.3, 230, 270, 292–299; also at 615.852 vs. 203.1, 234.131, 292–299; also at 616.86 vs. 158.1, 204.42, 248.8629, 292–299, 362.29

SUMMARY

297.01–.09	**Standard subdivisions**
.1	**Sources of Islam**
.2	**Islamic doctrinal theology ('Aqā'id and Kalām); Islam and secular disciplines; Islam and other systems of belief**
.3	**Islamic worship**
.4	**Sufism (Islamic mysticism)**
.5	**Islamic ethics and religious experience, life, practice**
.6	**Islamic leaders and organization**
.7	**Protection and propagation of Islam**
.8	**Islamic sects and reform movements**
.9	**Babism and Bahai Faith**

[.06]	Organizations and management
	Do not use; class in 297.6
.07	Education, research, related topics
.071	Education

Class here Islamic religion as an academic subject

Class comprehensive works on Islamic religious education, religious education to inculcate religious faith and practice in 297.77

See Manual at 207.5, 268 vs. 200.71, 230.071, 292–299

.09   Historical, geographic, persons treatment

               Class here religious aspects of Islamic fundamentalism

               Class political science aspects of Islam, of Islamic fundamentalism in 320

                    For religious aspects of Islamic fundamentalism in a specific sect or reform movement, see 297.8

                    See also 909.09767 for Islamic civilization

                    See Manual at 320.557 vs. 297.09, 297.272, 322.1

.092   Persons

               Class interdisciplinary works on caliphs as civil and religious heads of state with the subject in 940–990, e.g., Abu Bakr 953.02092

                    For Muslims primarily associated with a specific religious activity, see 297.1–297.7; for founders of Sufi orders, see 297.48; for Muḥammad the Prophet, see 297.63; for Muḥammad's family and companions (including religious biography of the first four caliphs), see 297.64; for Muslims primarily associated with a specific sect or reform movement, see 297.8

                    See Manual at 297.092

>   **297.1–297.8   Islam**

               Class comprehensive works in 297

>   **297.1–297.3   Sources of Islam; Islamic doctrinal theology ('Aqā'id and Kalām); Islam and secular disciplines; Islam and other systems of belief; Islamic worship**

               Class comprehensive works in 297

.1   **Sources of Islam**

                         SUMMARY

        297.12   **Koran and Hadith**
          .14   **Religious and ceremonial laws and decisions**
          .18   **Stories, legends, parables, proverbs, anecdotes told for religious edification**

.12   Koran and Hadith

               Class theology based on Koran and Hadith in 297.2

.122   Koran

.122 03   Topical dictionaries and encyclopedias

                         Do not use for concordances or non-topical dictionaries; class in 297.1224–297.1225

.122 09	Historical, geographic, persons treatment

Class here geography, history, chronology of the Middle East in Koran times in relation to the Koran

Class origin of Koran, commentary about historical occasions on which passages of Koran were revealed in 297.1221; class compilation and recording of Koran in 297.1224042; class comprehensive works on geography, history, chronology of the Middle East in Koran times in 939.4

.122 092	Persons

For Muḥammad, see 297.63; for Muḥammad's family and companions, see 297.64; for prophets prior to Muḥammad, see 297.246

.122 1	Origin and authenticity

Including inspiration, revelation, commentary about historic occasions on which passages were revealed; Koranic prophecy and prophecies

Class compilation and recording of Koran in 297.1224042

.122 2	Koran stories retold

Including picture books

\>   297.1224–297.1225   Texts

Class comprehensive works in 297.122

For texts accompanied by commentaries, see 297.1227

.122 4	Arabic texts

Class here textual criticism

Class Arabic texts accompanied by translations in 297.1225

.122 404	Special topics of Arabic texts
.122 404 2	Compilation and recording of Koran
.122 404 5	Recitation and readings

Standard subdivisions are added for either or both topics in heading

Class here art of melodic reading, tajwīd (adornment of recitation); qirā'āt (science of the readings, which treats various renditions of the text according to different oral traditions)

.122 5	Translations

Class here Arabic texts accompanied by translations

Add to base number 297.1225 notation 1–9 from Table 6, e.g., the Koran in English 297.122521

.122 6	Interpretation and criticism (Exegesis)

Class art of recitation in 297.1224045

For textual criticism, see 297.1224; for commentaries, see 297.1227

.122 601	Philosophy and theory

Class here hermeneutics, principles and methods of Koranic exegesis

.122 61	General introductions to the Koran

Including general introductions to the sciences necessary to study the Koran

.122 67	Historical criticism
.122 68	Allegorical and numerical interpretations
.122 7	Commentaries

Criticism and interpretation arranged in textual order

Class here texts accompanied by commentaries

.122 8	Nonreligious subjects treated in the Koran

Class a religious subject treated in the Koran with the subject, e.g., Islamic ethics 297.5

.122 800 01–.122 800 09	Standard subdivisions
.122 800 1–.122 899 9	Specific nonreligious subjects treated in the Koran

Add to base number 297.1228 notation 001–999, e.g., natural sciences in the Koran 297.12285

.122 9	Individual suras and groups of suras

Origins, authenticity; geography, history, chronology of Koran lands in Koran times; texts; criticism, interpretation; commentaries; nonreligious subjects treated in the suras

.124	Hadith (Traditions)

Including collection by Aḥmad ibn Ḥanbal

.124 001–.124 009	Standard subdivisions
.124 01–.124 08	Generalities

Add to base number 297.1240 the numbers following 297.122 in 297.1221–297.1228, e.g., origins 297.12401

>   297.1241–297.1248   Specific Hadith

       Add to each subdivision identified by * as follows:
          001–009   Standard subdivisions
          01–08   Generalities
               Add to 0 the numbers following 297.122 in
               297.1221–297.1228, e.g., criticism 06

       Class comprehensive works in 297.124

.124 1	*Al-Bukhārī, Muḥammad ibn Ismāʿīl
.124 2	*Abū Dāʾūd Sulaymān ibn al-Ashʿath al-Sijistānī
.124 3	*Muslim ibn al-Ḥajjāj al-Qushayrī
.124 4	*Al-Tirmidhī, Muḥammad ibn ʿĪsá
.124 5	*Al-Nasāʾī, Aḥmad ibn Shuʿayb
.124 6	*Ibn Mājah, Muḥammad ibn Yazīd
.124 7	Other Sunni Hadith
.124 8	Hadith of other sects

.14   Religious and ceremonial laws and decisions

       Class here fiqh in relation to religious and ceremonial laws and decisions, sharia in relation to religious and ceremonial laws and decisions

       Class Islamic law relating to secular matters, interdisciplinary works on Islamic law in 340.59. Class religious law on a specific topic with the topic, e.g., religious law concerning ḥajj 297.352

.18   Stories, legends, parables, proverbs, anecdotes told for religious edification

       Class here comprehensive works on Islamic legends

       Class Islamic folklore in 398.2088297

       For Islamic legends on a specific topic, see the topic, e.g., Islamic legends about pre-Islamic prophets 297.246

.2   **Islamic doctrinal theology (ʿAqāʾid and Kalām); Islam and secular disciplines; Islam and other systems of belief**

       Standard subdivisions are added for Islamic doctrinal theology, Islam and secular disciplines, Islam and other systems of belief together; for Islamic doctrinal theology alone

       Class Islamic ethics in 297.5; class doctrines concerning Muḥammad the Prophet in 297.63

*Add as instructed under 297.1241–297.1248

SUMMARY

297.204	**Doctrines of specific sects**
.21	**God and spiritual beings**
.22	**Humankind**
.23	**Eschatology**
.24	**Other doctrines**
.26	**Islam and secular disciplines**
.27	**Islam and social sciences**
.28	**Islam and other systems of belief**
.29	**Apologetics and polemics**

>   **297.204–297.24**   Islamic doctrinal theology ('Aqā'id and Kalām)

         Class comprehensive works in 297.2

         For apologetics and polemics, see 297.29; for shahāda (profession of faith), see 297.34

.204   Doctrines of specific sects

         Add to base number 297.204 the numbers following 297.8 in 297.81–297.87, e.g., doctrines of Shiites 297.2042

.21   God and spiritual beings

.211   God

.211 2   Attributes and names of God

         Class vindication of God's justice and goodness in permitting existence of evil and suffering in 297.2118

         For tawhid (unity of God), see 297.2113

.211 3   Tawhid (Unity of God)

.211 4   Relation to the world

         Including relation to and action in history

         For revelation, see 297.2115; for creation, see 297.242

.211 5   Revelation

         Including prophecy

         Class Koranic prophecy in 297.1221; class prophets and prophethood in 297.246

.211 8   Theodicy

         Vindication of God's justice and goodness in permitting existence of evil and suffering

.215   Angels

.216   Devils

.217   Jinn

.22	Humankind
	Including faith, repentance
	For eschatology, see 297.23
.221	Creation
	Class comprehensive works on creation in 297.242
.225	Nature
	Including soul
	Class free will and predestination in 297.227
.227	Free will and predestination
	Class here freedom of choice between good and evil
.23	Eschatology
	Including day of judgment, death, eternity, future life, heaven, hell, punishment, resurrection, rewards
	Class doctrines of Hidden Imam, of Mahdi in 297.24
.24	Other doctrines
	Including doctrines of Hidden Imam, of Mahdi
.242	Creation
	Including origin of life
	Class here Islamic cosmology
	For creation of humankind, see 297.221
.246	Prophets prior to Muḥammad
	Including Adam, Moses
	Class here comprehensive works on prophets and prophethood in Islam
	For Muḥammad the Prophet, see 297.63
.246 3	Abraham
.246 5	Jesus, son of Mary

.26 Islam and secular disciplines

Class here attitudes of Islam toward and influence on secular issues, Islamic views and teachings about secular disciplines

Class relation of a specific Islamic doctrine and a secular discipline with the doctrine in 297.2, e.g., relation of Islamic doctrine about creation and scientific theories about creation 297.242; class work influenced by Islam and Islamic theories within a secular discipline with the discipline, e.g., Islamic philosophy 181.07, architecture in the Islamic world 720.91767

For Islam and social sciences, see 297.27

See also 297.1228 for nonreligious subjects treated in Koran; also 297.12408 for nonreligious subjects treated in Hadith

See Manual at 297.26–297.27

.261 Islam and philosophy, parapsychology and occultism, psychology

.265 Islam and natural sciences, mathematics

.266 Islam and technology

.267 Islam and the arts

.27 Islam and social sciences

Attitudes of Islam toward and influence on social issues

Including environment, war and peace

Class here Islam and socioeconomic problems, Islamic social theology

Class Islamic view of marriage and family in 297.577

See Manual at 297.26–297.27

.272 Islam and politics

Including civil rights, international affairs, nationalism

Class political science view of religiously oriented political theories and ideologies in 320.55; class political science view of relation of state to religious organizations and groups in 322.1; class political science view of religious political parties in 324.2182

See Manual at 320.557 vs. 297.09, 297.272, 322.1

.273 Islam and economics

Including Islam and communism

See also 297.289 for Islam and atheism

.28 Islam and other systems of belief

Attitudes toward and relations with other systems of belief

Class apologetics and polemics in 297.29

.282 Islam and Judaism

Class Biblical figures as prophets prior to Muḥammad in 297.246

.283	Islam and Christianity

Class Biblical figures as prophets prior to Muḥammad in 297.246

.284	Islam and religions of Indic origin

Add to base number 297.284 the numbers following 294 in 294.3–294.6, e.g., Islam and Hinduism 297.2845

.289	Islam and irreligion

Including Islam and atheism

.29	Apologetics and polemics
.292	Polemics against Judaism
.293	Polemics against Christianity
.294	Polemics against religions of Indic origin
.298	Polemics against scientists and materialists

.3   Islamic worship

Including use of arts and symbolism in worship

Class here comprehensive works on Islamic worship, on non-Sufi worship, on Islamic private worship, on non-Sufi private worship, public worship

Class Pillars of Islam (Pillars of the Faith) in 297.31. Class specific applications of the arts and symbolism in worship with the application in 297.301–297.38, e.g., use of arts and symbolism in mosques 297.351

For Sufi worship, see 297.43

.300 1–.300 9	Standard subdivisions
.301–.307	Specific sects

Add to base number 297.30 the numbers following 297.8 in 297.81–297.87, e.g., Shiite rites 297.302

.31	Pillars of Islam (Pillars of the Faith)

Comprehensive works only

For shahāda (profession of faith), see 297.34; for ḥajj (pilgrimage to Mecca), see 297.352; for ṣawm Ramaḍān (annual fast of Ramadan), see 297.362; for ṣalāt (prayer five times daily), see 297.3822; for zakat, see 297.54

See also 297.72 for jihad

.34	Shahāda (Profession of faith)

.35   Sacred places and pilgrimages

> Standard subdivisions are added for sacred places and pilgrimages together, for sacred places alone
>
> Including non-Sufi pilgrimages, comprehensive works on Islamic pilgrimages
>
> Class here rites and ceremonies associated with sacred places and pilgrimages
>
> Class pilgrimages to specific places in 297.352–297.359
>
> *For Sufi pilgrimages, see 297.435*

[.350 93–.350 99]   Treatment by specific continents, countries, localities

> Do not use; class in 297.353–297.359

.351   Mosques

> Class here interdisciplinary works
>
> *For organizational role and function of mosques, see 297.65; for architecture of mosques, see 726.2*

[.351 093–.351 099]   Treatment by specific continents, countries, localities

> Do not use; class in 297.352–297.359

.352   Mecca

> Class here ḥajj (pilgrimage to Mecca)

.353–.359   Treatment by specific continents, countries, localities

> Add to base number 297.35 notation 3–9 from Table 2, e.g., Medina 297.35538, Jerusalem 297.35569442; however, for Mecca, see 297.352

.36   Special days and seasons

> Including Jum'ah (Friday prayer); 'Āshūrā' (Tenth of Muḥarram); Mawlid al-Nabī (Prophet's birthday); 'Īd al-Aḍḥā, 'Īd al-Fiṭr
>
> Class here rites and ceremonies associated with special days and seasons, Islamic religious calendar
>
> *See also 297.37 for sermons for special days and seasons*

.362   Ṣawm Ramaḍān (Annual fast of Ramadan)

> Including Laylat al-Qadr
>
> Class comprehensive works on fasting in 297.53

.37   Sermons and preaching

> Class sermons on a specific subject with the subject, e.g., sermons on day of judgment 297.23

.38   Rites, ceremonies, prayer, meditation

Conduct and texts

Including ablutions

Class ablutions associated with prayer and meditations in 297.382; class ablutions associated with burial and mourning in 297.385; class rites and ceremonies associated with sacred places and pilgrimages in 297.35; class rites and ceremonies associated with special days and seasons in 297.36

See also 297.37 for sermons and preaching

.382   Prayer and meditation

Standard subdivisions are added for prayer and meditation together, for prayer alone

Including dhikr (remembrance), qiblah (direction of prayer)

Class here practical works on prayer and meditation

Class prayer and meditation associated with sacred places and pilgrimages in 297.35; class prayer and meditation associated with special days and seasons in 297.36. Class prayer and meditation associated with specific rites and ceremonies with the rites and ceremonies, e.g., funerals in 297.385; class prayers and meditations on a specific subject with the subject, e.g., unity of God 297.2113

.382 2   Ṣalāt (Prayer five times daily)

For texts of prayers, see 297.3824

.382 4   Texts of prayers and meditations

Class here prayer books

.385   Burial and mourning rites

.39   Popular practices

Including controversial practices, e.g., divination and occultism

Class occult practices not regarded as Islamic practices in 130; class Islamic views of occultism regarded as a secular topic in 297.261; class sociological studies of Islamic popular practices in 306.69739. Class popular practices associated with a topic provided elsewhere with the topic, e.g., popular practices associated with burial and mourning 297.385

.4   Sufism (Islamic mysticism)

.41   Sufi doctrinal theology; Sufism and secular disciplines; Sufism and non-Islamic systems of belief

> Standard subdivisions are added for Sufi doctrinal theology, Sufism and secular disciplines, Sufism and non-Islamic systems of belief together; for Sufi doctrinal theology alone

> Add to base number 297.41 the numbers following 297.2 in 297.21–297.29, e.g., Sufi concept of God 297.4111

> Class Sufi doctrines concerning Muḥammad the Prophet in 297.4; class Sufi ethics in 297.45

.43   Sufi worship

> Add to base number 297.43 the numbers following 297.3 in 297.3001–297.38, e.g., Sufi pilgrimages 297.435, Sufi observance of ṣawm Ramaḍān 297.4362, Sufi prayer and meditation 297.4382

.44   Sufi religious life and practice

> Class here guides to Sufi religious life

> Class Sufi ethics in 297.45

> *For Sufi worship, see 297.43*

.446   Sufi individual observances

> Including Sufi ascetic practices, dietary laws and observance

> *For Sufi fasting, see 297.45*

.45   Sufi ethics

> Including Sufi almsgiving, fasting, ṣadaqah, zakat

> *For Sufi observance of ṣawm Ramaḍān, see 297.4362*

.48   Sufi orders

> Including Bektashi, Naqshabandiyah, Qādirīyah, Tijānīyah

> *See also 297.835 for Kadarites (Islamic sect)*

.482   Mevleviyeh

.5   **Islamic ethics and religious experience, life, practice**

> Standard subdivisions are added for ethics and religious experience, life, practice together; for ethics alone

> Including conscience; general works on duty, sin, vice, virtue

> Class a specific duty, sin, vice, virtue in 297.56

> *For Pillars of Islam (Pillars of the Faith), see 297.31; for jihad, see 297.72*

.53   Ṣawm (Fast)

> Class here comprehensive works on fasting

> *For ṣawm Ramaḍān (Annual Fast of Ramadan), see 297.362*

.54   Zakat

     Class here almsgiving, ṣadaqah

.56   Specific vices, virtues, moral issues

     Add to base number 297.56 the numbers following 17 in 172–179, e.g., Islamic sexual ethics 297.566; however, for almsgiving, see 297.54

     Class comprehensive works on vices, on virtues in 297.5

.57   Religious experience, life, practice

     Standard subdivisions are added for any or all topics in heading

     Class here non-Sufi and comprehensive works on Islamic religious experience, life, practice; non-Sufi and comprehensive guides to religious life

     Class Islamic ethics in 297.5

     For worship, see 297.3; for mysticism and Sufi religious experience, see 297.4; for Sufi life and practice, see 297.44

[.570 85]   Relatives   Parents

     Do not use; class in 297.577

.570 86   Persons by miscellaneous social characteristics

[.570 865 5]   Married persons

     Do not use; class in 297.577

.574   Conversion

     Class here conversion of non-Muslims to Islam

     Class da'wah in 297.74. Class conversion of Muslims to another religion with the religion, e.g., conversion of Muslims to Christianity 248.246

.576   Individual observances

     Including ascetic practices, dietary laws and observance, ritual slaughter of animals to conform with dietary laws

     For pilgrimages, see 297.35; for fasting, see 297.53; for almsgiving, see 297.54

.577   Marriage and family life

     Including Muslim child rearing

     Class here comprehensive works on marriage, on family life

     For ethics of marriage and family, see 297.563

.6 **Islamic leaders and organization**

.61 Leaders and their work

Role, function, duties

Class here ayatollahs, caliphate, caliphs, imamate, imams, ulama

For doctrine of Hidden Imam, see 297.24; for Muḥammad the Prophet, see 297.63; for Muḥammad's family and companions (including first four caliphs), see 297.64

[.610 92] Persons

Do not use for persons treatment of religious leaders primarily associated with a specific religious activity; class in 297.1–297.7, e.g., founders of Sufi orders 297.48. Do not use for persons treatment of Muḥammad; class in 297.63. Do not use for persons treatment of Muḥammad's family and companions (including first four caliphs); class in 297.64. Do not use for persons treatment of Islamic leaders primarily associated with a specific sect or reform movement; class in 297.8. Do not use for persons treatment of other religious leaders; class in 297.092

.63 Muḥammad the Prophet

Class here comprehensive works on Muḥammad and his family and companions

Class Hadith in 297.124

For Muḥammad's family and companions, see 297.64

.630 92 Persons

Do not use for Muḥammad the Prophet; class in 297.63

Class here scholars who specialize in the life and works of Muḥammad the Prophet

.632 Period prior to call to prophethood

Including birth, childhood

See also 297.36 for Mawlid al-Nabī (holiday of Prophet's birthday)

.633 Period at Mecca

Including Isrā' (Night Journey to Jerusalem) and Mi'rāj (Ascent to Heaven)

Class comprehensive works on prophetic career in 297.635

For period prior to call to prophethood, see 297.632

.634 Hijrah (Emigration from Mecca)

.635 Period at Medina

For emigration from Mecca to Medina, see 297.634

.64   Muḥammad's family and companions

> Standard subdivisions are added for family and companions together, for family alone

> Including descendants of Muḥammad

.642   Wives

.644   Daughters

.648   Ṣaḥābah (Companions)

> Including religious biography and theological discussion of the first four caliphs

> Class interdisciplinary biographies of the first four caliphs with the subject in 950, e.g., Abu Bakr 953.02092

.65   Organizations and organization

> Role and function

> Including associations, congregations, mosques

> Class Islamic organizations in relation to political affairs in 297.272; class a specific organization limited to a specific sect or reform movement in 297.8; class political science view of relation of state to religious organizations and groups in 322.1; class political science view of religious political parties in 324.2182; class interdisciplinary works on mosques in 297.351

.7   Protection and propagation of Islam

.72   Jihad

.74   Da'wah

> Class here call to Islam, missionary work

.77   Islamic religious education

> Class Islam as an academic subject in 297.071; class comprehensive works on madrasah education, treating both religious education and other subjects, in 371.077

> *For religious education at the level of higher education, see 297.0711*

> *See Manual at 207.5, 268 vs. 200.71, 230.071, 292–299*

.770 83   Young people

> Class here Islamic religious schools, religious education in Islamic schools that teach all subjects

> Class comprehensive works on Islamic schools that teach all subjects in 371.077

.8   **Islamic sects and reform movements**

Class specific aspects of sects and reform movements in 297.1–297.7; class secular view of relation of state to religious organizations and groups in 322.1; class secular view of religious political parties in 324.2182

For Sufism, see 297.4

.804   Special topics of Islamic sects and reform movements

.804 2   Relations among sects and reform movements

Class here relations between Sunni and Shia Islam

.81   Sunnites

Class relations between Sunnites and Shiites in 297.8042

.811   Hanafites

.812   Shafiites

.813   Malikites

.814   Hanbalites and Wahhābīyah

.82   Shiites

Class relations between Shiites and Sunnites in 297.8042

.821   Twelvers (Ithna Asharites)

.822   Seveners (Ismailites)

Including Mustalians, Nizaris

.824   Zaydites

.83   Other sects and reform movements

Including Kharijites

.833   Ibadites

.834   Motazilites

.835   Kadarites

See also 297.48 for Qādirīyah (Sufi order)

.837   Murjiites

.85   Druzes

.86   Ahmadiyya movement

.87   Black Muslim movement

Including American Muslim Mission, Nation of Islam, World Community of al-Islam in the West

.9   **Babism and Bahai Faith**

.92   Babism

| .93 | Bahai Faith |
| .931–.937 | Specific aspects |

        Add to base number 297.93 the numbers following 20 in 201–207, e.g., Bahai ethics 297.935

| .938 | Sources |
| .938 2 | Sacred books |

        For works by the Bab, see 297.92

.938 22	Works by Bahá'u'lláh
.938 24	Works by 'Abdu'l-Bahá
.938 6	Authoritative interpretation

        Class here works by Shoghi Effendi

| .938 7 | Elucidation and legislation |

        Class here works of the Universal House of Justice

(298) (Permanently unassigned)

(Optional number used to provide local emphasis and a shorter number for a specific religion other than Christianity; prefer the number for the specific religion elsewhere in 292–299; or optional number used for Christianity if option A under 290 is chosen. Other options are described at 290)

299 Religions not provided for elsewhere

Including Urantia, modern revivals of long dormant religions

Class syncretistic religious writings of individuals expressing personal views and not claiming to establish a new religion or to represent an old one in 200

If a religion not named in the schedule claims to be Christian, class it in 289.9 even if it is unorthodox or syncretistic

See Manual at 200.92 and 201–209, 292–299; also at 201–209 and 292–299; also at 203.6, 263.9, 292–299 vs. 394.265–394.267; also at 207.5, 268 vs. 200.71, 230.071, 292–299; also at 322.1 vs. 201.72, 261.7, 292–299; also at 398.2 vs. 201.3, 230, 270, 292–299; also at 615.852 vs. 203.1, 234.131, 292–299; also at 616.86 vs. 158.1, 204.42, 248.8629, 292–299, 362.29

(Options for giving local emphasis and shorter numbers for a specific religion are described at 290)

SUMMARY

299.1–.4	**Religions of Indo-European, Semitic, Non-Semitic Afro-Asiatic, North and West Asian, Dravidian origin**
.5	**Religions of East and Southeast Asian origin**
.6	**Religions originating among Black Africans and people of Black African descent**
.7	**Religions of North American native origin**
.8	**Religions of South American native origin**
.9	**Religions of other origin**

.1–.4 **Religions of Indo-European, Semitic, Non-Semitic Afro-Asiatic, North and West Asian, Dravidian origin**

> Not otherwise provided for
>
> Add to base number 299 the numbers following —9 in notation 91–94 from Table 5, e.g., Mithraism 299.15
>
> Class modern revivals of long dormant religions in 299

.1 **Religions of Indo-European origin**

> Number built according to instructions under 299.1–299.4

.16 **Celtic religion**

> Number built according to instructions under 299.1–299.4

.161 Specific aspects of Celtic religion

> Add to base number 299.161 the numbers following 20 in 201–209, e.g., Celtic mythology 299.16113

.3 **Religions of Non-Semitic Afro-Asiatic origin**

> Number built according to instructions under 299.1–299.4

.31 †Ancient Egyptian religion

> Number built according to instructions under 299.1–299.4

.5 **Religions of East and Southeast Asian origin**

> *See Manual at 200.9 vs. 294, 299.5*

.51 Religions of Chinese origin

.511 Specific aspects of Chinese religions

> Add to base number 299.511 the numbers following 20 in 201–209, e.g., Chinese gods and goddesses 299.511211

.512 †Confucianism

> Class the Four books of Confucius, interdisciplinary works on Confucianism in 181.112

.514 †Taoism

.54 Religions of Tibetan origin

> Class here Bon

.56 Religions of Japanese and Ryukyuan origin

.561 †Shinto

.57–.59 Other religions of East and Southeast Asian origin

> Add to base number 299.5 the numbers following —95 in notation 957–959 from Table 5, e.g., Caodaism 299.592

†Add as instructed under 290

.6   Religions originating among Black Africans and people of Black African descent

> *For Black Muslims, see 297.87; for religions originating among peoples who speak, or whose ancestors spoke, Ethiopian languages, see 299.28; for religions originating among Cushitic and Omotic peoples, see 299.35; for religions originating among the Hausa, see 299.37; for religions originating among the Malagasy, see 299.93*

[.609 61–.609 69]   Religions in specific areas in Africa

> Do not use; class in 299.691–299.699

.61   Specific aspects

> Add to base number 299.61 the numbers following 20 in 201–208, e.g., mythology and mythological foundations 299.6113 [*formerly* 299.62], doctrines 299.612 [*formerly* 299.63], practices 299.613 [*formerly* 299.64], rites and ceremonies 299.6138 [*formerly* 299.64]
>
> Class specific aspects of specific religions and movements, of religions of specific groups and peoples in 299.67–299.68

[.62]   Mythology and mythological foundations

> Mythology and mythological foundations relocated to 299.6113; mythology and mythological foundations of specific religions and movements relocated to 299.67; mythology and mythological foundations of religions of specific groups and peoples relocated to 299.68

[.63]   Doctrines

> Doctrines relocated to 299.612; doctrines of specific religions and movements relocated to 299.67; doctrines of religions of specific groups and peoples relocated to 299.68

[.64]   Practices, rites, ceremonies

> Practices relocated to 299.613; rites, ceremonies relocated to 299.6138; practices, rites, ceremonies of specific religions and movements relocated to 299.67; zombiism relocated to 299.675; practices, rites, ceremonies of religions of specific groups and peoples relocated to 299.68

.67   Specific religions and movements

> Class here mythology and mythological foundations [*formerly* 299.62]; doctrines [*formerly* 299.63]; practices, rites, ceremonies [*formerly* 299.64]; and other specific aspects of specific religions and movements

.672   †Umbanda

.673   †Candomblé

.674   †Santeria

---

†Add as instructed under 290

.675 †Voodoo

Including zombiism [*formerly* 299.64]

Class voodoo as an occult practice without regard to its religious significance in 133.4

.676 †Ras Tafari movement

.68 Religions of specific groups and peoples

Class here mythology and mythological foundations [*formerly* 299.62]; doctrines [*formerly* 299.63]; practices, rites, ceremonies [*formerly* 299.64]; and other specific aspects of religions of specific groups and peoples

Class specific religions and movements of specific groups and peoples in 299.67

.681 Religions of Khoikhoi and San

.683–.685 Religions of peoples who speak, or whose ancestors spoke, Niger-Congo, Nilo-Saharan languages

Add to base number 299.68 the numbers following —96 in notation 963–965 from Table 6, e.g., religion of the Yoruba 299.68333; then add further as follows:
001–008 Standard subdivisions [*formerly* 01–08]
009 Historical, geographic, persons treatment [*formerly* 09]
01–08 Specific aspects
Add to 0 the numbers following 20 in 201–208, e.g., mythology 013, Yoruba mythology 299.68333013; however, standard subdivisions relocated from 01–08 to 001–008
[09] Historical, geographic, persons treatment
Relocated to 009

.686–.688 Religions of national groups in Africa

Add to base number 299.68 the numbers following —6 in notation 66–68 from Table 2, e.g., religion of Ugandans 299.68761

Class national groups that predominate in specific areas in Africa in 299.69

.689 Religions of other national groups of largely African descent

Add to base number 299.689 notation 4–9 from Table 2, e.g., African religion of Haitians 299.6897294

Class religions of such national groups in areas where they predominate in 299.609, e.g., African religion of Haitians in Haiti 299.6097294

†Add as instructed under 290

.69   Religions of specific areas in Africa

Add to base number 299.69 the numbers following —6 in notation 61–69 from Table 2, e.g., religions of West Africa 299.696

Class specific aspects of religions of specific areas in 299.61; class specific religions and movements in specific areas in 299.67; class religions of specific groups and peoples in specific areas in 299.68

.7   Religions of North American native origin

[.709 71–.709 79]   Religions in specific areas in North America

Do not use; class in 299.791–299.799

.71   Specific aspects

Add to base number 299.71 the numbers following 20 in 201–208, e.g., mythology and mythological foundations 299.7113 [*formerly* 299.72], doctrines 299.712 [*formerly* 299.73], practices 299.713 [*formerly* 299.74], rites and ceremonies 299.7138 [*formerly* 299.74]

Class specific aspects of religions of specific groups and peoples in 299.78

[.72]   Mythology and mythological foundations

Mythology and mythological foundations relocated to 299.7113; mythology and mythological foundations of religions of specific groups and peoples relocated to the group or people in 299.78, plus notation 013 from table under 299.78

[.73]   Doctrines

Doctrines relocated to 299.712; doctrines of religions of specific groups and peoples relocated to the group or people in 299.78, plus notation 02 from table under 299.78

[.74]   Practices, rites, ceremonies

Practices relocated to 299.713; rites, ceremonies relocated to 299.7138; practices of religions of specific groups and peoples relocated to the group or people in 299.78, plus notation 03 from Table under 299.78; rites, ceremonies of religions of specific groups and peoples relocated to the group or people in 299.78, plus notation 038 from table under 299.78

[.77]   Specific cults

Number discontinued; class in 299.7

.78   Religions of specific groups and peoples

Add to base number 299.78 the numbers following —97 in notation 971–979 from Table 5, e.g., religion of Aztecs 299.78452; then add further as follows (*not* as instructed at Table 5):
     001–009   Standard subdivisions
     01–08   Specific aspects
           Add to 0 the numbers following 20 in 201–208, e.g., mythology and mythological foundations 013 [*formerly* 299.72], doctrines 02 [*formerly* 299.73], practices 03 [*formerly* 299.74], rites and ceremonies 038 [*formerly* 299.74], Aztec mythology 299.78452013

.79   Religions of specific areas in North America

> Add to base number 299.79 the numbers following —7 in notation 71–79 from Table 2, e.g., religions of Indians of Mexico 299.792

> Class religions of specific groups and peoples in specific areas in 299.78

.8   Religions of South American native origin

[.809 81–.809 89]   Religions of specific areas in South America

> Do not use; class in 299.891–299.899

.81   Specific aspects

> Add to base number 299.81 the numbers following 20 in 201–208, e.g., mythology and mythological foundations 299.8113 [*formerly* 299.82], doctrines 299.812 [*formerly* 299.83], practices 299.813 [*formerly* 299.84], rites and ceremonies 299.8138 [*formerly* 299.84]

> Class specific aspects of religions of specific groups and peoples in 299.88

[.82]   Mythology and mythological foundations

> Mythology and mythological foundations relocated to 299.8113; mythology and mythological foundations of religions of specific groups and peoples relocated to the group or people in 299.88, plus notation 013 from table under 299.88

[.83]   Doctrines

> Doctrines relocated to 299.812; doctrines of religions of specific groups and peoples relocated to the group or people in 299.88, plus notation 02 from table under 299.88

[.84]   Practices, rites, ceremonies

> Practices relocated to 299.813; rites, ceremonies relocated to 299.8138; practices of religions of specific groups and peoples relocated to the group or people in 299.88, plus notation 03 from Table under 299.88; rites, ceremonies of religions of specific groups and peoples relocated to the group or people in 299.88, plus notation 038 from table under 299.88

[.87]   Specific cults

> Number discontinued; class in 299.8

.88   Religions of specific groups and peoples

> Add to base number 299.88 the numbers following —98 in notation 982–989 from Table 5, e.g., religion of Incas 299.88323; then add further as follows (*not* as instructed at Table 5):
>   001–009   Standard subdivisions
>   01–08   Specific aspects
>   Add to 0 the numbers following 20 in 201–208, e.g., mythology and mythological foundations 013 [*formerly* 299.82], doctrines 02 [*formerly* 299.83], practices 03 [*formerly* 299.84], rites and ceremonies 038 [*formerly* 299.84], Inca mythology 299.88323013

.89	Religions of specific areas in South America

    Add to base number 299.89 the numbers following —8 in notation 81–89 from Table 2, e.g., religions of Indians of the Amazon 299.8911

    Class religions of specific groups and peoples in specific areas in 299.88

.9	**Religions of other origin**
.92	Religions of other ethnic origin

    Add to base number 299.92 the numbers following —99 in notation 991–999 from Table 5, e.g., religion of Polynesians 299.924

.93	Religions of eclectic and syncretistic origin

    Religions and applied religious philosophies of eclectic, syncretistic, universal nature

    Including Eckankar, a Course in Miracles, Great White Brotherhood, New Age religions, New Thought, systems of Bhagwan Shree Rajneesh and Meher Baba, United Church of Religious Science

    Class syncretistic religious writings of individuals expressing personal views and not claiming to establish a new religion or to represent an old one in 200

        See also 289.98 for Christian New Thought

        See Manual at 299.93; also at 201–209 and 292–299

.932	Gnosticism

    Including Manicheism

    Class Christian gnosticism in 273.1; class Christian Manicheism in 273.2

.933	Subud
.934	Theosophy
.935	Anthroposophy
.936	Scientology

    Including dianetics

.94	Religions based on modern revivals of witchcraft

    Class here neopaganism, wicca

Manual Notes
for 200 Religion

MANUAL NOTES
FOR 200 RELIGION

T1—0882 and 200

Religious groups and Religion

Use subdivisions of T1—0882 in 200 to represent official or semiofficial positions of denominations and sects, e.g., Catholic teachings on socioeconomic problems 261.8088282.

Do not use T1—0882 for works of an individual except in the rare cases in which an individual's view has become an official statement of a group. That is, use 261.8 (*not* 261.8088282) for writings on Christian attitudes towards socioeconomic problems by persons who happen to be Catholic.

130 vs. 200

Parapsychology and occultism vs. Religion

Use 130 for parapsychological and occult phenomena if they are not presented as religious, or if there is doubt as to whether they have been so presented. Use 200 for works about parapsychological or occult phenomena if the author describes them as religious, or the believers and practitioners consider them to be religious. If in doubt, prefer 130.

Use 130 for knowledge reputedly derived from secret and ancient religious texts but not applied for religious purposes; however, use 200 for editions of the texts, even if annotated from an occultist viewpoint, e.g., discussion of occult traditions derived from the Zohar 135.47, but the text of the Zohar 296.162.

200 vs. 100

Religion vs. Philosophy

Both religion and philosophy deal with the ultimate nature of existence and relationships, but religion treats them within the context of revelation, deity, worship. Philosophy of religion (210) does not involve revelation or worship but does examine questions within the context of deity.

Use 200 for any work that emphasizes revelation, deity, or worship, even if it uses philosophical methods, e.g., a philosophical proof of the existence of God 212.1. Use 180–190 for the thought of a religious tradition used to examine philosophical questions without reference to deity or religious topics, e.g., Jewish philosophy 181.06, Christian philosophy 190. However, use 200 for ethics based on a religion. If in doubt, prefer 200.

200.9 vs. 294, 299.5

Geographic treatment of religion vs. Religions of Indic and of East and Southeast Asian origin

Use 200.9 for works covering various religious traditions in an area, not just the religions that originated there, e.g., use 200.954 for the religions of India (including Christianity and Islam), use 200.951 for the religions of China (including Christianity and Buddhism). Use 294 and 299.5 for the religions that originated in particular geographic areas. Most of these religions have spread beyond the area where they originated. These areas also have adherents of religions that originated elsewhere, e.g., Buddhism (which originated in India) is present in China. If in doubt, prefer 200.9.

200.92 and 201–209, 292–299

Persons associated with religions other than Christianity

Persons associated with the religions in 292–299 are often identified with a number of religious functions and activities. For example, a Hindu guru may be thought of as a theologian, a teacher, a missionary, or a clergyman. If a religious leader cannot be identified primarily with one function, activity, or sect, class the leader's biography in the base number for the religion and add notation 092 from Table 1. Use 200.922 for collected biography of persons from many religions who are not identified with one function or activity. Use a number that corresponds to the number given in the table below for persons associated with a specific religion, e.g., a Buddhist member of a religious order 294.365092 (corresponds to 206.57092 in the table below). Use the following table of preference for comprehensive biographies of persons primarily identified with one function, activity, or sect:

Founders of religions	206.3
Founders of sects	209
Founders of religious orders	206.57092
Religious leaders (high ranking officials)	200.92
Of specific sects	209
Theologians	202.092
Moral theologians	205.092
Missionaries	207.2092
Martyrs, heretics, saints	200.92
Of specific sects	209
Teachers	207.5092
Members of religious orders	206.57092
Clergy	200.92
Of specific sects	209

Use the subdivisions of 206 for the nature, role, and function of religious leaders. Except for founders of religions (206.3) and founders and members of religious orders (206.57092), do not use the subdivisions of 206 for biography.

Class works dealing with only one aspect of a person's career with the aspect, e.g., Muḥammad as a moral theologian 297.5092 (*not* 297.63).

201–209 and 292–299

Comparative religion

Except for 296 Judaism and 297 Islam, the subdivisions of the various religions in 292–299 are based on 201–209. All topics in 201–209 are provided for under the separate religions in 292–299, either explicitly, by synthesis, or by implication, even if the order is sometimes different. What is said about 201–209, therefore, will also be true of 292–299.

Compare the topics in 201–209 with the subdivisions of Christianity for clues to placement of specific topics. A comparative list follows:

Social theologies	201.7	261
Doctrinal theologies	202	230
Public worship	203	246–247, 263–265
Religious experience, life, practice	204	242, 248
Religious ethics	205	241
Leaders and organizations	206	250, 262, 267
Pastoral theology and work	206.1	253
Missions, religious education	207	266, 268
Sources	208	220
Denominations, sects, reform movements	209	280

Denominations and sects

Class a denomination or sect with the religion to which its own members say it belongs.

Class the early history of a specific religion before its division into sects as general history of the religion, but class a comprehensive survey of the various sects in the number for the sects of the religion, e.g., the sects and reform movements of Buddhism 294.39. Class a work dealing with both early history and sects in the general number for history of the religion.

Class religious orders in 206.5 and similar numbers in 292–299, not with any sect within the religion to which the orders may belong.

203.6, 263.9, 292–299 vs. 394.265–.267

Customs associated with religious holidays

Use 203.6, 263.9, and similar numbers in 292–299 for the religious customs associated with religious holidays, e.g., sunrise Easter services 263.93, lighting the Hanukkah lamp 296.435. Use 394.265–.267 for the secular customs associated with religious holidays, e.g., Easter egg hunts 394.2667, eating latkes and spinning the Hanukkah top 394.267. If in doubt, prefer 203.6, 263.9, and similar numbers in 292–299.

207.5, 268 vs. 200.71, 230.071, 292–299

Religious education, Christian religious education vs. Education in religion, education in Christianity, in Christian theology

Use 207.5 (and similar numbers in 292–299, such as 294.575 Hindu religious education or 297.77 Islamic religious education) for works on how various religions educate their members (especially young members) to be good followers of their own religions, usually called "religious education." Such education stresses knowledge of the faith and living as a member of a religion, and is meant to instill the values of a particular religion, not to study it in a detached manner. Use 268 for religious education as a ministry of the Christian church for the purpose of confirming believers in Christian faith and life, and religious education programs sponsored by the local church.

Use 200.71 for works on education in and teaching of comparative religion, the religions of the world, and religion as an academic subject, usually called "religious studies." Use 230.071 for works on education in and teaching of Christianity as an academic subject, e.g., a course on Christianity in secular secondary schools 230.0712. Use a similar number in 292–299 for works on education in and teaching of another specific religion as an academic subject, e.g., a course on Hinduism in secular secondary schools 294.50712, on Islam 297.0712.

If in doubt as to which type of education is being treated, prefer 207.5 (or a similar number in 292–299) and 268.

Use 200.711 (*not* 207.5) for works on religious education at the level of higher education, and for works on the education of the clergy. Use 230.0711 (*not* 268) for works on higher education in both Christianity and Christian theology and for works on education of the clergy; all of this education usually takes place in divinity schools, theological seminaries, and graduate departments of theology or ministry in universities. Class education or training of the clergy for specialized work with the specialty, e.g., courses in Biblical studies 220.0711, programs in Christian pastoral counseling 253.50711. Use similar numbers from 292–299, e.g., university education in Islam 297.0711.

Class study and teaching of specific topics in comparative religion, Christianity, or the specific religions in 292–299, as follows:

Class works on teaching a specific topic to children of elementary-school age with works on religious education of children in general, e.g., Christian religious education courses on the Bible for children 268.432; Jewish religious education courses on the Tanakh (scriptures) for children 296.68.

Class works on teaching a specific topic to persons of secondary-school age and older with the topic using notation 071 from Table 1, e.g., study and teaching of Christian church history in secondary schools 270.0712; study of the Tanakh in Jewish colleges and universities 221.0711.

Use 268.434 for Christian religious education of adults, other than in the setting of formal higher education, e.g., works on adult education in parish religious education programs or Sunday schools.

220.92

Biography of individual persons in Bible

Class a comprehensive biography of a Biblical person with the book or books with which the person is most closely associated, usually the historical part of the Bible in which the person's life is narrated, e.g., Solomon, King of Israel, in 1st Kings 222.53092. Solomon's association with 223 Poetic books is weaker. However, some Biblical persons are more closely associated with nonhistorical books, e.g., class Isaiah and Timothy with the books that bear their names, 224.1092 and 227.83092, respectively. Although they appear briefly in historical narratives, their lives are not narrated in full there. Use 225.92 for the apostles John, Peter, and Paul, since each is associated with a number of books in the New Testament, but use 226.092 for the other apostles, associated primarily with Gospels and Acts.

See also discussion at 230–280.

221

Optional numbers for books of Old Testament (Tanakh)

Alphabetic index

Each of the books of the Old Testament (Tanakh) and the combination of them can have one of three different numbers depending on whether one chooses the preferred arrangement at 222–224 or one of the two optional arrangements. Optional numbers showing the books in the order found in Jewish Bibles appear in Appendix A (Option A) and at 296.11 (Option B). The following alphabetic listing gives the three numbers for each book or combination of books:

Book	Preferred	Option A	Option B
Amos	224.8	223.63	296.1143
Canticle of Canticles	223.9	224.41	296.11641
Chronicles	222.6	224.8	296.1168
Chronicles 1	222.63	224.81	296.11681
Chronicles 2	222.64	224.82	296.11682
Daniel	224.5	224.5	296.1165
Deuteronomy	222.15	222.5	296.1125
Ecclesiastes	223.8	224.44	296.11644
Exodus	222.12	222.2	296.1122
Esther	222.9	224.45	296.11645
Ezekiel	224.4	223.5	296.1139
Ezra	222.7	224.6	296.1166
Five scrolls	221.044	224.4	296.1164
Former Prophets	222	223.1	296.1131
Genesis	222.11	222.1	296.1121
Habakkuk	224.95	223.68	296.1148
Haggai	224.97	223.72	296.1152
Hosea	224.6	223.61	296.1141
Isaiah	224.1	223.3	296.1137

Jeremiah	224.2	223.4	296.1138
Job	223.1	224.3	296.1163
Joel	224.7	223.62	296.1142
Jonah	224.92	223.65	296.1145
Joshua	222.2	223.11	296.1132
Judges	222.32	223.12	296.1133
Ketuvim	223	224	296.116
Kings	222.5	223.14	296.1135
Kings 1	222.53	223.141	296.11351
Kings 2	222.54	223.142	296.11352
Kohelet	223.8	224.44	296.11644
Lamentations	224.3	224.43	296.11643
Later Prophets	224	223.2	296.1136
Leviticus	222.13	222.3	296.1123
Malachi	224.99	223.74	296.1154
Megillot	221.044	224.4	296.1164
Micah	224.93	223.66	296.1146
Minor Prophets	224.9	223.6	296.114
Nahum	224.94	223.67	296.1147
Nehemiah	222.8	224.7	296.1167
Nevi'im	224	223	296.113
Numbers	222.14	222.4	296.1124
Obadiah	224.91	223.64	296.1144
Pentateuch	222.1	222	296.112
Prophetic books	224	223	296.113
Proverbs	223.7	224.2	296.1162
Pslams	223.2	224.1	296.1161
Qohelet	223.8	224.44	296.11644
Ruth	222.35	224.42	296.11642
Samuel	222.4	223.13	296.1134
Samuel 1	222.43	223.131	296.11341
Samuel 2	222.44	223.132	296.11342
Song of Solomon	223.9	224.41	296.11641
Song of Songs	223.9	224.41	296.11641
Torah	222.1	222	296.112
Writings	223	224	296.116
Zechariah	224.98	223.73	296.1153
Zephaniah	224.96	223.71	296.1151

230–280

Persons associated with Christianity

Use the following table of preference for comprehensive biographies:

Jesus Christ, Mary, Joseph, Joachim, Anne, John the Baptist	232.9
Other persons in the Bible	220
Founders of denominations	280
Founders of religious orders	271
Higher clergy (e.g., popes, metropolitans, archbishops, bishops) prior to 1054	270.1–.3
Higher clergy subsequent to 1054	280
Theologians	230
Moral theologians	241
Missionaries	266
Evangelists	269.2
Persons noted for participation in associations for religious work	267
Martyrs	272
Heretics	273
Saints	270
Saints prior to 1054	270.1–.3
Saints subsequent to 1054	280
Mystics	248.22
Hymn writers	264.23
Religious educators	268
Members of religious orders	271
Clergy prior to 1054	270.1–.3
Clergy subsequent to 1054	280
Members of the early church to 1054	270.1–.3
Members of denominations	280
Christian biography of persons who fall in none of the above categories	270

Add notation 092 from Table 1 as appropriate, e.g., collected biography of saints 270.0922; Pope Gregory the Great 270.2092.

Use numbers in the range 220–269 other than those listed in the table of preference above for comprehensive biographies of persons with specialized religious careers, or for works treating only one aspect of a person's life and work, e.g., a Biblical scholar 220.092.

Use subdivisions of 230 for biography and criticism of individual theologians, e.g., Saint Thomas Aquinas 230.2092. Use 230.044092 for Protestant theologians who are not connected with a specific denomination or who are important and influential enough to transcend their own denominations, e.g., Karl Barth 230.044092. Use 230.092 for theologians not connected with any specific type of theology. If in doubt, prefer 230.092. Class critical appraisal of an individual theologian's thought on a specific topic with the topic, e.g., on justification 234.7092.

Do not use 248.2 Religious experience or its subdivisions except 248.22 for comprehensive biographies, e.g., a biography of Teresa of Avila's religious life 282.092 (*not* 248.2092). However, use 248.2 for biographical accounts written for devotional purposes, not as comprehensive accounts of a person's life, e.g., the story of one's conversion 248.246092.

Do not use 253, 255, and 262.1 for biographies of the kinds of persons listed in the table of preference above.

Class biographies of members of specific denominations and sects with the main branch of the denomination rather than with the most specific organization or area, e.g., a biography of a member of the Lutheran Church in America 284.1092 (*not* 284.133092); a biography of a clergyman of the African Methodist Episcopal Church 287.8092 (*not* 287.83); a biography of a Russian clergyman of the Eastern Orthodox Church 281.9092 (*not* 281.947092); collected biography of Catholics in the United States 282.092273.

Use 280 without subdivision for members of nondenominational and interdenominational Christian churches. Also use 280 without subdivision if a person living after 1054 belongs to a Christian church, but it cannot be determined which denomination.

If a person does not belong to a church, or if it cannot be determined whether the person belongs to a church, use the historical period that most closely matches the individual's life span or the time period of the individual's greatest prominence in 270 and the country if known, e.g., biography of a 20th-century Christian 270.82092, biography of a 20th-century United States Christian 277.3082092.

See also discussion at 220.92.

231.7652 vs. 213, 500, 576.8

Relation of scientific and Christian viewpoints of origin of universe vs. Creation in philosophy of religion vs. Natural sciences and mathematics vs. Evolution

Evolution versus creation

Use 231.7652 for works on creation science or creationism written by Christians who assume that the Bible provides a chronology of natural history and who rely upon religious premises in responding to theories from the natural sciences. Similarly, use 231.7652 for works that attempt to refute creation science, unless they take the writings of creationists as a starting point from which to demonstrate the case for evolution. On the other hand, use 500 for works by creationist authors that attempt to refute evolution theory by examining the writings, hypotheses, and findings of scientists.

The difficulty stems from the fact that on the question of evolution the *pro* and *con* positions differ so radically that they normally belong in different disciplines, science and religion, respectively. However, when a religious author is trying to enlighten scientists on a specific scientific matter, class the work with science, while if a scientist is trying to enlighten the religious on a specific religious matter, class the work with religion. The correct classification is determined by the intent of the author, and the interest of the readers that the author is seeking to reach, not by the truth, falsity, or validity of interpretations and premises.

Use 231.7652 for comprehensive works including both religion and science.

Use 213 for works that consider the relation between divine creation and evolution as a philosophical problem, without appealing to a particular religion or scripture. If in doubt between 213 and 231.7652, prefer 231.7652.

The most common focus of interest of works belonging in 500 is on biological evolution. Use 576.8 for these works. Use 523.88 if the emphasis of a work is mainly on stellar evolution, 530 if on basic physical principles, 551.7 if on historical geology, and 560 if on paleontology. Use 500 if there is no clear emphasis on a specific branch of science.

241 vs. 261.8

Christian ethics vs. Christian social theology

Some topics are covered in both religious ethics and social theology, e.g., war and peace (241.6242, 261.873). Use 241 for works that focus on what conduct is right or wrong. Use 261.8 for works that may discuss right and wrong, but treat the topic in a broader context as a problem in society and discuss Christian attitudes toward and influence on the problem. Use 241 for works that emphasize what the individual should do. Use 261.8 for works that stress what the church's stance should be, what response the church or Christian community should make to alleviate the problem, or the church's view on problems transcending individual conduct. If in doubt, prefer 241.

260 vs. 251–254, 259

Christian social and ecclesiastical theology vs. Local church and Pastoral care of specific kinds of persons

The local church is the group in which individual believers can meet regularly face to face for worship, fellowship, and church activities—for example, a congregation, a college church group.

Among the more recent forms of the local church are the small groups called basic Christian communities or basic ecclesial communities. These are smaller than parishes or congregations, but, like other forms of the local church, are organized for the general religious welfare of their members, not just for special projects or functions. Class these in the same way as parishes, i.e., class comprehensive works in 250 (or in 262.26 when treated as part of ecclesiology), and class specific aspects with the aspect in the subdivisions of 250.

Use either 250 or 260 for activities undertaken by the church, depending on the context. Use 250 for works intended for the individual practitioner in the local setting. This may be as small as a parish youth group or as large as a counseling program that serves a metropolitan area. Use 261 for the church's attitude to cultural and social problems, and its activities regarding them, unless the context is limited to the local church, e.g., a practical work for the prison chaplain 259.5, but the church's attitude to the treatment of criminals 261.8336. If in doubt, prefer 260.

Use 260 for some activities that can be conducted by the local church, e.g., public worship (264–265), religious education (268), spiritual renewal and evangelism (269), as the context of works on these subjects is often broader than the local church.

Use 262 for church organization, unless the scope is limited to administration of the local church (254).

261.5

Christianity and secular disciplines

Use 261.5 for personal Christian views and church teachings about secular disciplines as a whole, their value, how seriously a Christian should take them, how far the disciplines should affect faith. Class Christian philosophy of a secular discipline with the discipline, e.g., a Christian philosophy of psychology 150.1. In some cases specific provision is made for use of secular disciplines for religious purposes, e.g., use of drama 246.72. If in doubt, class with the secular discipline.

270, 230.11–.14 vs. 230.15–.2, 281.5–.9, 282

Early church to 1054 vs. Eastern churches, Roman Catholic Church

Use 270.1–.3 (*not* 281.1–.4) for the history of the Church prior to 1054, because the early church is considered to be undivided by denominations until the schism of 1054. Use 274–279 for the history of specific churches prior to 1054.

Use 270.1–.3 or 274–279 for the history of the Eastern and Roman Catholic churches before 1054. Use 281.5–.9 or 282 for works on later history or works that cover both the early and later history. If in doubt for works about both Eastern and Roman Catholic churches, prefer 270. If in doubt for works about a specific denomination, prefer 281.5–.9 or 282.

Use 230.11–.14 for theology of Eastern and Roman Catholic churches before 1054. Use 230.15–.2 for later theology.

280.042 vs. 262.0011

Relations between denominations vs. Ecumenism

Use 280.042 for works on the ecumenical movement and interdenominational cooperation. Use 280.042 also for works on relations between two or more specific denominations having notation that differs in the first three digits, e.g., relations between Roman Catholics (282) and Lutherans (284.1). Class works about relations among denominations having the same notation in the first three digits in the most specific number that includes them all, e.g., relations among the various Baptist denominations, between Baptists and Disciples of Christ 286. Class works about relations between one denomination and several others with the denomination emphasized, e.g., relations between Baptists and other denominations 286. Class discussions among denominations on a specific subject with the subject, e.g., the Eucharist 234.163. Use 262.0011 for theoretical works on ecumenism. If in doubt, prefer 280.042.

283–289

Protestant and other denominations

Under the general name of some denominations, e.g., Presbyterian churches of United States origin 285.1, notation is provided for specific denominations, e.g., 285.13. The specific denominations are named church bodies uniting a number of individual local churches, e.g., the Presbyterian Church (U.S.A.) 285.137, the Associate Presbyterian Church of North America 285.13 (the latter denomination is not listed in the schedule). Along with notation for specific denominations, a span for treatment of the denomination by continent, country, or locality will also be provided, e.g., 285.14–.19. Use the notation for specific denominations if the denominations are treated with regard to all or nearly all the geographic area they cover, but use the span for treatment by continent, country, or locality for works on a specific denomination covering a smaller area, e.g., use 286.132 for the Southern Baptist Convention, but use 286.1768 for a state association of Southern Baptist churches in Tennessee (286.1 plus notation 768 for Tennessee from Table 2). Use the span for treatment by continent, country, or locality for individual local churches, regardless of the specific denomination to which they belong. Also use the span for treatment by continent, country, or locality for a work about several specific denominations in one country by area, e.g., a work describing the various Presbyterian denominations in the United States 285.173 (*not* 285.13).

Where the notation for specific denominations is limited to churches that originated in the United States or the British Commonwealth, e.g., the numbers following 284.1, 285.1, 285.2 and 287.5, use the span for treatment by continent, country, or locality for specific denominations in other areas, e.g., use 284.135 for the Evangelical Lutheran Church in America, but use 284.1485 (284.1 plus notation 485 for Sweden from Table 2) for the Lutheran Church of Sweden.

297.092

Persons associated with Islam

Use the following table of preference for comprehensive biographies of persons associated with an identifiable function, activity, or sect in Islam:

Muḥammad the Prophet	297.63
Muḥammad's family	297.64
Muḥammad's companions	297.648
Prophets prior to Muḥammad	297.246092
Other persons in Koran	297.122092
Founders of sects and reform movements	297.8
Founders of Sufi orders	297.48
Higher non-Sufi religious leaders	297.092
Of specific sects and movements	297.8
Theologians	297.2092
Moral theologians	297.5092
Da'wah workers	297.74
Leaders and members of Sufi orders	297.48
Other Sufis (mystics)	297.4
Religious educators	297.77092
Mosque officers	297.092
Of specific sects and movements	297.8
Members of sects and movements	297.8

Use 297.61 Leaders and their work for the role, function, and duties of religious leaders, not for biography of religious leaders.

Class works dealing with only one specialized aspect of a person's career or religious experience with the aspect, e.g., an account of conversion to Islam 297.574092.

Use 297.092 if a Muslim cannot be identified primarily with one function, activity, or sect.

297.26–.27

Islam and secular disciplines

Use numbers outside 200 for works that focus on issues of importance to practitioners of a secular discipline and for works that describe achievements of Muslims working within the discipline, but use 297.26–.27 for works that focus on Islamic theological issues in relation to secular disciplines. For example, class works describing achievements of Islamic arts with art, but use 297.267 for Islamic attitudes toward the arts, e.g., what kinds of music and visual arts are consistent with Islamic beliefs. Use 320.91767 (political situation and conditions in the Islamic world) or another subdivision of 320 for a work on Islam and politics that emphasizes issues primarily of concern to political scientists, but use 297.272 for a work on Islam and politics that emphasizes Islamic religious issues. If in doubt, prefer a number outside 297.

299.93

New Age religions

Class New Age perspectives on health and medicine, environmentalism, gardening, and other activities and areas of knowledge with the subject and discipline under discussion, even if the discussion rejects some of the main tenets of the discipline, e.g., using mental energy to cure illness 615.851.

Use 130 and its subdivisions for New Age literature mostly concerned with psychic and paranormal phenomena.

Use 201–209 for works on some aspects of religion from a New Age perspective if the works do not attempt to speak for a particular known religion or to establish a new religion or sect, e.g., use 204 for a New Age perspective on spirituality.

Use 299.93 for works concerned with several New Age religions, but use 200 if the work includes sects of the more established religions, e.g., sects of Buddhism, Hinduism, Native American religion, etc.

Use 299.93 for comprehensive works on the New Age as a whole or as a movement.

320.557 vs. 297.09, 297.272, 322.1

Islamism and Islamic fundamentalism

Use 320.557 for works emphasizing the religiously oriented political ideologies of Islamism or Islamic fundamentalism; and for works on Islamism or Islamic fundamentalism that emphasize political aspects from a secular viewpoint.

Use 297.09 and other subdivisions of 297 only for works that emphasize religious aspects of Islamism or Islamic fundamentalism, such as a concern to maintain and hand down a pure version of the Islamic faith, a mindfulness to follow the strict letter of the Koran and Hadith, an attempt to generate a religious reawakening through preaching, teaching, and other forms of religious communication. Use 297.272 only for works that treat politics from the religious point of view.

Use 322.1 for works emphasizing the political role of Islamist or Islamic fundamentalist organizations and groups in relation to the state.

If in doubt, prefer in the following order: 320.557; 322.1; a subdivision of 297.

322.1 vs. 201.72, 261.7, 292–299

Politics and religion

Use 322.1 for works discussing the relationships between religious organizations or movements and states or governments from a secular perspective. Use 201.72, 261.7, and similar numbers in 292–299 for works on the position that religious people and organizations take or should take toward political affairs (including the state). If in doubt, prefer 322.1.

398.2 vs. 201.3, 230, 270, 292–299

Myths and legends

Use 398.2 for myths or mythology presented in terms of cultural entertainment or, especially, as representative of the early literary expression of a society, even if they are populated by gods and goddesses. Use 201.3 and similar numbers elsewhere in 200 for mythology presented from a strictly theological point of view or presented as an embodiment of the religion of a people. For example, use 398.2 for Greco-Roman myths retold for a juvenile audience; but use 294.382325 for Jataka tales illustrating the character of the Buddha.

Use 398.2 for mythology having a nonreligious basis that deals with beliefs and stories that can be referred to as superstitions, legends, fairy tales, etc., where the religious content or interest is not apparent. Use 201.3 and similar numbers elsewhere in 200 for mythology having a religious basis that deals with the most basic beliefs of people and with religious beliefs and practices.

Class specific myths and legends presented as examples of a people's religion with the subject in religion, e.g., legends of Jesus' coming to Britain 232.9.

Use 398.2 for interdisciplinary works on mythology, since this number includes folk narratives with a broader focus than religion alone. If in doubt, prefer 398.2.

615.852 vs. 203.1, 234.131, 292–299

Religious and psychic therapy vs. Religious healing and Christian gift of healing

Use 615.852 for works on healing and medicine that focus on religious practices as a part of the medical practice. Use 203.1, 234.131, and similar numbers in 292–299 for works on healing as a religious practice, including such topics as religious beliefs about illness, rituals and prayers for healing, miraculous cures by charismatic leaders or saints, e.g., healing in religions of North American native peoples 299.7131 (number built with 31 from 203.1). Works on healing as a religious practice may also be concerned with emotional or spiritual healing as well as physical healing, or in place of physical healing. Use 615.8528 for works on the use of psychic and paranormal powers in healing that do not mention a religious context. If in doubt, prefer 615.852.

Class other works concerning illness or medicine and religion as follows:

Religion and the art and science of medicine	201.661
Christianity	261.561
Other religions	292–299
Religion and health and illness and the social questions and programs concerning them	201.7621
Christianity	261.8321
Other religions	292–299
Discussion of whether cures are miracles	202.117
Christianity	231.73
Philosophy of religion	212

616.86 vs. 158.1, 204.42, 248.8629, 292–299, 362.29

Recovery from addiction

Use 616.86 for self-help programs for individuals recovering from substance abuse and interdisciplinary works about recovery programs that focus on the individual's life with addiction, covering the individual's experience with both social and medical aspects. Use 204.42, 248.8629, and similar numbers in 292–299 for religious guides and inspirational works for the recovering addict. Use 362.29 for works on organizations providing recovery programs, including administration of the program, and interdisciplinary works that cover both organizational and therapeutic aspects of recovery programs. If in doubt, prefer 616.86.

Class works that treat recovery programs for persons recovering from a specific kind of substance abuse as a medical service with the substance in 616.86, plus notation 06 Therapy or notation 03 Rehabilitation from the table under 616.1–.9, whether the programs are run by professionals, such as psychiatrists or clinical psychologists, or whether they are self-help programs run by laypersons. Use notation 06 for programs to arrest the illness and begin recovery, e.g., twelve step programs. Use notation 03 for programs to help the individual remain in recovery. If in doubt, prefer notation 06.

Class works that treat recovery programs for those recovering from a specific kind of substance abuse as a social service, with the substance in 362.29, plus notation 86 Counseling and guidance from the table under 362–363. Such works typically emphasize the organizational or institutional aspects of the program.

For example, use 616.86103 for interdisciplinary works on life as a recovering alcoholic; 616.86106 for the twelve step Alcoholics Anonymous program; 204.42 for a general guide for a recovering alcoholic on how to live a religious life; 248.86292 for a guide for a recovering alcoholic on how to live a Christian life; 362.29286 for comprehensive works on Alcoholics Anonymous, the organization that provides the twelve step program and places for individuals in the program to meet.

Do not use 158.1 for works on recovery from addiction, because psychology applied to a medical problem is classed with the medical problem, not in 150.

Appendixes

Appendix A

Optional numbers for books of Bible as arranged in Tanakh (Jewish Bible, Hebrew Bible) (Option A)

The following schedule is an optional arrangement for books of the Bible as found in Jewish Bibles. The preferred arrangement is at 222–224 in the regular schedule. Option B is given at 296.11 in the regular schedule.

> **(222–224) Optional numbers for books of Bible as arranged in Tanakh (Jewish Bible, Hebrew Bible)**

Class comprehensive works in 221

For Apocrypha, pseudepigrapha, see 229

See Manual at 221: Optional numbers for books of Bible

(222) *Torah (Pentateuch)

(Optional number; prefer standard 222.1)

(.1) *Genesis

(Optional number; prefer standard 222.11)

(.2) *Exodus

(Optional number; prefer standard 222.12)

For Ten Commandments, see 222.6

(.3) *Leviticus

(Optional number; prefer standard 222.13)

(.4) *Numbers

(Optional number; prefer standard 222.14)

(.5) *Deuteronomy

(Optional number; prefer standard 222.15)

For Ten Commandments, see 222.6

(.6) *Ten Commandments (Decalogue)

(Optional number; prefer standard 222.16)

(223) *Prophetic books (Nevi'im)

(Optional number; prefer standard 224)

(.1) *Former Prophets (Nevi'im rishonim)

(Optional number; prefer standard 222)

(.11) *Joshua

(Optional number; prefer standard 222.2)

(.12) *Judges

(Optional number; prefer standard 222.32)

---

*Add as instructed under 221–229

(.13)   *Samuel

> (Optional number; prefer standard 222.4)

(.131)   *Samuel 1

> (Optional number; prefer standard 222.43)

(.132)   *Samuel 2

> (Optional number; prefer standard 222.44)

(.14)   *Kings

> (Optional number; prefer standard 222.5)

(.141)   *Kings 1

> (Optional number; prefer standard 222.53)

(.142)   *Kings 2

> (Optional number; prefer standard 222.54)

(.2)   *Later Prophets (Nevi'im aḥaronim)

> (Optional number; prefer standard 224)
>
> *For Isaiah, see 223.3; for Jeremiah, see 223.4; for Ezekiel, see 223.5; for Minor Prophets, see 223.6*

(.3)   *Isaiah

> (Optional number; prefer standard 224.1)

(.4)   *Jeremiah

> (Optional number; prefer standard 224.2)

(.5)   *Ezekiel

> (Optional number; prefer standard 224.4)

(.6)   *Minor prophets

> (Optional number; prefer standard 224.9)
>
> *For Zephaniah, Haggai, Zechariah, Malachi, see 223.7*

(.61)   *Hosea

> (Optional number; prefer standard 224.6)

(.62)   *Joel

> (Optional number; prefer standard 224.7)

(.63)   *Amos

> (Optional number; prefer standard 224.8)

*Add as instructed under 221–229

(.64)   *Obadiah

(Optional number; prefer standard 224.91)

(.65)   *Jonah

(Optional number; prefer standard 224.92)

(.66)   *Micah

(Optional number; prefer standard 224.93)

(.67)   *Nahum

(Optional number; prefer standard 224.94)

(.68)   *Habakkuk

(Optional number; prefer standard 224.95)

(.7)   *Zephaniah, Haggai, Zechariah, Malachi

(Optional number; prefer standard 224.9)

(.71)   *Zephaniah

(Optional number; prefer standard 224.96)

(.72)   *Haggai

(Optional number; prefer standard 224.97)

(.73)   *Zechariah

(Optional number; prefer standard 224.98)

(.74)   *Malachi

(Optional number; prefer standard 224.99)

(224)   *Writings (Ketuvim)

(Optional number; prefer standard 223)

(.1)   *Psalms

(Optional number; prefer standard 223.2)

(.2)   *Proverbs

(Optional number; prefer standard 223.7)

(.3)   *Job

(Optional number; prefer standard 223.1)

(.4)   *Megillot (Five scrolls)

(Optional number; prefer standard 221.044)

*Add as instructed under 221–229

(.41)   *Song of Solomon (Canticle of Canticles, Song of Songs)

        (Optional number; prefer standard 223.9)

(.42)   *Ruth

        (Optional number; prefer standard 222.35)

(.43)   *Lamentations

        (Optional number; prefer standard 224.3)

(.44)   *Ecclesiastes (Kohelet, Qohelet)

        (Optional number; prefer standard 223.8)

(.45)   *Esther

        (Optional number; prefer standard 222.9)

(.5)   *Daniel

        (Optional number; prefer standard 224.5)

(.6)   *Ezra

        (Optional number; prefer standard 222.7)

(.7)   *Nehemiah

        (Optional number; prefer standard 222.8)

(.8)   *Chronicles

        (Optional number; prefer standard 222.6)

(.81)   *Chronicles 1

        (Optional number; prefer standard 222.63)

(.82)   *Chronicles 2

        (Optional number; prefer standard 222.64)

*Add as instructed under 221–229

Appendix B:
170 Ethics

Some entries in the index have been built by adding *unabridged* numbers from *outside the 200 class*.

Since many of these entries have been built with numbers from 172–179 Applied ethics, class 170 from Edition 22 has been included for your use. An example of such a built number follows:

> Civil disobedience
> > ethics
> > > religion   205.621

The built number 205.621 is made up of two elements: 205.6 Specific moral issues, sins, vices, virtues + 21 (last two digits from 172.1 Relation of individuals to the state).

Instructions on how to build such numbers are provided in the 200 schedule.

170 Ethics (Moral philosophy)

Class here ethics of specific subjects and disciplines, interdisciplinary works on social ethics

For religious ethics, see 205; for social ethics as a method of social control, see 303.372. For ethics of a specific religion, see the religion, e.g., Christian ethics 241

SUMMARY

170.1–.9	Standard subdivisions and special topics
171	Ethical systems
172	Political ethics
173	Ethics of family relationships
174	Occupational ethics
175	Ethics of recreation, leisure, public performances, communication
176	Ethics of sex and reproduction
177	Ethics of social relations
178	Ethics of consumption
179	Other ethical norms

.4 Special topics

.42 Metaethics

Class bases for specific systems in 171

.44 Normative ethics

[.440 8] History and description with respect to kinds of persons

Do not use; class in 170.8

.8 History and description with respect to kinds of persons

[.88] Occupational and religious groups

Do not use for ethics of occupational groups; class in 174. Do not use for ethics of religious groups; class in 205

.9 Historical, geographic, persons treatment

.92 Persons

See Manual at 170.92 vs. 171

171 Ethical systems

Regardless of time or place

Class a specific topic in ethics, regardless of the system within which it is treated, with the topic in 172–179, e.g., professional ethics 174

See Manual at 170.92 vs. 171

.1 Systems based on authority

.2   **Systems based on intuition, moral sense, reason**

Including empiricism, existentialism, humanism, natural law, naturalism, stoicism

For systems and doctrines based on conscience, see 171.6

See also 171.7 for systems based on biology, genetics, evolution; also 340.112 for natural law in legal theory

.3   **Perfectionism**

Systems based on self-realization, personal fulfillment

.4   **Hedonism**

Systems based on achievement of individual pleasure or happiness

.5   **Consequentialism and utilitarianism**

Standard subdivisions are added for either or both topics in heading

.6   **Systems based on conscience**

Including casuistry, conflict of duties

.7   **Systems based on biology, genetics, evolution, education, social factors**

Including communist ethics, relativism, situation ethics, sociobiological ethics

See also 171.2 for systems based on natural law, naturalism

.8   **Systems based on altruism**

For utilitarianism, see 171.5

.9   **Systems based on egoism**

For hedonism, see 171.4

>   ## 172–179   Applied ethics (Social ethics)

Ethics of specific human qualities, relationships, activities

Class comprehensive works in 170

172   Political ethics

.1   **Relation of individuals to the state**

Including civic and political activity, military service, obedience to law, payment of taxes, resistance, revolution, civil war

.2   **Duties of the state**

Duties of government toward citizens, e.g., education, freedom, personal security, welfare; duties of officeholders and officials

Class here justice

.4   **International relations**

> Including conduct of foreign affairs, disarmament, espionage

.42   War and peace

> Standard subdivisions are added for either or both topics in heading
>
> Including conscientious objection, just war theory, pacifism, ways and means of conducting warfare
>
> Class occupational ethics of military personnel in 174.9355
>
> *For civil war, see 172.1*

.422   Nuclear weapons and nuclear war

> Standard subdivisions are added for either or both topics in heading

173   Ethics of family relationships

> Including ethics of marriage, divorce, separation, parent-child relationships, sibling relationships
>
> Class ethics of sex and reproduction in 176

174   Occupational ethics

> Class here economic, professional ethics; ethics of work

.1   **Clergy**

.2   **Medical professions**

> Class medical ethics related to human reproduction in 176; class comprehensive works on bioethics in 174.957

.22   Hippocratic oath

[.24]   Questions of life and death

> Relocated to 179.7

[.25]   Innovative procedures

> Relocated to 174.29

.26   Economic questions

> Including advertising, fee splitting

.28   Experimentation

> Including embryo research
>
> Class here experimentation on human subjects
>
> Class embryo research relating to human reproduction in 176
>
> *For experimentation on animals, see 179.4*

.29   Specific topics and branches of medicine

Class here innovative procedures [*formerly* 174.25]

Add to base number 174.29 the numbers following 61 in 610–618, e.g., organ transplants 174.297954 [*formerly* 174.25], gene therapy 174.295895 [*formerly* 174.25], nursing ethics 174.29073, pharmaceutical ethics 174.2951, psychiatric ethics 174.29689; however, for experimentation on human subjects and comprehensive works on medical experimentation, see 174.28; for human reproduction, see 176; for animal experimentation, see 179.4; for questions of life and death, see 179.7

.3   **Legal professions**

.4   **Business ethics**

Including industrial espionage

Class here ethics of finance, manufacturing, trade

.6   **Gambling business**

Including lottery management

See also 175 for gambling

.9   **Other professions and occupations**

Add to base number 174.9 notation 001–999, e.g., bioethics 174.957; however, for ethics of public administration and public office, see 172.2
Notation 001–999 replaces notation 09–99 from Table 7 with the result that many numbers have been reused with new meanings

175   Ethics of recreation, leisure, public performances, communication

Including ethics of dancing, gambling, music, television; fair play, sportsmanship

Class occupational ethics for those involved in the recreation industry with the industry in 174, e.g., occupational ethics for professional athletes 174.9796

For ethics of hunting, see 179.3

176   Ethics of sex and reproduction

Including artificial insemination, celibacy, chastity, cloning used for human reproduction, contraception, embryo transfer, homosexuality, premarital and extramarital relations, promiscuity, surrogate motherhood

For abortion, see 179.76

See also 174.28 for embryo research not for purpose of human reproduction; also 177.65 for ethics of courtship; also 177.7 for ethics of love

.5   **Prostitution**

.7 **Obscenity and pornography**

Standard subdivisions are added for either or both topics in heading

For obscenity and pornography in literature, see 176.8; for obscenity in speech, see 179.5

.8 **Obscenity and pornography in literature**

Standard subdivisions are added for either or both topics in heading

177 Ethics of social relations

Limited to the topics provided for below

.1 **Courtesy, hospitality, politeness**

Class etiquette in 395

.2 **Conversation**

Including gossip

.3 **Truthfulness, lying, slander, flattery**

.4 **Personal appearance**

Including exposure of person, ostentatious dress

.5 **Discriminatory practices and slavery**

Standard subdivisions are added for either or both topics in heading

.6 **Friendship and courtship**

.62 Friendship

.65 Courtship

Class sexual ethics in courtship in 176

.7 **Love**

Including benevolence, caring, charity, kindness, liberality, philanthropy

See also 128.46 for love as human experience

178 Ethics of consumption

Including abstinence, gluttony, greed, overindulgence, temperance

Class here use of natural resources, of wealth

Class environmental and ecological ethics, respect for nature in 179.1; class consumption of meat in 179.3

.1 **Consumption of alcoholic beverages**

.7 **Consumption of tobacco**

.8 **Consumption of narcotics**

179 Other ethical norms

Class here cruelty

[.01–.09]   Standard subdivisions

Do not use; class in 170

.1   Respect for life and nature

Standard subdivisions are added for either or both topics in heading

Class here environmental and ecological ethics

For ethics of consumption, see 178; for treatment of animals, see 179.3; for respect for human life, see 179.7

.2   Treatment of children

For parent-child relationships, see 173

.3   Treatment of animals

Including ethics of hunting; vegetarianism

For experimentation on animals, see 179.4

.4   Experimentation on animals

Including vivisection

.5   Blasphemy, profanity, obscenity in speech

Standard subdivisions are added for any or all topics in heading

.6   Courage and cowardice

.7   Respect and disrespect for human life

Standard subdivisions are added for either or both topics in heading

Including questions of life and death in medical ethics [*formerly* 174.24], capital punishment, dueling, euthanasia, genocide, homicide, suicide

Class here comprehensive works on ethics of violence, of nonviolence

Class ethics of contraception in 176; class comprehensive works on medical ethics in 174.2

For ethics of violence, of nonviolence in political activity, see 172; for ethics of civil war, see 172.1; for ethics of war, see 172.42; for treatment of children, see 179.2

.76   Abortion

.8   Vices, faults, failings

Not otherwise provided for

Including anger, cheating, covetousness, envy, hatred, jealousy, pride, sloth

.9   Virtues

Not otherwise provided for

Including cheerfulness, gentleness, gratitude, honesty, humility, modesty, patience, prudence, self-control, self-reliance, toleration

Class here virtue

Relative Index

A

Abbeys
  church history   271
  religious significance of
    buildings   246.97
Abdias (Biblical book)   224.91
'Abdu'l-Bahá
  works by   297.938 24
Abel (Biblical person)
  Bible stories   222.110 950 5
Abhidhammapiṭaka   294.382 4
Abhidharmapiṭaka   294.382 4
Ablutions
  Islam   297.38
Abodah Zarah   296.123 4
  Babylonian Talmud   296.125 4
  Mishnah   296.123 4
  Palestinian Talmud   296.124 4
Abortion
  ethics
    religion   205.697 6
      Buddhism   294.356 976
      Christianity   241.697 6
      Hinduism   294.548 697 6
      Islam   297.569 76
      Judaism   296.369 76
  social theology   201.763 46
    Christianity   261.836
    Judaism   296.38
Aboth   296.123 47
Abraham (Patriarch)
  Bible   222.110 92
  Islam   297.246 3
Absolution (Christian rite)   234.166
  public worship   265.64
  theology   234.166
Abstinence
  religious practice   204.47
    Buddhism   294.344 47
    Christianity   248.47
    Hinduism   294.544 7
    Islam   297.576
    Judaism   296.7
Abū Dā'ūd Sulaymān ibn
  al-Ash'ath al-Sijistānī
  Hadith   297.124 2
Abused children
  social theology   201.762 76
    Christianity   261.832 71
Accountability
  Christian doctrines   233.4

Acolytes   253
  public worship
    Christianity   264
Acts of the Apostles   226.6
  pseudepigrapha   229.925
Actual grace   234.1
Adam
  Bible stories   222.110 950 5
  Islam   297.246
Addiction
  devotional literature   204.32
    Christianity   242.4
  pastoral theology   206.1
    Christianity   259.429
  religious guidance   204.42
    Christianity   248.862 9
  social theology   201.762 29
    Christianity   261.832 29
Adi Granth   294.682
Adolescent boys
  guides to religious life   204.408 351
    Christianity   248.832
Adolescent girls
  guides to religious life   204.408 352
    Christianity   248.833
Adolescents
  Bible   220.830 523 5
  religion   200.835
    Christianity   270.083 5
      devotional literature   242.63
      guides to Christian life   248.83
      pastoral care of   259.23
      religious education   268.433
      sermons   252.55
    guides to life   204.408 35
    Judaism   296.083 5
      guides to life   296.708 35
      religious education   296.680 835
Adoption
  religion   204.41
Adoration of magi   232.923
Adoration of shepherds   232.922
Adult baptism   234.161 3
  public worship   265.13
  theology   234.161 3
Adult child abuse victims
  social theology   201.762 764
    Christianity   261.832 73
Adult child sexual abuse
  victims
  social theology   201.762 764
    Christianity   261.832 73

Adultery
  ethics
    religion   205.66
      see also Sexual
      relations — ethics —
      religion
  social theology   201.7
    Christianity   261.835 736
Adults
  guides to religious life   204.4
  religion   200
    Christianity   230
      guides to Christian life   248.84
      religious education   268.434
Advent   263.912
  devotional literature   242.332
  sermons   252.612
Advent Christian Church   286.73
  see also Adventists
Adventists   286.7
  biography   286.709 2
  church government   262.067
    parishes   254.067
  church law   262.986 7
  doctrines   230.67
    catechisms and creeds   238.67
  guides to Christian life   248.486 7
  missions   266.67
  moral theology   241.046 7
  public worship   264.067
  religious associations   267.186 7
  religious education   268.867
  seminaries   230.073 67
  theology   230.67
African American Methodist
  churches   287.8
  see also Methodist Church
African independent churches   289.93
  see also Christian
    denominations
African Methodist Episcopal
  Church   287.83
  see also Methodist Church
African Methodist Episcopal
  Zion Church   287.83
  see also Methodist Church
African religions   299.6
Agama   294.482
Agapes (Christian rites)   265.9
Aged persons
  religion   200.846
    see also Older persons —
      religion

Aggadah   296.19
  Midrash   296.142
  Talmud   296.127 6
Aggeus (Biblical book)   224.97
Agnosticism   211.7
  Christian polemics   239.7
  philosophy of religion   211.7
Agnostics   211.709 2
Agnus Dei   264.36
Agrapha   229.8
Agriculture
  Bible   220.863
  Koran   297.122 863
Aharonim   296.180 92
Ahilot   296.123 6
Ahimsa   294.548 697
  Buddhism   294.356 97
  Hinduism   294.548 697
  Jainism   294.456 97
Ahmadiyya movement   297.86
  doctrines   297.204 6
AIDS (Disease)
  church work with patients   259.419 697 92
  social theology   201.762 196 979 2
    Christianity   261.832 196 979 2
Akan (African people)
  religion   299.683 385
Albigensianism   273.6
  denomination   284.4
    see also Christian
      denominations
  persecution of   272.3
Alcoholic beverages
  ethics
    religion   205.681
      Christianity   241.681
      Islam   297.568 1
      Judaism   296.368 1
Alcoholism
  pastoral theology   206.1
    Christianity   259.429 2
  social theology   201.762 292
    Christianity   261.832 292
Algonquian Indians
  religion   299.783
All Saints' Day   263.98
All Souls' Day   263.97
Allah   297.211
Allegory
  Biblical   220.68
  Koran   297.122 68
Almsgiving   204.46
  Christianity   248.46
  Islam   297.54

Altar railings	247.1
Altar screens	247.1
Altars	203.7
Christianity	247.1
American Baptist Association	286.136
see also Baptists	
American Baptist Churches in	
the U.S.A.	286.131
see also Baptists	
American Baptist Convention	286.131
see also Baptists	
American Evangelical	
Lutheran Church	284.133 2
see also Lutheran church	
American Lutheran Church	284.131
see also Lutheran church	
American Muslim Mission	297.87
American native peoples	
religion	299.7
North America	299.7
South America	299.8
American Reformed Church	285.7
see also Reformed Church	
(American Reformed)	
American Revised version	
Bible	220.520 4
American Standard version	
Bible	220.520 4
Amish	
biography	289.709 2
Amish churches	289.73
see also Mennonite Church	
Amoraim	296.120 092
Amos (Biblical book)	224.8
Amulets	
Islamic popular practices	297.39
religious significance	203.7
Anabaptists	284.3
see also Christian	
denominations	
Ancestors	
objects of worship	202.13
Angels	202.15
Christianity	235.3
Islam	297.215
Judaism	296.315
Anger	
ethics	
religion	205.698
see also Vices — religion	

Anglican Communion	283
church government	262.03
parishes	254.03
church law	262.983
doctrines	230.3
catechisms and creeds	238.3
general councils	262.53
guides to Christian life	248.483
liturgy	264.03
missions	266.3
moral theology	241.043
persecution by Queen Mary	272.6
public worship	264.03
religious associations	267.183
religious education	268.83
religious orders	255.83
church history	271.83
women	255.983
church history	271.983
seminaries	230.073 3
theology	230.3
Anglican sacred music	
public worship	
religion	264.030 2
Anglicans	
biography	283.092
Animal sacrifice	203.4
Animals	
Bible	220.859
Hadith	297.124 085 9
Koran	297.122 859
religious worship	202.12
treatment of	
ethics	
religion	205.693
Buddhism	294.356 93
Christianity	241.693
Hinduism	294.548 693
Judaism	296.369 3
Animism	
comparative religion	202.1
Anne (Mother of the Virgin	
Mary), Saint	232.933
private prayers to	242.75
Annihilationism	236.23
Annunciation to Mary	232.912
Anointing of the sick	234.167
public worship	265.7
theology	234.167
Ante-Nicene church	270.1
Anthropology	
theological anthropology	202.2
see also Humans — religion	

Anthropomorphism
  comparative religion 202.112
  philosophy of religion 211
Anthroposophy 299.935
Anti-mission Baptists 286.4
  see also Baptists
Anti-Semitism
  social theology 201.5
    Christianity 261.26
Anti-Trinitarianism 289.1
Antichrist 236
Antimission Baptists 286.4
  see also Baptists
Antinomianism 273.6
Antinuclear movement
  social theology 201.727 5
    Christianity 261.873 2
    Judaism 296.382 7
Antiochian school (Christian
  theology) 230.14
Antonines 255.18
  church history 271.18
Apocalypse (Biblical book) 228
Apocalypses (Biblical literature) 220.046
  New Testament pseudepigrapha 229.94
  Old Testament pseudepigrapha 229.913
Apocrypha (Bible) 229
Apocryphal wisdom literature 229.3
Apologetics 202
  Christianity 239
  Islam 297.29
  Judaism 296.35
Apostates
  Christian polemics 239.7
Apostles 225.92
Apostles' Creed 238.11
Apostleship (Spiritual gift) 234.13
Apostolic Church 270.1
Apostolic succession 262.11
Apostolicity 262.72
Apparitions of Mary 232.917
'Aqā'id (Islam) 297.2
Arabic language
  Biblical texts 220.46
  Hadith texts 297.124 04
  Koran texts 297.122 4
Arakhin 296.123 5
  Babylonian Talmud 296.125 5
  Mishnah 296.123 5
Aramaic languages
  Biblical texts 220.42
  Midrashic texts 296.140 4
  Talmudic texts 296.120 4
Aranyakas 294.592 1

Arapaho Indians
  religion 299.783 54
Archaeology
  Bible 220.93
  religion 201.693 01
Archbishops 270.092
  biography 270.092
    specific denominations 280
    see Manual at 230–280
  ecclesiology 262.12
Architecture
  religious significance 203.7
    Christianity 246.9
    see also Arts — religious
      significance
Ari liturgy 296.450 4
Arianism 273.4
Ark of the Covenant 296.493
Armageddon 236.9
Armenian Church 281.62
  see also Eastern churches
Armenian language
  Biblical texts 220.49
Arminians 284.9
  see also Christian
    denominations
Arms race
  ethics
    religion 205.624 22
      Christianity 241.624 22
      Judaism 296.362 422
  social theology 201.727 5
    Christianity 261.873 2
Art and religion 201.67
  see also Arts and religion
Artificial insemination
  ethics
    religion 205.66
      see also Reproduction —
        ethics — religion
Arts
  religious significance 203.7
    Buddhism 294.343 7
    Christianity 246
    Hinduism 294.537
    Islam 297.3
    Judaism 296.46
    Native American religions 299.713 7
Arts and religion 201.67
  Buddhism 294.336 7
  Christianity 261.57
  Islam 297.267
  Judaism 296.377
Arya-Samaj 294.556 3

Ascension Day	263.93
see also Ascensiontide	
Ascension of Jesus Christ	232.97
Ascension of Mary	232.914
Ascensiontide	263.93
devotional literature	242.36
sermons	252.63
Ascent to Heaven of Muḥammad	297.633
Asceticism	204.47
Buddhism	294.344 47
Christianity	248.47
Hinduism	294.544 7
Islam	297.576
Sufi	297.446
Judaism	296.7
Ash Wednesday	263.925
devotional literature	242.35
sermons	252.625
Ashkenazic liturgy	296.45
'Āshūrā'	297.36
Assemblies of God	289.94
see also Christian	
denominations	
Assisted suicide	
ethics	
religion	205.697
see also Right to die —	
ethics — religion	
Associations for religious	
work	206.5
Christianity	267
Judaism	296.67
Assumption of Mary	232.914
Assurance (Christian theology)	234
Assyrians	
religion	299.21
Astrolatry	202.12
Astrology and religion	201.613 35
Christianity	261.513
Astronomical interpretation	
Bible	220.68
Astronomy and religion	201.652
Christianity	261.55
philosophy of religion	215.2
Asvamedha	294.534
Athanasian Creed	238.144
Atharvaveda	294.592 15
Atheism	211.8
Christian polemics	239.7
Islamic view	297.289
Atheistic religions	201.4
Atheists	211.809 2

Atonement	202.2
Christianity	234.5
Islam	297.22
Judaism	296.32
Atonement Day	
Judaism	296.432
liturgy	296.453 2
Atonement of Jesus Christ	232.3
Atsina Indians	
religion	299.783 54
Attributes of God	212.7
Christianity	231.4
comparative religion	202.112
Islam	297.211 2
Judaism	296.311 2
philosophy of religion	212.7
Attributes of the Church	262.72
Audiovisual materials	
Christian religious education	268.635
Augsburg Confession	238.41
Augustana Evangelical	
Lutheran Church	284.133 3
see also Lutheran church	
Augustinians	255.4
church history	271.4
Australian Aborigines	
religion	299.921 5
Authority	
ethical systems	
Christianity	241.2
religion	206.5
Christianity	262.8
Judaism	296.67
Authorized version (Bible)	220.520 3
Authorship of Bible	220.66
Avarice	
moral theology	205.68
see also Greed — moral	
theology	
Ave Maria	242.74
Avesta	295.82
Avodah Zarah	296.123 4
Babylonian Talmud	296.125 4
Mishnah	296.123 4
Palestinian Talmud	296.124 4
Avot	296.123 47
Ayatollahs	297.092
biography	297.092
specific sects	297.8
role and function	297.61
see Manual at 297.092	
Aztecs	
religion	299.784 52

B

Baba Batra	296.123 4
Babylonian Talmud	296.125 4
Mishnah	296.123 4
Palestinian Talmud	296.124 4
Baba Kamma	296.123 4
Babylonian Talmud	296.125 4
Mishnah	296.123 4
Palestinian Talmud	296.124 4
Baba Meẓia	296.123 4
Babylonian Talmud	296.125 4
Mishnah	296.123 4
Palestinian Talmud	296.124 4
Babism	297.92
Babists	
biography	297.920 92
Babylon (Extinct city)	
Bible	228.064
Babylonian Talmud	296.125
Babylonians	
religion	299.21
Bahai ethics	297.935
Bahai Faith	297.93
Bahais	
biography	297.930 92
Bahá'u'lláh	297.930 92
works by	297.938 22
Baptism	234.161
public worship	265.1
theology	234.161
Baptism in the Holy Spirit	234.13
Baptism of Jesus Christ	232.95
Baptismal fonts	247.1
Baptist General Conference	
of America	286.5
see also Baptists	
Baptist sacred music	
public worship	
religion	264.060 2
Baptists	286
biography	286.092
church government	262.06
parishes	254.06
church law	262.986
doctrines	230.6
catechisms and creeds	238.6
general councils	262.56
guides to Christian life	248.486
missions	266.6
moral theology	241.046
persecution of	272.8
public worship	264.06
religious associations	267.186

Baptists (continued)	
religious education	268.86
seminaries	230.073 6
theology	230.6
Bar mitzvah	296.442 4
liturgy	296.454 24
Baraita	296.126 3
Barnabites	255.52
church history	271.52
Baruch (Bible)	229.5
Basic Christian communities	250
ecclesiology	262.26
see Manual at 260 vs. 251–254, 259	
Basilians	255.17
church history	271.17
Bat mitzvah	296.443 4
liturgy	296.454 34
Bava Batra	296.123 4
Babylonian Talmud	296.125 4
Mishnah	296.123 4
Palestinian Talmud	296.124 4
Bava Kamma	296.123 4
Babylonian Talmud	296.125 4
Mishnah	296.123 4
Palestinian Talmud	296.124 4
Bava Meẓia	296.123 4
Babylonian Talmud	296.125 4
Mishnah	296.123 4
Palestinian Talmud	296.124 4
Beatification of saints	235.24
Beatitudes	226.93
Christian moral theology	241.53
Bekhorot	296.123 5
Babylonian Talmud	296.125 5
Mishnah	296.123 5
Bektashi	297.48
Bel and the Dragon (Bible)	229.6
Benedictines	255.1
church history	271.1
women	255.97
church history	271.97
Benedictions	203.8
Christianity	264.13
Judaism	296.45
Benedictus	264.36
Berakhot	296.123 1
Babylonian Talmud	296.125 1
Mishnah	296.123 1
Palestinian Talmud	296.124 1
Bereavement	
pastoral theology	206.1
Christianity	259.6
Judaism	296.61

Bereavement (continued)
religion   204.42
  Christianity
    devotional literature   242.4
    personal religion   248.866
    rites   265.85
    devotional literature   204.32
  Judaism
    personal religion   296.7
    rites   296.445
     liturgy   296.454 5
    sermons   296.47
  personal religion   204.42
  rites   203.88
Berit milah   296.442 2
  liturgy   296.454 22
Beẓah   296.123 2
  Babylonian Talmud   296.125 2
  Mishnah   296.123 2
  Palestinian Talmud   296.124 2
Bhagavad Gita   294.592 4
Bhakti Yoga   294.543 6
Bible   220
  biography   220.92
  see Manual at 220.92
  English   220.52
    American Revised   220.520 4
    American Standard   220.520 4
    Authorized   220.520 3
    Challoner   220.520 2
    Confraternity   220.520 5
    Coverdale   220.520 1
    Douay   220.520 2
    English Revised   220.520 4
    Good News Bible   220.520 82
    Jerusalem Bible   220.520 7
    King James   220.520 3
    Living Bible   220.520 83
    New American   220.520 5
    New English   220.520 6
    New International Version 220.520 81
    New Jerusalem Bible   220.520 7
    New King James   220.520 8
    New Living Translation   220.520 83
    New Revised Standard   220.520 43
    Revised   220.520 4
    Revised English   220.520 6
    Revised standard   220.520 42
    Rheims   220.520 2
    Today's English   220.520 82
    Tyndale   220.520 1
    Wycliffe   220.520 1

Bible (continued)
  gay interpretations   220.608 664
  homiletical use   251
  use in public worship   264.34
Bible Christians (Methodist
  denomination)   287.53
  see also Methodist Church
Bible colleges   230.071 1
Bible meditations   242.5
Bible prayers   242.722
Bible stories   220.950 5
Bible study   220.07
Bible. N.T.   225
  Acts of the Apostles   226.6
  Apocalypse   228
  Catholic epistles   227.9
  Colossians   227.7
  Corinthians   227.2
  Ephesians   227.5
  Epistles   227
    exegesis   227.06
  Epistles of John   227.94
  Epistles of Paul   227
    exegesis   227.06
  exegesis   225.6
  Galatians   227.4
  Gospels   226
    biography   226.092
    exegesis   226.06
  Hebrews   227.87
  James   227.91
  John   226.5
    exegesis   226.506
  Jude   227.97
  Luke   226.4
    exegesis   226.406
  Mark   226.3
    exegesis   226.306
  Matthew   226.2
  Pastoral Epistles   227.83
  Peter   227.92
  Philemon   227.86
  Philippians   227.6
  Revelation   228
  Romans   227.1
  Thessalonians   227.81
  Timothy   227.83
  Titus   227.85

Bible. O.T.	221	Bible. O.T. (continued)	
Amos	224.8	Minor Prophets	224.9
Apocrypha	229	Nahum	224.94
Baruch	229.5	Nehemiah	222.8
Bel and the Dragon	229.6	Nevi'im	224
Ecclesiasticus	229.4	Numbers	222.14
Epistle of Jeremiah	229.5	Obadiah	224.91
Esdras	229.1	Pentateuch	222.1
Esther	229.27	Poetic books	223
Judith	229.24	Prophets	224
Maccabees	229.73	Proverbs	223.7
Prayer of Manasseh	229.6	Psalms	223.2
Sirach	229.4	exegesis	223.206
Song of the Three Children	229.6	Qohelet	223.8
Susanna	229.6	Ruth	222.35
Tobit	229.22	Samuel	222.4
Wisdom of Solomon	229.3	Song of Solomon	223.9
Canticle of Canticles	223.9	Song of Songs	223.9
Chronicles	222.6	Ten Commandments	222.16
Daniel	224.5	Torah	222.1
Deuteronomy	222.15	Twelve prophets	224.9
Ecclesiastes	223.8	Wisdom literature	223
English	221.52	Zechariah	224.98
Jewish Publication Society		Zephaniah	224.96
Bible	221.520 8	*see Manual at* 221	
see also Bible — English		Biblical events	220.95
Esther	222.9	Biblical moral precepts	
exegesis	221.6	Christianity	241.5
Exodus	222.12	Judaism	296.36
Ezekiel	224.4	Biblical persons	
Ezra	222.7	biography	220.92
Former Prophets	222	*see Manual at* 220.92	
Genesis	222.11	Biblical theology	
exegesis	222.110 6	Christianity	230.041
Habakkuk	224.95	Judaism	296.3
Haggai	224.97	Bikkurim	296.123 1
Hexateuch	222.1	Mishnah	296.123 1
Historical books	222	Palestinian Talmud	296.124 1
Hosea	224.6	Bioethics	
Isaiah	224.1	religion	205.649 57
Jeremiah	224.2	Christianity	241.649 57
Job	223.1	Judaism	296.364 957
Joel	224.7	*see also* Ethical problems —	
Jonah	224.92	religion	
Joshua	222.2	Biological warfare	
Judges	222.32	ethics	
Ketuvim	223	religion	205.624 2
Kings	222.5	*see also* War — ethics —	
Kohelet	223.8	religion	
Lamentations	224.3	social theology	201.727 3
Later Prophets	224	*see also* War — social	
Leviticus	222.13	theology	
Malachi	224.99		
Micah	224.93		

Biology and religion — 201.657
  Christianity — 261.55
  philosophy of religion — 215.7
Bird watching
  religion — 201.659 807 234
Birth control
  ethics
    religion — 205.66
      Buddhism — 294.356 6
      Christianity — 241.66
      Hinduism — 294.548 66
      Islam — 297.566
      Judaism — 296.366
  social theology — 201.7
    Christianity — 261.836
    Judaism — 296.38
Birth of Jesus Christ — 232.92
Birth rites
  religion — 203.81
Birthday of the Buddha — 294.343 6
Bishops — 270.092
  biography — 270.092
    specific denominations — 280
    see Manual at 230–280
  ecclesiology — 262.12
Bishops' thrones — 247.1
Black Methodist churches — 287.8
  see also Methodist Church
Black Muslim religion — 297.87
Black Muslims
  biography — 297.870 92
Black theology — 202.089 96
  Christianity — 230.089 96
    United States — 230.089 960 73
Blasphemy — 205.695
  Christianity — 241.695
  Islam — 297.569 5
  Judaism — 296.369 5
Blavatsky, H. P. (Helena Petrovna) — 299.934 092
Blessings — 203.8
  Christianity — 264.13
  Judaism — 296.45
Blindness
  Bible — 220.836 241
Bo tree
  Buddhism — 294.343 5
Body (Human)
  religion — 202.2
    Christianity — 233.5
    see also Humans — religion

Body and soul
  religion — 202.2
    Christianity — 233.5
    Islam — 297.225
    Judaism — 296.32
  philosophy of religion — 218
  see also Humans — religion
Bon (Tibetan religion) — 299.54
Book of Common Prayer — 264.03
Book of Mormon — 289.322
Books of Hours — 242
Brahma Samaj — 294.556 2
Brahmanas — 294.592 1
Brahmanism — 294.5
Brahmans
  biography — 294.509 2
Brethren churches — 286.5
Breviaries — 264.15
  Roman Catholic — 264.020 15
  texts — 264.024
Brothers (Christian religious orders) — 255.092
  biography — 271.092 02
  church history — 271.092
Brothers Hospitallers of St. John of God — 255.49
  church history — 271.49
Brownists — 285.8
Buddha — 294.363
Buddhism — 294.3
  Islamic polemics — 297.294
Buddhism and Islam — 294.335
  Buddhist view — 294.335
  Islamic view — 297.284 3
Buddhist calendar
  religion — 294.343 6
Buddhist education — 294.375
Buddhist ethics — 294.35
Buddhist fundamentalism — 294.309
Buddhist holidays — 294.343 6
  see Manual at 203.6, 263.9, 292–299 vs. 394.265–.267
Buddhist monasteries — 294.365 7
Buddhist temples and shrines — 294.343 5
Buddhists
  biography — 294.309 2
Bukhārī, Muḥammad ibn Ismāʻīl
  Hadith — 297.124 1
Bullfighting and religion — 201.679 182
Bulls (Papal documents) — 262.91
Burial of Jesus Christ — 232.964

Business
  social theology   201.73
    Christianity   261.85
    Judaism   296.383
Business ethics
  religion   205.644
    Christianity   241.644
    Islam   297.564 4
    Judaism   296.364 4
    see also Ethical problems —
      religion
Byzantine art
  religious significance   246.1
Byzantine rite churches   281.5
  see also Eastern churches

C

Cabala   296.16
  Jewish mysticism
    experience   296.712
    movement   296.833
  Jewish religious sources   296.16
Cain (Biblical person)
  Bible stories   222.110 950 5
Calendars
  religion   203.6
    Christianity   263.9
    Islam   297.36
    Judaism   296.43
Calendars (Liturgical books)   264
  Anglican   264.031
  Roman Catholic   264.021
Caliphate   297.61
Caliphs
  companions of Muḥammad   297.648
  role and function   297.61
Call to Islam   297.74
Calvin, Jean   284.209 2
Calvinism   284.2
  see also Reformed Church
Calvinistic Baptists   286.1
  biography   286.109 2
  see also Baptists
Calvinistic churches   284.2
  see also Reformed Church
Calvinistic Methodist Church
  of Wales   285.235
  see also Presbyterian Church
Calvinists
  biography   284.209 2
Camillians   255.55
  church history   271.55

Camp meetings
  Christian religious practices   269.24
Camp programs
  church work   253.7
  Jewish religious work   296.67
Campbellites   286.6
  biography   286.609 2
  see also Disciples of Christ
Campus Crusade for Christ   267.61
Campus ministry   259.24
Candlemas   263.97
Candomblé   299.673
Canon law   262.9
Canon of Bible   220.12
Canonization of saints   235.24
Canons regular   255.08
  church history   271.08
  women   255.908
    church history   271.908
Canticle of Canticles   223.9
Cantors (Judaism)
  biography   296.462 092
Capital punishment
  ethics
    religion   205.697
      Buddhism   294.356 97
      Christianity   241.697
      Hinduism   294.548 697
      Islam   297.569 7
      Judaism   296.369 7
    social theology   201.764
      Christianity   261.833 66
Capitalism
  social theology   201.73
    Christianity   261.85
    Islam   297.273
    Judaism   296.383
Capuchins   255.36
  church history   271.36
Caracciolini   255.56
  church history   271.56
Cardinal sins   241.3
Cardinals (Clergy)   282.092
  biography   282.092
  ecclesiology   262.135
Cargo cults
  Melanesian religion   299.92
Caring
  ethics
    religion   205.677
      see also Love — ethics —
        religion

Carmelite Nuns | 255.971
church history | 271.971
Carmelites | 255.73
church history | 271.73
women | 255.971
church history | 271.971
Caro, Joseph
Jewish legal codes | 296.182
Carthusians | 255.71
church history | 271.71
women | 255.97
church history | 271.97
Catechetics | 268
Catechisms | 202
Christianity | 238
Catechists | 268.092
biography | 268.092
see Manual at 230–280
role and function | 268.3
Catechumenate | 265.13
Catharism | 273.6
denomination | 284.4
see also Christian
denominations
persecution of | 272.3
Cathedral systems
Christian ecclesiology | 262.3
Cathedrals
religious significance | 246.96
Catholic Church | 282
see also Roman Catholic
Church
Catholic epistles | 227.9
Catholicity | 262.72
Catholics | 282.092
Celestial Church of Christ | 289.93
see also Christian
denominations
Celestines | 255.16
church history | 271.16
Celibacy
ethics
religion | 205.66
Buddhism | 294.356 6
Christianity | 241.66
Hinduism | 294.548 66
religious practice | 204.47
Buddhism | 294.344 47
Christianity | 248.47
clergy | 253.25
Hinduism | 294.544 7
Celtic religion | 299.16
Ceremonials | 264.022

Ceremonies
religion | 203.8
see also Rites — religion
Chabad Lubavitch Hasidism | 296.833 22
Chakras
Hinduism | 294.543
Chaldeans (Religious order) | 255.18
church history | 271.18
Challoner Bible | 220.520 2
Ch'an Buddhism | 294.392 7
Chancel railings | 247.1
Chanukah | 296.435
liturgy | 296.453 5
Chaplaincy | 206.1
Christianity | 253
Judaism | 296.61
Chaplains | 200.92
Christian | 270.092
Charismatic gifts | 234.13
Charismatic movement | 270.82
Protestantism | 280.4
Charismatic spiritual renewal | 269
Charity
ethics
religion | 205.677
see also Love — ethics —
religion
Chastity
ethics
religion | 205.66
Buddhism | 294.356 6
Christianity | 241.66
Hinduism | 294.548 66
Judaism | 296.366
religious practice | 204.47
Buddhism | 294.344 47
Christianity | 248.47
Hinduism | 294.544 7
Cheerfulness
moral theology | 205.699
see also Virtues — religion
Cherubim and Seraphim Church | 289.93
see also Christian
denominations
Chibcha Indians
religion | 299.882
Child abuse
social theology | 201.762 76
Christianity | 261.832 71
Child rearing
personal religion | 204.41
Christianity | 248.845
Islam | 297.577
Judaism | 296.74

Childhood of Jesus Christ	232.927
Children	
religion	200.83
Christianity	270.083
devotional literature	242.62
guides to Christian life	248.82
pastoral care of	259.22
prayer books	242.82
religious education	268.432
sermons	252.53
guides to life	204.408 3
Judaism	296.083
guides to life	296.708 3
religious education	296.680 83
Children's church	264.008 3
Children's sermons	204.3
Christianity	252.53
Chinese calendar	
religion	299.511 36
Chinese religions	299.51
Choir stalls	247.1
Chorti Indians	
religion	299.784 28
Chosen people (Judaism)	296.311 72
Christening	265.1
Christian and Missionary	
Alliance	289.9
see also Christian	
denominations	
Christian art	
religious significance	246
Christian biography	270.092
specific denominations	280
Christian Brothers	255.78
church history	271.78
Christian calendars	
religion	263.9
Christian church	260
history	270
local	250
specific denominations	280
see Manual at 260 vs.	
251–254, 259	
Christian Church (Disciples	
of Christ)	286.63
see also Disciples of Christ	
Christian college students	
guides to Christian life	248.834
Christian denominations	280
church government	262.01–.09
parishes	254.01–.09
church law	262.98
doctrines	230.1–.9
catechisms and creeds	238.1–.9

Christian denominations (continued)	
general councils	262.51–.59
guides to Christian life	248.48
missions	266.1–.9
moral theology	241.04
public worship	264.01–.09
religious associations	267.18
religious education	268.8
religious orders	255
church history	271
women's	255.9
seminaries	230.073
theology	230.1–.9
see Manual at 283–289	
Christian doctrine	230
Christian education	268
see Manual at 207.5, 268 vs.	
200.71, 230.071, 292–299	
Christian ethics	241
see Manual at 241 vs. 261.8	
Christian holidays	263.9
devotional literature	242.3
sermons	252.6
see Manual at 203.6, 263.9,	
292–299 vs. 394.265–.267	
Christian initiation	265.1
Christian leadership	262.1
local church	253
Christian life	248.4
Christian-Marxist dialogue	
Christian theology	261.21
Christian Methodist	
Episcopal Church	287.83
see also Methodist Church	
Christian Reformed Church	285.731
see also Reformed Church	
(American Reformed)	
Christian sacred music	
public worship	
religion	264.2
religious symbolism	246.75
Christian Science	289.5
see also Christian	
denominations	
Christian Scientists	
biography	289.509 2
Christianity	230
art representation	
religious significance	246
arts	
religious significance	246
Islamic polemics	297.293
Christianity and anti-Semitism	261.26
Christianity and atheism	261.21

Christianity and culture	261
Christianity and Islam	261.27
Christian view	261.27
Islamic view	297.283
Christianity and Judaism	261.26
Christian view	261.26
Jewish view	296.396
Christianity and occultism	261.513
Christianity and other	
religions	261.2
Christianity and politics	261.7
Christianity and secular	
disciplines	261.5
see Manual at 261.5	
Christianity and the arts	261.57
Christians	270.092
biography	270.092
specific denominations	280
specific denominations	280
see Manual at 230–280	
Christmas	263.915
devotional literature	242.335
sermons	252.615
Christmas story	232.92
Christology	232
Chronicles (Biblical books)	222.6
Chuang-Tzu. Nan-hua ching	299.514 82
Church	260
ecclesiology	262
history	270
specific denominations	280
local	250
Church administration	262
local church	254
Church and state	
social theology	201.72
Christianity	261.7
see Manual at 322.1 vs. 201.72,	
261.7, 292–299	
Church and the poor	261.832 5
Church authority	262.8
Church buildings	
management	254.7
religious significance	246.9
Church calendar	263.9
Church controversies	262.8
local church	250
specific denominations	280
Church fathers	270
biography	270.092
Church finance	262.006 81
local church	254.8
Church furniture	247.1
Church government	262
local church	254
Church group work	253.7
Church growth	
local church	254.5
missionary work	266
Church history	270
specific denominations	280
Church holidays	263.9
devotional literature	242.3
sermons	252.6
see Manual at 203.6, 263.9,	
292–299 vs. 394.265–.267	
Church law	262.9
Church membership	
local church	254.5
Church of Christ, Scientist	289.5
see also Christian	
denominations	
Church of England	283.42
church government	262.034 2
parishes	254.034 2
church law	262.983 42
doctrines	230.3
catechisms and creeds	238.3
guides to Christian life	248.483
liturgy	264.03
missions	266.3
moral theology	241.043
persecution by Queen Mary	272.6
religious associations	267.183 42
religious education	268.834 2
religious orders	255.83
church history	271.83
women	255.983
church history	271.983
seminaries	230.073 342
theology	230.3
Church of God General	
Conference	286.73
see also Adventists	
Church of God in Christ,	
Mennonites	289.73
see also Mennonite Church	
Church of Jesus Christ of	
Latter-Day Saints	289.332
see also Mormon Church	
Church of North India	287.95
see also Christian	
denominations	
Church of Scotland	285.233
see also Presbyterian Church	

Church of South India	287.94
see also Christian	
denominations	
Church of the Brethren	286.5
see also Baptists	
Church of the Nazarene	287.99
see also Christian	
denominations	
Church of the New Jerusalem	289.4
see also Christian	
denominations	
Church organization	262
Church polity	262
Church renewal	262.001 7
Church services	264
Church work (Pastoral care)	253
Church work with children	259.22
Church work with disabled	
persons	259.44
Church work with families	259.1
Church work with juvenile	
delinquents	259.5
Church work with lepers	259.419 699 8
Church work with older persons	259.3
Church work with sick children	259.419 892
Church work with the sick	259.4
Church work with unmarried	
mothers	259.086 947
Church work with victims of	
crime	259.086 949
Church work with young adults	259.25
Church work with youth	259.23
Church year	263.9
devotional literature	242.3
sermon preparation	251.6
sermons	252.6
Church youth groups	259.23
Churches of Christ	286.63
see also Disciples of Christ	
Churches of Christ in	
Christian Union	289.9
see also Christian	
denominations	
Churches of God	289.9
see also Christian	
denominations	
Ciphers (Cryptography)	
Bible	220.68
Circumcision	
Jewish rites	296.442 2
liturgy	296.454 22
Circumcision of Jesus Christ	232.92

Cistercians	255.12
church history	271.12
women	255.97
church history	271.97
Citizenship	
ethics	
religion	205.621
Christianity	241.621
Judaism	296.362 1
social theology	201.723
Christianity	261.7
Judaism	296.382
City churches	250.917 32
administration	254.22
pastoral theology	253.091 732
City missions	266.022
Civil disobedience	
ethics	
religion	205.621
Buddhism	294.356 21
Christianity	241.621
Hinduism	294.548 621
Judaism	296.362 1
social theology	201.72
Christianity	261.7
Judaism	296.382
Civil rights	
social theology	201.723
Buddhism	294.337 23
Christianity	261.7
Hinduism	294.517 23
Islam	297.272
Judaism	296.382
Civil war	
ethics	
religion	205.621
Buddhism	294.356 21
Christianity	241.621
Hinduism	294.548 621
Judaism	296.362 1
social theology	201.72
Buddhism	294.337 2
Christianity	261.7
Hinduism	294.517 2
Judaism	296.382 7
Civilization	
Bible	220.95
Classical religion	292

Clergy	200.92
biography	200.92
Christian	270.092
biography	270.092
specific denominations	280
see Manual at 230–280	
ecclesiology	262.1
occupational ethics	241.641
pastoral theology	253
personal religion	248.892
training	230.071 1
occupational ethics	
religion	205.641
role and function	206.1
see also Rabbis;	
Religious leaders	
see Manual at 200.92 and	
201–209, 292–299	
Clergymen's wives	
Christianity	253.22
see also Spouses of clergy —	
Christianity	
Clerical celibacy	
Christianity	253.25
Clerks regular	255.5
church history	271.5
Clerks Regular of Somaschi	255.54
church history	271.54
Clerks Regular of the Mother	
of God	255.57
church history	271.57
Cloning	
human reproduction	
ethics	
religion	205.66
see also Reproduction —	
ethics — religion	
Cluniacs	255.14
church history	271.14
Coaching (Sports)	
religion	201.679 607 7
Code of Manu	294.592 6
Codependency	
devotional literature	204.32
Christianity	242.4
pastoral theology	206.1
Christianity	259.429
religious guidance	204.42
Christianity	248.862 9
social theology	201.762 29
Christianity	261.832 29
Codes of conduct	
moral theology	205
Christianity	241.5
Judaism	296.36
Codex iuris canonici (1917)	262.93
Codex iuris canonici (1983)	262.94
College students	
guides to religious life	
Christianity	248.834
pastoral care	
Christianity	259.24
Color	
religious significance	203.7
Christianity	246.6
see also Symbolism —	
religious significance	
Colossians (Biblical book)	227.7
Commandments	
Jewish law	296.18
moral theology	205
Christianity	241.5
Judaism	296.36
Common lectionary	264.34
preaching	251.6
Common of the mass	264.36
Common Worship	264.03
Communication	
ethics	
religion	205.65
Christianity	241.65
Communications media	
religion	201.7
see also Mass media —	
religion	
Communion (Part of service)	264.36
Communion of saints	262.73
Communion service	264.36
Communism and Christianity	261.21
Communism and Islam	297.273
Community of Christ	289.333
see also Mormon Church	
Companions of Muḥammad	297.648
Comparative religion	200
see Manual at 201–209 and	
292–299	
Compline	264.15
see also Liturgy of the hours	
Computer science and religion	201.600 4
Condemnation of Jesus Christ	232.962
Conditional immortality	236.23

Conduct of life	
ethics	
religion	205
see also Religious ethics	
personal religion	204.4
Buddhism	294.344 4
Christianity	248.4
Hinduism	294.544
Islam	297.57
Sufi	297.44
Judaism	296.7
Confederated Benedictines	255.11
church history	271.11
Confession (Christian rite)	234.166
public worship	265.62
theology	234.166
Confessionals	247.1
Confessions of faith	202
Christianity	238
Confirmation (Religious rite)	203.8
Christianity	234.162
public worship	265.2
theology	234.162
Judaism	296.442 4
liturgy	296.454 24
women's	296.443 4
liturgy	296.454 34
Conflict	
Bible	220.830 36
Confraternities	267
Confraternity Bible	220.520 5
Confucianism	
religion	299.512
Confucianists	
biography	
religion	299.512 092
Congregational Christian	
Churches of the United	
States	285.833
see also Congregationalism	
Congregational Churches of	
the United States	285.832
see also Congregationalism	
Congregational Methodist	
Church	287.2
see also Methodist Church	
Congregational systems	
Christian ecclesiology	262.4
Congregationalism	285.8
church government	262.058
parishes	254.058
church law	262.985 8
doctrines	230.58
catechisms and creeds	238.58

Congregationalism (continued)	
general councils	262.558
guides to Christian life	248.485 8
missions	266.58
moral theology	241.045 8
public worship	264.058
religious associations	267.185 8
religious education	268.858
seminaries	230.073 58
theology	230.58
Congregationalists	
biography	285.809 2
Congregations	
Christianity	
denominations	280
local church	250
papal administration	262.136
Judaism	296.65
religion	206.5
Conscience	
religion	205
Buddhism	294.35
Christianity	241.1
Hinduism	294.548
Islam	297.5
Judaism	296.36
Conscientious objection	
ethics	
religion	205.624 2
see also War — ethics —	
religion	
social theology	201.727 3
see also War — social	
theology	
Consecrations (Christian rites)	265.92
Conservation of natural	
resources	
social theology	201.77
Christianity	261.88
Conservative Judaism	296.834 2
liturgy	296.450 47
Consolatory devotions	204.32
Christianity	242.4
Judaism	296.72
Constantinopolitan Creed	238.14
Constitutional Church	284.8
Consumption	
ethics	
religion	205.68
Buddhism	294.356 8
Christianity	241.68
Hinduism	294.548 68
Islam	297.568
Judaism	296.368

Contemplation 204.3
  Christianity 248.34
Contemplative religious
  orders 255.01
  church history 271.01
  women 255.901
  church history 271.901
Contextual theology 202
  Christianity 230
    ethnic context 230.089
    feminist context 230.082
    geographic context 230.09
Contraception
  ethics
    religion 205.66
      Christianity 241.66
      Islam 297.566
      Judaism 296.366
  social theology 201.7
    Christianity 261.836
    Judaism 296.38
Contrition (Christian rite) 234.166
  public worship 265.61
  theology 234.166
Convents 206.57
  Christianity 255.9
    church history 271.9
    religious significance of
      buildings 246.97
Conventuals 255.37
  church history 271.37
Conversation
  ethics
    religion 205.672
      Christianity 241.672
      Judaism 296.367 2
    see also Ethical
      problems — religion
Conversion (Religious experience) 204.2
  Christianity 248.24
  Islam 297.574
  Judaism 296.714
Converts 204.2
  Judaism 296.714
    outreach activity for 296.69
  missions for 207.2
Coptic Church 281.72
  liturgy 264.017 2
  public worship 264.017 2
  see also Eastern churches
Coptic language
  Biblical texts 220.49
Coptic Orthodox Church 281.72
  see also Eastern churches

Corinthians (Biblical books) 227.2
Corpus iuris canonici 262.923
Cosmology
  religion 202.4
    Christianity 231.765
    comparative religion 202.4
    Hinduism 294.524
    Islam 297.242
    Judaism 296.3
    Mískito Indians 299.788 820 24
    Mosquito Indians 299.788 820 24
    philosophy of religion 215.2
Councils
  Christian ecclesiology 262.5
Counseling
  pastoral theology 206.1
    Christianity 253.5
    Judaism 296.61
Counter-Reformation 270.6
Countess of Huntingdon's
  Connexion 285.23
  see also Presbyterian Church
Country music and religion 201.678 164 2
Course in Miracles 299.93
Courtship
  ethics
    religion 205.676 5
      Christianity 241.676 5
      Judaism 296.367 65
Covenant relationship with God
  Christianity 231.76
  Judaism 296.311 72
Covenanters (Presbyterianism)
  Scotland 285.241 1
Coverdale Bible 220.520 1
Creation
  religion 202.4
    Christianity 231.765
    comparative religion 202.4
    Islam 297.242
    Judaism 296.34
    philosophy of religion 213
Creation science 231.765 2
  see Manual at 231.7652 vs.
    213, 500, 576.8
Creationism 231.765 2
  see Manual at 231.7652 vs.
    213, 500, 576.8
Credibility
  Christian church 262.72
Credo 264.36
Creeds 202
  Christianity 238

Crime
  social theology 201.764
    Christianity 261.833
Crosier Fathers 255.19
  church history 271.19
Crosses
  religious significance 246.558
Crucifixes
  religious significance 246.558
Crucifixion of Jesus Christ 232.963
Cruelty
  ethics
    religion 205.69
Cruelty to animals
  ethics
    religion 205.693
      see also Animals —
        treatment of —
        ethics — religion
Crusades
  church history 270.4
Cults 209
  see Manual at 201–209 and
    292–299; *also at* 299.93
Cumberland Presbyterian
  Church 285.135
  see also Presbyterian Church
Curia Romana 262.136

D

Daily devotions 204.46
  Christianity 242.2
  Judaism 296.45
Dakota Indians
  religion 299.785 243
Dalits
  religion 200.869 4
    Hinduism 294.508 694
Dancing
  religious significance 203.7
    Christianity 246.7
    see also Arts — religious
      significance
Daniel (Biblical book) 224.5
Dao de jing 299.514 82
David, King of Israel
  Biblical leader 222.409 2
David and Goliath story 222.430 950 5
Da'wah 297.74
Day of the Lord
  Christianity 236.9

Deacons 270.092
  biography 270.092
    specific denominations 280
    see Manual at 230–280
  ecclesiology 262.14
  pastoral theology 253
  see also Clergy — Christian
Dead
  objects of worship 202.13
Dead Sea Scrolls 296.155
  Old Testament works in 221.44
  pseudepigrapha 229.91
  Qumran community writings 296.155
Deadly sins 241.3
Death
  ethics
    religion 205.697
      Buddhism 294.356 97
      Christianity 241.697
      Hinduism 294.548 697
      Islam 297.569 7
      Judaism 296.369 7
  medical ethics
    religion 205.697
  religion 202.3
    Buddhism 294.342 3
    Christianity 236.1
    Hinduism 294.523
    Islam 297.23
    Judaism 296.33
    philosophy of religion 218
  religious rites 203.88
    Christianity 265.85
    Islam 297.385
    Judaism 296.445
      liturgy 296.454 5
    see also Rites — religion
Death of Jesus Christ 232.963
Decalogue 222.16
  moral theology
    Christianity 241.52
    Judaism 296.36
Dedications (Christian rites) 265.92
Defenseless Mennonites 289.73
  biography 289.709 2
  see also Mennonite Church
Deism 211.5
Deists 211.509 2
Deities 202.11
  see also Gods and goddesses
Delaware Indians
  religion 299.783 45
  religious rites 299.783 450 38

Demai	296.123 1
Mishnah	296.123 1
Palestinian Talmud	296.124 1
Demoniac possession	
religion	204.2
Demonology	
religion	202.16
Hinduism	294.521 6
Demons	
religion	202.16
Christianity	235.4
Demythologizing (Bible)	220.68
Denominations	209
Christianity	280
see also Christian	
denominations	
Judaism	296.8
see Manual at 201–209 and	
292–299	
Descent into hell of Jesus Christ	232.967
Destiny	
religion	202.2
Christianity	234.9
Determinism	
religion	
Islam	297.227
Deuteronomy (Bible)	222.15
Devil	202.16
Christianity	235.4
Islam	297.216
Judaism	296.316
Devil worship	202.16
Devotional calendars	242.2
Devotional literature	204.32
Buddhism	294.344 32
Christianity	242
Hinduism	294.543 2
Islam	297.382
Sufi	297.438 2
Judaism	296.72
Devotional theology	204
Buddhism	294.344
Christianity	240
Hinduism	294.54
Islam	297.57
Sufi	297.4
Judaism	296.7
Dhammapada	294.382 322
Dharma	
Hinduism	294.548
Dharmacakra	294.343 7
Dharmasastras	294.592 6
Dhikr	297.382
Dianetics	299.936
Diatessaron	226.1
Dietary laws	
Islam	297.576
Judaism	296.73
Dietary limitations	
religion	204.46
Hinduism	294.544 6
Judaism	296.73
Digambara (Jainism)	294.493
Dioceses	
Christian ecclesiology	262.3
Directors of religious	
education	207.509 2
biography	207.509 2
Christianity	268.092
biography	268.092
see Manual at 230–280	
role and function	268.3
Judaism	296.680 92
biography	296.680 92
role and function	296.68
Disabled persons	
pastoral care	
Christianity	259.44
Disarmament	
ethics	
religion	205.624
see also International	
relations — ethics —	
religion	
social theology	201.727 3
see also Peace — social	
theology	
Disciples of Christ	286.6
biography	286.609 2
church government	262.066
parishes	254.066
church law	262.986 6
doctrines	230.66
catechisms and creeds	238.66
guides to Christian life	248.486 6
missions	266.66
moral theology	241.046 6
public worship	264.066
religious associations	267.186 6
religious education	268.866
seminaries	230.073 66
theology	230.66

Discrimination
  ethics
    religion — 205.675
      Buddhism — 294.356 75
      Christianity — 241.675
      Islam — 297.567 5
      Judaism — 296.367 5
    religion — 200.8
      Christianity — 270.08
      Judaism — 296.08
Diseases
  humans
    pastoral theology — 206.1
      Christianity — 259.41
    religious rites — 203.8
      Christianity — 265.82
    social theology — 201.762 1
      Christianity — 261.832 1
Dispensationalist theology — 230.046 3
Dissenters (Protestant churches) — 280.4
  see also Protestantism
Distributive justice
  ethics
    religion — 205.622
      Buddhism — 294.356 22
      Christianity — 241.622
      Hinduism — 294.548 622
      Islam — 297.562 2
      Judaism — 296.362 2
Divali — 294.536
Divination
  religion — 203.2
    African religions — 299.613 2
Divine law
  Christianity — 241.2
Divine Light Mission — 294
Divine office (Religion) — 264.15
  Anglican — 264.030 15
  Roman Catholic — 264.020 15
  texts — 264.024
Divinities — 202.11
  see also Gods and goddesses
Divinity of Jesus Christ — 232.8
Divinity schools — 230.071 1
Divorce
  ethics
    religion — 205.63
      Buddhism — 294.356 3
      Christianity — 241.63
      Hinduism — 294.548 63
      Islam — 297.563
      Judaism — 296.363
  Judaism — 296.444 4
  religion — 204.41

Divorce (continued)
  social theology — 201.7
    Christianity — 261.835 89
Divorced men
  guides to Christian life — 248.842 3
Divorced persons
  Christian devotional
    literature — 242.646
  guides to religious life — 204.41
    Christianity — 248.846
Divorced women
  guides to Christian life — 248.843 3
Doctrinal controversies
  Christian church history — 273
Doctrinal theology — 202
  Buddhism — 294.342
  Christianity — 230
  Hinduism — 294.52
  Islam — 297.2
    Sufi — 297.41
  Judaism — 296.3
  philosophy of religion — 210
Doctrine and Covenants
  (Mormon sacred book) — 289.32
Documentary hypothesis
  (Pentateuchal criticism) — 222.106 6
Dogma — 202
Dominican Sisters — 255.972
  church history — 271.972
Dominicans — 255.2
  church history — 271.2
  women — 255.972
    church history — 271.972
Dominion theology — 230.046
Donatism — 273.4
Douay Bible — 220.520 2
Doxologies
  Christian private prayer — 242.72
Drama in Christian education — 268.67
Dreamtime (Mythology) — 299.921 5
Druidism — 299.16
Druzes (Islamic sect) — 297.85
Dualism (Concept of God) — 211.33
  classes of religions — 201.4
  philosophy of religion — 211.33
Dukhobors — 289.9
  see also Christian
    denominations
Dunkers — 286.5
  see also Baptists
Dutch Reformed Church in
  North America — 285.732
  see also Reformed Church
    (American Reformed)

Duty
  religion 205
  Islam 297.5
Dwellings
  Bible 220.839 236
Dying patients
  pastoral theology 206.1
    Christianity 259.417 5
  social theology 201.762 175
    Christianity 261.832 175
Dysfunctional families
  pastoral theology 206.1
    Christianity 259.1
  social theology 201.7
    Christianity 261.835 85

E

E document (Biblical criticism) 222.106 6
Early Christian art
  religious significance 246.2
Early Church 270.1
  see Manual at 270,
    230.11–.14 vs.
    230.15–.2, 281.5–.9, 282
Easter 263.93
  devotional literature 242.36
  sermons 252.63
Easter story 232.97
Eastern churches 281.5
  church government 262.015
    parishes 254.015
  church law 262.981 5
  doctrines 230.15
    catechisms and creeds 238.19
  general councils 262.515
  guides to Christian life 248.481 5
  liturgy 264.015
  missions 266.15
  monasticism 255.81
    church history 271.81
    women 255.981
      church history 271.981
  moral theology 241.041 5
  public worship 264.015
  religious associations 267.181 5
  religious education 268.815
  seminaries 230.073 15
  theology 230.15
  see Manual at 270, 230.11–.14
    vs. 230.15–.2, 281.5–.9, 282

Eastern Orthodox Christians
  biography 281.909 2
Eastern Orthodox Church 281.9
  church government 262.019
    parishes 254.019
  church law 262.981 9
  doctrines 230.19
    catechisms and creeds 238.19
  general councils 262.519
  guides to Christian life 248.481 9
  liturgy 264.019
  missions 266.19
  monasticism 255.819
    church history 271.819
    women 255.981 9
      church history 271.981 9
  moral theology 241.041 9
  public worship 264.019
  religious associations 267.181 9
  religious education 268.819
  seminaries 230.073 19
  theology 230.19
  see Manual at 270, 230.11–.14
    vs. 230.15–.2, 281.5–.9, 282
Eastern Orthodox sacred music
  public worship
    religion 264.019 02
Eastern rite Catholics 281.5
  see also Eastern churches
Eastern rite churches 281.5
  see also Eastern churches
Eastertide 263.93
  devotional literature 242.36
  sermons 252.63
Ecclesiastes 223.8
Ecclesiastical law 262.9
Ecclesiasticus (Bible) 229.4
Ecclesiology
  Christianity 262
Eckankar 299.93
Ecology
  ethics
    religion 205.691
      Buddhism 294.356 91
      Christianity 241.691
      Hinduism 294.548 691
      Islam 297.569 1
      Judaism 296.369 1
  social theology 201.77
    Christianity 261.88
    Judaism 296.38

Economics	
social theology	201.73
Christianity	261.85
Islam	297.273
see Manual at 297.26–.27	
Judaism	296.383
Ecumenical councils	262.5
Christian church history	270.2
modern period	270.82
Ecumenical movement	280.042
see Manual at 280.042 vs. 262.0011	
Ecumenism	262.001 1
see Manual at 280.042 vs. 262.0011	
Eddy, Mary Baker	289.509 2
Christian Science writings	289.52
Eden	
Bible stories	222.110 950 5
Eduyyot	296.123 4
Babylonian Talmud	296.125 4
Mishnah	296.123 4
Palestinian Talmud	296.124 4
Eglise de Jésus-Christ sur la terre par le prophète Simon Kimbangu	289.93
see also Christian denominations	
Egyptians (Ancient)	
religion	299.31
Elderly persons	
religion	200.846
see also Older persons — religion	
Election (Christian doctrine)	234
Election sermons	204.3
Christianity	252.68
Embryo transfer	
ethics	
religion	205.66
see also Reproduction — ethics — religion	
Emigration from Mecca	297.634
Emperor worship	202.13
Encyclicals	262.91
End of the world	
religion	202.3
Christianity	236.9
Islam	297.23
English Revised version Bible	220.520 4

Enlightenment	
religion	204.2
Buddhism	294.344 2
Hinduism	294.542
Islam	297.57
Enoch (Pseudepigrapha)	229.913
Entertainments (Parties)	
religion	201.679 32
Environment	
ethics	
religion	205.691
Buddhism	294.356 91
Christianity	241.691
Hinduism	294.548 691
Islam	297.569 1
Judaism	296.369 1
social theology	201.77
Christianity	261.88
Islam	297.27
Judaism	296.38
Environmental abuse	
social theology	201.77
Christianity	261.88
Envy	
ethics	
religion	205.698
see also Vices — religion	
Ephesians (Biblical book)	227.5
Epiphany	263.915
devotional literature	242.335
sermons	252.615
Episcopacy	262.12
Episcopal Church	283.73
church government	262.037 3
parishes	254.037 3
church law	262.983 73
doctrines	230.3
catechisms and creeds	238.3
guides to Christian life	248.483
liturgy	264.03
missions	266.3
moral theology	241.043
religious associations	267.183 73
religious education	268.837 3
religious orders	255.83
church history	271.83
women	255.983
church history	271.983
seminaries	230.073 373
theology	230.3
Episcopal systems	
Christian ecclesiology	262.3
Episcopalians	
biography	283.092

Epistle of Jeremiah (Bible)   229.5
Epistles (Bible)   227
  exegesis   227.06
  pseudepigrapha   229.93
Equality
  religion   200.8
    Christianity   270.08
    Judaism   296.08
Equipment
  local Christian parishes   254.7
Eremitical religious orders   255.02
  church history   271.02
  women   255.902
    church history   271.902
Eruvin   296.123 2
  Babylonian Talmud   296.125 2
  Mishnah   296.123 2
  Palestinian Talmud   296.124 2
Eschatology   202.3
  Buddhism   294.342 3
  Christianity   236
  Germanic religion   293.23
  Hinduism   294.523
  Islam   297.23
  Judaism   296.33
  philosophy of religion   218
Esdras (Deuterocanonical book)   229.1
Espionage
  ethics
    religion   205.624
      see also International
        relations — ethics —
        religion
  social theology   201.727
      see also International
        relations — social
        theology
Essenes   296.814
Esther (Biblical book)   222.9
Esther (Deuterocanonical book)   229.27
Eternity
  religion   202.3
    Christianity   236.21
    Islam   297.23
    Judaism   296.33
Ethical problems
  religion   205.6
    Buddhism   294.356
    Christianity   241.6
    Hinduism   294.548 6
    Islam   297.56
    Judaism   296.36
Ethical wills
  Judaism   296.36

Ethics
  religion   205
    Bahai Faith   297.935
    Buddhism   294.35
    Christianity   241
        see Manual at
          241 vs. 261.8
    Hinduism   294.548
    Islam   297.5
      Sufi   297.45
    Judaism   296.36
Ethics of the Fathers   296.123 47
Ethiopian Church   281.75
    see also Eastern churches
Ethiopian Orthodox Church   281.75
    see also Eastern churches
Ethiopic language
  Biblical texts   220.46
Ethnic groups
  religion   200.89
    Christianity   270.089
Eucharist   234.163
  public worship   264.36
    Anglican   264.030 36
      texts   264.03
    Roman Catholic   264.020 36
      texts   264.023
  theology   234.163
Eucharistic Liturgy   264.36
    see also Eucharist — public
      worship
Euthanasia
  ethics
    religion   205.697
      see also Death — ethics —
        religion
Eutychian Church   281.6
    see also Christian
      denominations
Evangelical and Reformed
    Church   285.734
    see also Reformed Church
      (American Reformed)
Evangelical churches   289.95
    see also Christian
      denominations
Evangelical Congregational
    Church   289.9
    see also Christian
      denominations
Evangelical Free Church of
    America   289.95
    see also Christian
      denominations

Evangelical Lutheran Church 284.131 2
  see also Lutheran church
Evangelical Lutheran Church
  in America 284.135
  see also Lutheran church
Evangelical Lutheran
  Synodical Conference of
  North America 284.132
  see also Lutheran church
Evangelical theology 230.046 24
Evangelical United Brethren
  Church 289.9
  see also Christian
    denominations
Evangelicalism 270.82
  independent denominations 289.95
  Protestantism 280.4
Evangelische Kirche in
  Deutschland 284.094 3
  see also Lutheran church
Evangelism 269.2
Evangelistic sermons 252.3
Evangelistic writings 243
Evangelists 269.209 2
Evangelization 266
Eve (Biblical person)
  Bible stories 222.110 950 5
Evening prayer 264.15
  Anglican 264.030 15
  texts 264.034
Evensong 264.030 15
  texts 264.034
Evil (Concept)
  ethics
    religion 205
      Christianity 241.3
      Islam 297.5
      Judaism 296.36
  religion 202.118
    Christianity 231.8
      freedom of choice 233.7
    comparative religion 202.118
    Islam 297.211 8
    Judaism 296.311 8
    philosophy of religion 214
Evil spirits
  religion 202.16
Evolution versus creation 202.4
  Christianity 231.765 2
    see Manual at 231.7652 vs.
      213, 500, 576.8
  Islam 297.242
  Judaism 296.34
  philosophy of religion 213

Excommunication
  Catholic Church 262.9
  Judaism 296.67
Executives
  Christian pastoral theology 259.088 658
Exegesis
  sacred books 208.2
    Bible 220.6
    Bible. N.T. 225.6
    Bible. O.T. 221.6
    Koran 297.122 6
    Talmud 296.120 6
Existence of God 212.1
  Christianity 231
  comparative religion 202.11
  Islam 297.211
  Judaism 296.311
  philosophy of religion 212.1
Existentialist theology 230.046
Exodus (Bible) 222.12
Exorcism
  religious rite 203.8
    Christianity 265.94
    see also Rites — religion
Exorcists 200.92
  biography 200.92
  religious role and function 206.1
  see Manual at 200.92 and
    201–209, 292–299
Experience
  religion 204.2
    see also Religious experience
Extramarital relations
  ethics
    religion 205.66
      see also Sexual relations —
        ethics — religion
    social theology 201.7
      Christianity 261.835 736
Extreme unction 234.167
  public worship 265.7
  theology 234.167
Ezekiel (Biblical book) 224.4
Ezra (Biblical book) 222.7

F

Faith
  religion 202.2
    Christianity 234.23
      knowledge of God 231.042
    Islam 297.22
    Judaism 296.32
    philosophy of religion 218

Faith and reason	210
Christianity	231.042
Judaism	296.311
philosophy of religion	210
Faith healing	
religion	203.1
Christianity	234.131
see also Spiritual healing —	
religion	
see Manual at 615.852 vs.	
203.1, 234.131, 292–299	
Fall of humankind	233.14
Families	
religion	
guides to life	204.41
Christianity	248.4
see also Family life —	
religion	
pastoral theology	206.1
Christianity	259.1
social theology	201.7
Christianity	261.835 85
worship	204.3
Christianity	249
Judaism	296.45
Families of clergy	
Christianity	
pastoral theology	253.22
Family counseling	
Christian pastoral	
counseling	259.12
Family ethics	
religion	205.63
Buddhism	294.356 3
Christianity	241.63
Hinduism	294.548 63
Islam	297.563
Judaism	296.363
Family life	
religion	204.41
Buddhism	294.344 41
Christianity	248.4
Hinduism	294.544 1
Islam	297.577
Judaism	296.74
Family planning	
ethics	
religion	205.66
Christianity	241.66
Islam	297.566
Judaism	296.366
social theology	201.7
Christianity	261.836
Judaism	296.38
Family purity	
Judaism	296.742
Family violence	
social theology	201.762 829 2
Christianity	261.832 7
Fast days	203.6
Christianity	263.9
devotional literature	242.3
sermons	252.6
Islam	297.53
Judaism	296.43
see also Holy days	
Fasting	
religious practice	204.47
Buddhism	294.344 47
Christianity	248.47
Hinduism	294.544 7
Islam	297.53
Sufi	297.45
Judaism	296.7
Fatalism	
religion	202.2
Islam	297.227
Father (God)	
Christian doctrines	231.1
Jewish doctrine	296.311 2
Fathers	
Christian devotional	
literature	242.642 1
guides to Christian life	248.842 1
Fathers of the Church	270.1
Feast days	
Christianity	263.9
devotional literature	242.3
sermons	252.6
religion	203.6
see also Holy days	
Fellowship of Grace Brethren	
Churches	286.5
Female goddesses	202.114
Femininity of God	202.114
Christianity	231.4
Judaism	296.311 2
Feminism	
religion	200.82
Christianity	270.082
Judaism	296.082
Feminist theology	202.082
Christianity	230.082
Judaism	296.308 2

Fertilization in vitro
ethics
   religion   205.66
   see also Reproduction —
     ethics — religion
Festivals
  religion   203.6
   Christianity   263
   Judaism   296.43
  see also Holy days
Fetishism
  religion   202.1
Finance
  churches   262.006 81
  local church   254.8
Finnish Evangelical Lutheran
  Church   284.133 4
  see also Lutheran church
Fiqh
  religious law   297.14
Fire
  religious worship   202.12
Five Confucian Classics   299.512 82
Five pillars of Islam   297.31
Five scrolls (Bible)   221.044
Flight from Mecca   297.634
Flight into Egypt   232.92
Fly fishing
  religion   201.679 912 4
Food taboos
  religion   204.46
   Hinduism   294.544 6
   Islam   297.576
   Judaism   296.73
Foot washing
  Christian rite   265.9
Foreign missions
  Christianity   266.023
Forensic medicine and
  religion   201.661 41
Foreordination (Christian
  doctrine)   234.9
Forgiveness
ethics
   religion   205.699
   see also Virtues —
     religion
  religious doctrine   202.2
   Christianity   234.5
Form criticism
  sacred books   208.2
   Bible   220.663
   Talmud   296.120 663

Forty Hours devotion
  Roman Catholic liturgy   264.027 4
Founders of religions   206.3
Four Noble Truths   294.342
Franciscans   255.3
  church history   271.3
  women   255.973
   church history   271.973
Free Church of Scotland   285.234
  see also Presbyterian Church
Free churches   280.4
  see also Protestantism
Free Methodist Church of
  North America   287.2
  see also Methodist Church
Free thought   211.4
Free will
  religion   202.2
   Christianity   233.7
    soteriology   234.9
   Islam   297.227
   Judaism   296.32
Freedom of religion
  social theology   201.723
   Christianity   261.72
  see also Politics and
    religion — social
    theology
Freethinkers   211.409 2
Freewill Baptists   286.2
  see also Baptists
Friaries
  church history   271
  religious significance of
   buildings   246.97
Friday
  Islamic observance   297.36
Friends (Religious society)   289.6
  biography   289.609 2
  see also Society of Friends
Friendship
ethics
   religion   205.676 2
    Christianity   241.676 2
    Islam   297.567 62
    Judaism   296.367 62
Fringes (Judaism)   296.461
Fruit of the Spirit   234.13
Fund raising
  local Christian church   254.8
  synagogues   296.65
Fundamental theology
  (Christianity)   230.01

Fundamentalism
  Buddhism   294.309
  Christianity   270.82
    independent denominations   289.95
    Protestantism   280.4
  Islam
    religion   297.09
    see Manual at 320.557 vs.
        297.09, 297.272, 322.1
Fundamentalist theology   230.046 26
Funeral sermons
  Christianity   252.1
Funerals
  Buddhist rites   294.343 88
  Christian rites   265.85
  Hindu rites   294.538 8
  Islamic rites   297.385
  Jewish rites   296.445
    liturgy   296.454 5
  religious rites   203.88
Future life
  religion   202.3
  Buddhism   294.342 3
  Christianity   236.2
  Hinduism   294.523
  Islam   297.23
  Judaism   296.33
Future punishment   202.3
  Islam   297.23

G

Galatians (Biblical book)   227.4
Gallican schismatic churches   284.8
  see also Old Catholic churches
Gambling
  ethics
    religion   205.65
      see also Recreation —
        ethics — religion
Games
  religion   201.679 01
Ganapataism   294.551 5
Gaonim   296.120 092
Gardens
  Bible   220.863 5
Gathas   295.82
Gautama Buddha   294.363
Gay marriage
  religion   204.41
Gay men
  religion   200.866 42
    Christianity   270.086 642
      pastoral theology   259.086 642

Gay women
  religion   200.866 43
    see also Lesbians — religion
Gays
  religion   200.866 4
    Christianity   270.086 64
      pastoral theology   259.086 64
    guides to life   204.408 664
    Judaism   296.086 64
Ge'ez language
  Biblical texts   220.46
General Conference Mennonite
  Church   289.73
  see also Mennonite Church
Genesis (Bible)   222.11
  exegesis   222.110 6
Genetic engineering and
  religion   201.666 065
Gentleness
  moral theology   205.699
  see also Virtues — religion
Geography
  Bible   220.91
Geonim   296.120 092
German Reformed Church (U.S.)   285.733
  see also Reformed Church
    (American Reformed)
Germanic religion   293
Gestures
  preaching   251.03
Ghost Dance   299.798 090 34
Gifts of the Holy Spirit   234.13
Gittin   296.123 3
  Babylonian Talmud   296.125 3
  Mishnah   296.123 3
  Palestinian Talmud   296.124 3
Gloria   264.36
Glossolalia   234.132
Gluttony
  moral theology   205.68
    see also Consumption —
      ethics — religion
Gnosticism   299.932
  Christian heresy   273.1
God   211
  Buddhism   294.342 11
  Christianity   231
  comparative religion   202.11
  Hinduism   294.521 1
  Islam   297.211
  Judaism   296.311
  philosophy of religion   211
Goddess religions   201.43

Goddesses	202.114	Good Friday	263.925
Greek	292.211 4	devotional literature	242.35
Roman	292.211 4	sermons	252.625
see also Gods and goddesses		Good News Bible	220.520 82
Gods	202.11	Good spirits	202.15
Egyptian	299.312 113	Goodness of God	214
Greek	292.211 3	Christianity	231.8
male	202.113	comparative religion	202.112
Roman	292.211 3	Islam	297.211 2
see also Gods and goddesses		Judaism	296.311 2
Gods and goddesses	202.11	philosophy of religion	214
African	299.612 11	Gospel of Thomas	229.8
Algonquian	299.783 021 1	Gospel stories retold	226.095 05
Australian	299.921 5	Gospels (Bible)	226
Buddhist	294.342 11	exegesis	226.06
Celtic	299.161 211	pseudepigrapha	229.8
Chinese	299.511 211	Gossip	
classical	292.211	ethics	
Egyptian	299.312 11	religion	205.672
Germanic	293.211	Christianity	241.672
Greek	292.211	Judaism	296.367 2
Hawaiian	299.924 2	*see also* Ethical	
Hindu	294.521 1	problems — religion	
Native American	299.712 11	Gothic art	
North American	299.712 11	religious significance	246.1
South American	299.812 11	Grace (Religious doctrine)	202.2
Norse	293.211	Christianity	234
Phoenician	299.26	Grace at meals	204.3
Polynesian	299.924	Christianity	242.72
Pueblo	299.784 021 1	Gradual	264.36
Roman	292.211	Gratitude	
Scandinavian	293.211	moral theology	205.699
Semitic	299.2	*see also* Virtues — religion	
Shinto	299.561 211	Great Awakening	277.307
Golden Rule		Great schism, 1054	270.38
Christianity	241.54	Great Western Schism,	
Judaism	296.36	1378–1417	282.090 23
Good and evil		Great White Brotherhood	299.93
ethics		Greed	
religion	205	moral theology	205.68
Christianity	241	Buddhism	294.356 8
Islam	297.5	Christianity	241.3
Judaism	296.36	Hinduism	294.548 68
religion	202.118	Islam	297.568
Christianity	231.8	Judaism	296.368
freedom of choice	233.7	Greek language	
comparative religion	202.118	Biblical texts	220.48
Islam	297.2	Greek religion	292.08
freedom of choice	297.227	Greeks (Ethnic group)	
theodicy	297.211 8	ancient	
Judaism	296.311 8	religion	292.08
freedom of choice	296.32		
philosophy of religion	214		

Grief
  at death
    Christianity
      pastoral theology   259.6
      personal religion   248.866
      prayers and meditations   242.4
Guaraní Indians
  religion   299.883 82
Guides to religious life   204.4
  Buddhism   294.344 4
  Christianity   248.4
  Hinduism   294.544
  Islam   297.57
    Sufi   297.44
  Judaism   296.7
Guilt
  religion   202.2
    Christianity   233.4
    Judaism   296.32
Guru Granth   294.682
Gurus   200.92
  biography   200.92
  Buddhist   294.309 2
    biography   294.309 2
      specific sects   294.39
    role and function   294.361
  Hindu   294.509 2
    biography   294.509 2
      specific sects   294.55
    role and function   294.561
  role and function   206.1
  Sikh   294.609 2
    biography   294.609 2
    role and function   294.663
  see Manual at 200.92 and
    201–209, 292–299

H

Habad Lubavitch Hasidism   296.833 22
Habakkuk (Biblical book)   224.95
Hades   202.3
  see also Hell
Hadith   297.124
Ḥadj   297.352
Haggadah (Passover)   296.453 71
Haggadot   296.453 71
Haggai (Biblical book)   224.97
Ḥagigah   296.123 2
  Babylonian Talmud   296.125 2
  Mishnah   296.123 2
  Palestinian Talmud   296.124 2
Hagiographa (Bible)   223

Hagiography   200.92
  Christianity   270.092
Hail Mary   242.74
Haitian religion   299.689 729 4
Ḥajj   297.352
Halakhah   296.18
  Midrash   296.141
  Talmud   296.127 4
Ḥallah   296.123 1
  Mishnah   296.123 1
  Palestinian Talmud   296.124 1
Hanafites (Islamic sect)   297.811
Hanbalites (Islamic sect)   297.814
Hanukkah   296.435
  liturgy   296.453 5
Hard-Shell Baptists   286.4
  see also Baptists
Hare Krishna movement   294.551 2
Harmonies of Bible   220.65
Harmonies of Gospels   226.1
Hasidism   296.833 2
  liturgy   296.450 44
Hatred
  religion   205.698
  see also Vices — religion
Hawaiian religion   299.924 2
Healing
  religion   203.1
  see also Spiritual healing —
    religion
  see Manual at 615.852 vs.
    203.1, 234.131, 292–299
Health
  social theology   201.762 1
    Christianity   261.832 1
    Judaism   296.38
Health services
  pastoral theology   206.1
    Christianity   259.41
  social theology   201.762 1
    Christianity   261.832 1
Heaven   202.3
  Christianity   236.24
  Islam   297.23
  Judaism   296.33
Hebrew language
  Biblical texts   220.44
  Midrashic texts   296.140 4
  Talmudic texts   296.120 4
Hebrew schools   296.680 83
Hebrews (Biblical book)   227.87
Hegirah   297.634

Hell	202.3
Christianity	236.25
Islam	297.23
Hellenistic movement (Judaism)	296.81
Heresy	
Christianity	262.8
church history	273
polemics	239
Islam	
polemics	297.29
Judaism	296.67
polemics	296.35
religious authority	296.67
Hermanos Penitentes	267.242 789
Hermeneutics	
sacred books	208.2
Bible	220.601
Koran	297.122 601
Talmud	296.120 601
Heroes	
objects of worship	202.13
Hexateuch (Bible)	222.1
Hidden Imam	297.24
Hierotherapy	
religion	203.1
see Manual at 615.852 vs.	
203.1, 234.131, 292–299	
High Holy Days	296.431
liturgy	296.453 1
Higher criticism	
Bible	220.66
Bible. N.T.	225.66
Bible. O.T.	221.66
Highway safety	
social theology	201.763 125
Hijrah	297.634
Hinayana Buddhism	294.391
Hindu calendar	
religion	294.536
Hindu demonology	294.521 6
Hindu education	294.575
Hindu ethics	294.548
Hindu holidays	294.536
see Manual at 203.6, 263.9,	
292–299 vs. 394.265–.267	
Hindu sacred music	
public worship	
religion	294.538
religion	294.537
Hindu temples and shrines	294.535
Hinduism	294.5
Islamic polemics	297.294
Hinduism and Islam	294.515
Hindu view	294.515
Islamic view	297.284 5
Hindus	
biography	294.509 2
Historians of religion	200.92
Historical books (Old Testament)	222
Historical books	
(Pseudepigrapha)	229.911
Historical criticism	
sacred books	208.2
Bible	220.67
Koran	297.122 67
Talmud	296.120 67
Historicity of Jesus Christ	232.908
History	
Biblical events	220.95
History (Theology)	202.117
Christianity	231.76
Islam	297.211 4
Judaism	296.311 7
History and religion	201.69
Hobbies	
religion	201.679 013
Holī (Hindu festival)	294.536
Holidays	
religion	203.6
see also Holy days	
Holiness	202.2
Christian church attribute	262.72
Christian doctrine	234.8
Holiness churches	289.94
Holocaust, 1933–1945	
Christian theology	231.76
interreligious relations	261.26
Jewish theology	296.311 74
Holy, The	211
Holy Communion	234.163
public worship	264.36
Anglican	264.030 36
texts	264.03
Roman Catholic	264.020 36
texts	264.023
theology	234.163

ɔly days	203.6
Buddhism	294.343 6
Christianity	263.9
devotional literature	242.3
sermons	252.6
Hinduism	294.536
Islam	297.36
Judaism	296.43
liturgy	296.453
see Manual at 203.6, 263.9, 292–299 vs. 394.265–.267	
ɔly Family	232.92
ɔly Ghost	231.3
ɔly Hours	264.7
ɔly Orders	234.164
public worship	265.4
theology	234.164
ɔly places	203.5
see also Sacred places	
ɔly Roman Empire	
church history	270
ɔly See	262.13
acts	262.91
ɔly Shroud	232.966
ɔly Spirit	231.3
baptism in	234.13
ɔly war (Islam)	297.72
ɔly Week	263.925
devotional literature	242.35
Roman Catholic liturgy	264.027 2
sermons	252.625
ɔme missions	266.022
ɔmeless persons	
social theology	201.762 5
Christianity	261.832 5
ɔmiletic illustrations	
Christianity	251.08
ɔmiletics	206.1
Christianity	251
see also Preaching	
ɔmilies	204.3
Christianity	252
ɔmosexuality	
ethics	
religion	205.66
see also Sexual relations — ethics — religion	
religion	200.866 4
Christianity	270.086 64

Homosexuals	
religion	200.866 4
Christianity	270.086 64
pastoral theology	259.086 64
Judaism	296.086 64
Honesty	
moral theology	205.699
see also Virtues — religion	
Hope	
Christianity	234.25
Hopi Indians	
magic	
religious practice	299.784 580 3
religion	299.784 58
Horayot	296.123 4
Babylonian Talmud	296.125 4
Mishnah	296.123 4
Palestinian Talmud	296.124 4
Hosea (Biblical book)	224.6
Hospices (Terminal care facilities)	
pastoral theology	206.1
Christianity	259.417 56
social theology	201.762 175 6
Christianity	261.832 175 6
Hospital chaplaincy	206.1
Christianity	259.411
Judaism	296.610 877
Hospitalers of St. John of Jerusalem	255.791 2
church history	271.791 2
Hospitals	
pastoral theology	206.1
Christianity	259.411
social theology	201.762 11
Christianity	261.832 11
House churches	250
Huguenots	284.5
biography	284.509 2
persecution of	272.4
see also Christian denominations	
Hullin	296.123 5
Babylonian Talmud	296.125 5
Mishnah	296.123 5
Human cloning	
ethics	
religion	205.66
see also Reproduction — ethics — religion	
Human ecology	
social theology	201.77
Christianity	261.88
Judaism	296.38

Human embryo
  transplantation
    ethics
      religion   205.66
      see also Reproduction —
        ethics — religion
Human life
  origin
    religion   202.2
      Christianity   233.11
      Islam   297.221
      Judaism   296.32
      philosophy of religion   213
  respect for
    ethics
      religion   205.697
        Buddhism   294.356 97
        Christianity   241.697
        Hinduism   294.548 697
        Islam   297.569 7
        Judaism   296.369 7
Human reproductive technology
  ethics
    religion   205.66
    see also Reproduction —
      ethics — religion
Human sacrifice
  religion   203.42
Humanism
  philosophy of religion   211.6
Humanistic Judaism   296.834
Humanity of Jesus Christ   232.8
Humans
  religion   202.2
    Buddhism   294.342 2
    Christianity   233
    Hinduism   294.522
    Islam   297.22
    Judaism   296.32
    philosophy of religion   218
Humility
  moral theology   205.699
  see also Virtues — religion
Hunger
  social theology   201.763 8
    Christianity   261.832 6
Hunting
  ethics
    religion   205.693
      see also Animals —
        treatment of —
        ethics — religion

Husbands
  Christian devotional
    literature   242.642 5
    guides to Christian life   248.842 5
Hussites   284.3
  see also Christian
    denominations
Hutterite Brethren   289.73
  biography   289.709 2
  see also Mennonite Church
Hymns
  religion   203.8
    Christianity   264.23
    Judaism   296.462
    private devotions   204.3
Hypostatic union   232.8

I

I ching
  religion   299.512 82
Ibadites   297.833
Iblīs   297.216
Ibn Ḥanbal, Aḥmad ibn
  Muḥammad
    Hadith   297.124
Ibn Mājah, Muḥammad ibn Yazīd
  Hadith   297.124 6
Ibrāhīm (Patriarch)
  Islam   297.246 3
Icons
  religious significance   203.7
    Christianity   246.53
    see also Symbolism —
      religious significance
'Īd al-Aḍḥā   297.36
'Īd al-Fiṭr   297.36
Idolatry   202.18
Idols   202.18
Igbo (African people)
  religion   299.683 32
Images
  religious significance   203.7
    Christianity   246.53
    see also Symbolism —
      religious significance
  religious worship   202.18
Imamate   297.61
Imams   297.092
  biography   297.092
    specific sects   297.8
  role and function   297.61
  see Manual at 297.092

Immaculate Conception of Mary	232.911
Immorality	
religion	205
see also Moral theology	
Immortality	
religion	202.3
Christianity	236.22
Islam	297.23
Judaism	296.33
philosophy of religion	218
In vitro fertilization	
ethics	
religion	205.66
see also Reproduction —	
ethics — religion	
Incarnation of Jesus Christ	232.1
Independent Catholic churches	284.8
Independent Fundamental	
Churches of America	289.95
see also Christian	
denominations	
Independent Fundamentalist	
and Evangelical churches	289.95
see also Christian	
denominations	
Independent Methodists	287.533
see also Methodist Church	
Indians of North America	
religion	299.7
Indians of South America	
religion	299.8
Indic religions	294
Islamic polemics	297.294
see Manual at 200.9 vs. 294,	
299.5	
Indic religions and Islam	294
Indic view	294
Islamic view	297.284
Indulgences (Christian rite)	265.66
Inequality	
religion	200.8
Christianity	270.08
Judaism	296.08
Inerrancy (Bible)	220.132
Infallibility	
Christian church	262.72
pope	262.131
Infancy of Jesus Christ	232.92
Infant baptism	234.161 2
public worship	265.12
theology	234.161 2
Information theory	
religion	201.600 354
Initiation rites	
Christianity	234.161
public worship	265.1
theology	234.161
religion	203.82
Innate virtues (Christian	
doctrine)	234
Inquisition (Church history)	272.2
Insignia	
religious significance	203.7
Christianity	246.56
Inspiration	
Bible	220.13
Koran	297.122 1
Intercession of Jesus Christ	232.8
Interdenominational cooperation	280.042
Interfaith marriage	
Judaism	296.444 3
religion	204.41
social theology	201.7
Christianity	261.835 843
Interfaith relations	201.5
see also Interreligious relations	
Intermediate state	
(Christian doctrine)	236.4
International relations	
ethics	
religion	205.624
Christianity	241.624
Islam	297.562 4
Judaism	296.362 4
social theology	201.727
Buddhism	294.337 27
Christianity	261.87
Islam	297.272
Judaism	296.382 7
International Society for	
Krishna Consciousness	294.551 2
Interpretation of tongues	234.13
Interreligious marriage	
Judaism	296.444 3
religion	204.41
social theology	201.7
Christianity	261.835 843
Interreligious relations	201.5
Buddhism	294.335
Christianity	261.2
Hinduism	294.515
Islam	297.28
Judaism	296.39
Intrafamily relationships	
Bible	220.830 687
Introit	264.36

Iroquois Indians	
religion	299.785 5
Irreligion	
religious attitude toward	201.5
Christianity	261.21
Isaac (Biblical patriarch)	222.110 92
Isagogics	
Bible	220.61
Isaiah (Biblical book)	224.1
Islam	297
Islam and atheism	
Islamic view	297.289
Islam and Buddhism	294.335
Buddhist view	294.335
Islamic view	297.284 3
Islam and Christianity	261.27
Christian view	261.27
Islamic view	297.283
Islam and Hinduism	294.515
Hindu view	294.515
Islamic view	297.284 5
Islam and Indic religions	294
Indic view	294
Islamic view	297.284
Islam and Judaism	296.397
Islamic view	297.282
Jewish view	296.397
Islam and occultism	297.261
Islam and politics	297.272
Islam and Sikhism	294.615
Islamic view	297.284 6
Sikh view	294.615
Islamic calendar	
religion	297.36
Islamic education	297.77
see Manual at 207.5, 268 vs.	
200.71, 230.071, 292–299	
Islamic ethics	297.5
Islamic fundamentalism	
religion	297.09
see Manual at 320.557 vs.	
297.09, 297.272, 322.1	
Islamic giving	297.54
Islamic holidays	297.36
see Manual at 203.6, 263.9,	
292–299 vs. 394.265–.267	
Islamic law	
religion	297.14
Islamic legends	297.18
Islamic New Year	297.36
Islamic shrines	297.35
Ismailis (Islamic sect)	297.822
Isrā'	297.633
Israel	
Biblical geography and history	220.9
Christian theology	231.76
Jewish theology	296.311 73
Ithna Asharites (Islamic sect)	297.821

J

J document (Biblical criticism)	222.106 6
Jacob (Biblical patriarch)	222.110 92
Jacobite Church	281.63
see also Eastern churches	
Jain temples and shrines	294.435
Jaina Agama	294.482
Jainism	294.4
Jains	
biography	294.409 2
James (Biblical book)	227.91
Jansenism	273.7
denominations	284.84
Japanese religions	299.56
Jatakas	294.382 325
Jealousy	
Bible	220.815 248
ethics	
religion	205.698
see also Vices — religion	
Jehovah's Witnesses	289.92
biography	289.920 92
see also Christian	
denominations	
Jeremiah (Biblical book)	224.2
Jerusalem	
sacred place	
Christianity	263.042 569 44
Islam	297.355 694 42
Judaism	296.482
Jerusalem Bible	220.520 7
Jerusalem Talmud	296.124
Jesuits	255.53
church history	271.53
Jesus Christ	232
biography	232.901
Gospel text and criticism	226
see Manual at 230–280	
Islam	297.246 5
Jewish interpretations	232.906
rationalistic interpretations	232.9
Jewish apocalypses	
pseudepigrapha	229.913
Jewish Bible	221
see Manual at 221	
Jewish calendar	
religion	296.43

Jewish-Christian dialogue 261.26
  Christian theology 261.26
  Jewish theology 296.396
Jewish Christians (Sects) 289.9
  see also Christian
    denominations
Jewish education 296.68
  see Manual at 207.5, 268 vs.
    200.71, 230.071, 292–299
Jewish holidays 296.43
  liturgy 296.453
  see Manual at 203.6, 263.9,
    292–299 vs. 394.265–.267
Jewish law
  religion 296.18
Jewish Publication Society Bible 221.520 8
Jewish religious schools 296.680 83
Jewish sacred music
  public worship
    religion 296.462
Jews (Religious group)
  biography 296.092
    specific denominations 296.8
  role of leaders 296.61
Jihad 297.72
Jinn 297.217
Jnana yoga 294.543 6
Joachim, Saint 232.933
  private prayers to 242.75
Job (Biblical book) 223.1
Joel (Biblical book) 224.7
John (Biblical books) 226.5
  Epistles 227.94
  gospel 226.5
    exegesis 226.506
  Revelation 228
John, the Baptist, Saint 232.94
Jonah (Biblical book) 224.92
Joseph (Son of Jacob) 222.110 92
Joseph, Saint 232.932
  private prayers to 242.75
Joshua (Biblical book) 222.2
Judaism 296
  Christian polemics 239.2
  Islamic polemics 297.292
Judaism and Christianity 261.26
  Christian view 261.26
  Jewish view 296.396
Judaism and Islam 296.397
  Islamic view 297.282
  Jewish view 296.397
Judaism and occultism 296.371
Judas Iscariot 226.092
Judas's betrayal of Jesus Christ 232.961

Jude (Biblical book) 227.97
Judges (Biblical book) 222.32
Judgment Day 202.3
  Christianity 236.9
  Islam 297.23
Judith (Deuterocanonical book) 229.24
Jum'ah 297.36
Just war theory
  ethics
    religion 205.624 2
      Christianity 241.624 2
      see also War — ethics —
        religion
Justice
  ethics
    religion 205.622
      Buddhism 294.356 22
      Christianity 241.622
      Hinduism 294.548 622
      Islam 297.562 2
      Judaism 296.362 2
  social theology 201.76
    Christianity 261.8
    Islam 297.27
    Judaism 296.38
Justice of God 214
  Islam 297.211 2
  see also Theodicy
Justification (Christian doctrine) 234.7
Juvenile delinquents
  pastoral care
    Christianity 259.5

K

Kabbalah 296.16
  see also Cabala
Kachina dolls 299.784
Kadarites (Islamic sect) 297.835
Kalām (Islam) 297.2
Karaites 296.81
Karma 202.2
  Buddhism 294.342 2
  Hinduism 294.522
Karma yoga 294.543 6
Karo, Joseph ben Ephraim
  Jewish legal codes 296.182
Kashrut 296.73
Kelim 296.123 6
Keritot 296.123 5
  Babylonian Talmud 296.125 5
  Mishnah 296.123 5
Kethubim 223

Ketubbot	296.123 3
Babylonian Talmud	296.125 3
Mishnah	296.123 3
Palestinian Talmud	296.124 3
Ketuvim	223
Kharijites	297.83
Khuddakanikāya	294.382 32
Khuṭbah	297.37
Kiddushin	296.123 3
Babylonian Talmud	296.125 3
Mishnah	296.123 3
Palestinian Talmud	296.124 3
Kilayim	296.123 1
Mishnah	296.123 1
Palestinian Talmud	296.124 1
Kindness	
ethics	
religion	205.677
see also Love — ethics — religion	
King James version (Bible)	220.520 3
Kingdom of God	231.72
eschatology	236
Kings (Biblical books)	222.5
Kingship of Jesus Christ	232.8
Kinnim	296.123 5
Knighthood orders	
Christian religious orders	255.791
church history	271.791
Knights Hospitalers of St. John of Jerusalem	255.791 2
church history	271.791 2
Knights of Malta	255.791 2
church history	271.791 2
Knights Templars	255.791 3
church history	271.791 3
Knowability of God	212.6
see also Knowledge of God	
Knowledge of God	212.6
Christianity	231.042
comparative religion	202.11
philosophy of religion	212.6
Knox, John	285.209 2
Kodashim	296.123 5
Babylonian Talmud	296.125 5
Mishnah	296.123 5
Palestinian Talmud	296.124 5
Kohelet	223.8
Kongo (African people)	
religion	299.683 931
Koran	297.122
Koran stories	297.122 2
Kosher observance	296.73

Kundalini yoga	
comparative religion	204.36
Hinduism	294.543 6
Kyrie	264.36

L

Labor	
ethics	
religion	205.64
Christianity	241.64
Islam	297.564
Judaism	296.364
religion	201.73
Christianity	261.85
guides to life	248.88
Judaism	296.383
Laboring class	
religion	200.862 3
Christianity	270.086 24
Lag b'Omer	296.439
liturgy	296.453 9
Laity (Church members)	262.15
biography	270.092
specific denominations	280
church government	262.15
pastoral theology	253
Lamaism	294.392 3
Lamentations (Bible)	224.3
Lao-tzu. Tao te ching	299.514 82
Last Judgment	
Christianity	236.9
Last Supper	232.957
Later Prophets (Biblical books)	224
Latin language	
Biblical texts	220.47
Latter-Day Saints	
biography	289.309 2
Latter-Day Saints Church	289.3
see also Mormon Church	
Lauds	264.15
see also Liturgy of the hours	
Law	
religious	208.4
see also Religious law	
Law (Theology)	
Christianity	241.2
Judaism	296.18
Law and gospel	241.2
Law of God	
Christianity	241.2
Lay brothers	
religious orders	255.093
church history	271.093

Lay ministry	253
ecclesiology	262.15
pastoral theology	253
Lay sisters	
religious orders	255.909 3
church history	271.909 3
Laying on of hands	
(Christian rite)	265.9
Laylat al-Barā'ah	297.36
Laylat al-Mi'rāj	297.36
Laylat al-Qadr	297.362
Laymen (Church members)	262.15
see also Laity (Church	
members)	
Lazarists	255.77
church history	271.77
Leadership	
Christian church	262.1
local church	253
Lectionaries (Public worship)	264.34
Anglican	264.030 34
texts	264.032
preaching	251.6
Roman Catholic	264.020 34
texts	264.029
Lecture method	
Christian religious education	268.632
Lent	263.92
devotional literature	242.34
sermons	252.62
Lesbianism	
religion	200.866 43
Christianity	270.086 643
Lesbians	
religion	200.866 43
Christianity	270.086 643
pastoral theology	259.086 643
Leviticus	222.13
Liberal Catholic Church	284.8
see also Old Catholic churches	
Liberal theology	230.046
Liberation theology	230.046 4
political aspects	261.7
Roman Catholic	230.2
socioeconomic aspects	261.8
Libraries and religion	201.602

Life	
medical ethics	
religion	205.697
Christianity	241.697
respect for	
ethics	
religion	205.691
Buddhism	294.356 91
Christianity	241.691
Hinduism	294.548 691
Judaism	296.369 1
Life after death	
religion	202.3
Christianity	236.2
Islam	297.23
Judaism	296.33
philosophy of religion	218
Life sciences and religion	201.657
Christianity	261.55
philosophy of religion	215.7
Lighting	
religious significance	203.7
Christianity	246.6
see also Symbolism —	
religious significance	
Limbo	236.4
Lingayats	294.551 3
Litanies	264.13
Roman Catholic	264.027 4
Literary criticism	
sacred books	208.2
Bible	220.66
Bible. N.T.	225.66
Bible. O.T.	221.66
Talmud	296.120 66
Literary genres	
sacred books	208.2
Bible	220.66
Talmud	296.120 66
Literature and religion	201.68
Christianity	261.58
Little Church of France	284.8
see also Christian	
denominations	
Little Sisters of the Poor	255.95
church history	271.95
Liturgical dance	246.7
Liturgical objects	203.7
Christianity	247
Judaism	296.461
Liturgical renewal	264.001
Liturgical year	263.9
devotional literature	242.3
sermons	252.6

Liturgy	203.8
see also Public worship	
Liturgy of the hours	264.15
Anglican	264.030 15
Roman Catholic	264.020 15
texts	264.024
Living Bible	220.520 83
Local Christian church	250
ecclesiology	262.2
specific denominations	280
see Manual at 260 vs.	
251–254, 259	
Local religious organizations	206.5
Logos	232.2
Lollards	284.3
Lord's Prayer	226.96
private devotions	242.722
Lord's Supper	234.163
public worship	264.36
theology	234.163
Lourdes, Our Lady of	232.917 094 478
Love	
ethics	
religion	205.677
Buddhism	294.356 77
Christianity	241.4
Hinduism	294.548 677
Islam	297.567 7
Judaism	296.367 7
God's love	212.7
Christianity	231.6
comparative religion	202.112
philosophy of religion	212.7
Love feasts	
Christian rite	265.9
Lower criticism	
Bible	220.404 6
Lubavitch Hasidism	296.833 22
Lucifer	
Christianity	235.47
Islam	297.216
Luke (Gospel)	226.4
exegesis	226.406
Lust	
ethics	
religion	205.66
Christianity	241.3
see also Sexual	
relations — ethics —	
religion	
Luther, Martin	284.109 2

Lutheran church	284.1
church government	262.041
parishes	254.041
church law	262.984 1
doctrines	230.41
catechisms and creeds	238.41
general councils	262.541
guides to Christian life	248.484 1
missions	266.41
moral theology	241.044 1
public worship	264.041
religious associations	267.184 1
religious education	268.841
seminaries	230.073 41
theology	230.41
Lutheran Church in America	284.133
see also Lutheran church	
Lutheran Church—Missouri	
Synod	284.132 2
see also Lutheran church	
Lutheran Free Church	284.131 4
see also Lutheran church	
Lutheran sacred music	
public worship	
religion	264.041 02
Lutherans	
biography	284.109 2

M

Ma'aser Sheni (Tractate)	296.123 1
Mishnah	296.123 1
Palestinian Talmud	296.124 1
Ma'aserot (Tractate)	296.123 1
Mishnah	296.123 1
Palestinian Talmud	296.124 1
Maccabees (Biblical books)	229.7
Madhyamika Buddhism	294.392
Magi (Christian doctrines)	232.923
Magic	
religious practice	203
Magicians (Religious leaders)	200.92
biography	200.92
role and function	206.1
see Manual at 200.92 and	
201–209, 292–299	
Magisterium	262.8
Mahabharata	294.592 3
Mahasanghika Buddhism	294.391
Mahayana Buddhism	294.392
Mahdi	
Islamic theology	297.24
Mahomet, Prophet	297.63
Mahzorim	296.453

Maimonides, Moses	
Jewish legal writings	296.181
Major Prophets (Biblical	
books)	224
Makhshirin	296.123 6
Makka (Saudi Arabia)	
Islamic religion	297.352
Makkot	296.123 4
Babylonian Talmud	296.125 4
Mishnah	296.123 4
Palestinian Talmud	296.124 4
Malachi (Biblical book)	224.99
Male gods	202.113
Malikites (Islamic sect)	297.813
Mandalas	203.7
Buddhism	294.343 7
Hinduism	294.537
Manicheism	299.932
Christian heresy	273.2
Mantras	203.7
Buddhism	294.343 7
Hinduism	294.537
Maori	
religion	299.924 42
Mar Thoma Church	281.5
see also Eastern churches	
Mariology (Christian doctrines)	232.91
Mark (Gospel)	226.3
exegesis	226.306
Maronites	281.5
Maronites (Religious order)	255.18
church history	271.18
Marriage	
ethics	
religion	205.63
Buddhism	294.356 3
Christianity	241.63
Hinduism	294.548 63
Islam	297.563
Judaism	296.363
personal religion	204.41
Buddhism	294.344 41
Christianity	248.4
Hinduism	294.544 1
Islam	297.577
Judaism	296.74
religion	204.41
Christianity	248.4
Islam	297.577
Judaism	296.74
religious doctrine	202.2
Christianity	234.165
Marriage (continued)	
religious law	208.4
Christianity	262.9
Judaism	296.444
rites	203.85
Christianity	265.5
Judaism	296.444
liturgy	296.454 4
see also Public worship	
social theology	201.7
Christianity	261.835 81
Marriage counseling	
pastoral theology	206.1
Christianity	259.14
Judaism	296.61
Marriage service	203.85
Christianity	265.5
Married men	
Christian devotional	
literature	242.642 5
guides to Christian life	248.842 5
Married persons	
Christian devotional	
literature	242.644
guides to religious life	204.41
Christianity	248.844
Islam	297.577
Judaism	296.74
see also Marriage — personal	
religion	
Married women	
Christian devotional	
literature	242.643 5
guides to Christian life	248.843 5
Martyrs	200.92
biography	200.92
Christian	272.092
see Manual at 230–280	
role and function	206.1
see Manual at 200.92 and	
201–209, 292–299	
Marxist-Christian dialogue	
Christian theology	261.21
Mary, Blessed Virgin, Saint	232.91
private prayers to	242.74
see Manual at 230–280	
Mary Magdalene, Saint	226.092
Masai (African people)	
religion	299.685
Masorah	221.44

Mass (Christian rite)	264.36
Anglican	264.030 36
texts	264.03
Roman Catholic	264.020 36
texts	264.023
Mass media	
religion	201.7
Christianity	261.52
evangelism	269.26
use by local Christian	
church	253.78
administration	254.3
Judaism	296.37
Massacre of innocents	232.92
Materialism	
Christian polemics	239.7
Islamic polemics	297.298
Matins	264.15
Anglican	264.030 15
texts	264.033
see also Liturgy of the hours	
Matrimony	
sacrament	234.165
public worship	265.5
theology	234.165
see also Marriage	
Matthew (Gospel)	226.2
Maundy Thursday	263.925
devotional literature	242.35
sermons	252.625
Mawlid al-Nabī	297.36
Maya Indians	
religion	299.784 2
Mazdaism	295
Mecca (Saudi Arabia)	
Islamic religion	297.352
Mechitarists	255.17
church history	271.17
Medals	
religious significance	203.7
see also Symbolism —	
religious significance	
Medical ethics	
religion	205.642
Buddhism	294.356 42
Christianity	241.642
Hinduism	294.548 642
Islam	297.564 2
Judaism	296.364 2
Medical missionaries	
Christian	266.009 2
Medical missions	
Christian	266

Medicine and religion	201.661
Christianity	261.561
Judaism	296.376
Medieval period	
church history	270.3
Medina (Saudi Arabia)	
Islamic religion	297.355 38
Meditation	
religion	204.35
Buddhism	294.344 35
Christianity	248.34
Hinduism	294.543 5
Islam	297.382
Sufi	297.438 2
Judaism	296.72
Meditations	
religion	204.32
Buddhism	294.344 32
Christianity	242
Hinduism	294.543 2
Islam	297.382 4
Sufi	297.438 24
Judaism	296.72
Megillah (Tractate)	296.123 2
Babylonian Talmud	296.125 2
Mishnah	296.123 2
Palestinian Talmud	296.124 2
Megillot (Bible)	221.044
Meher Baba	299.93
Me'ilah	296.123 5
Babylonian Talmud	296.125 5
Mishnah	296.123 5
Melodic reading	
Koran	297.122 404 5
Men	
Bible	220.830 53
religion	200.81
Christianity	270.081
devotional literature	242.642
guides to Christian life	248.842
preaching	251.008 1
guides to life	204.408 1
Islam	297.081
guides to life	297.570 81
Judaism	296.081
guides to life	296.708 1
Menaḥot	296.123 5
Babylonian Talmud	296.125 5
Mishnah	296.123 5
Mendicant religious orders	255.06
church history	271.06

Mennonite Church   289.7
   church government   262.097
     parishes   254.097
   church law   262.989 7
   doctrines   230.97
     catechisms and creeds   238.97
   general councils   262.597
   guides to Christian life   248.489 7
   missions   266.97
   moral theology   241.049 7
   public worship   264.097
   religious associations   267.189 7
   religious education   268.897
   seminaries   230.073 97
   theology   230.97
Mennonites   289.7
   biography   289.709 2
Mental health services
   pastoral theology   206.1
     Christianity   259.42
   social theology   201.762 2
     Christianity   261.832 2
Mental illness
   Christian religious guidance   248.862
   pastoral theology   206.1
     Christianity   259.42
   social theology   201.762 2
     Christianity   261.832 2
Mentally ill persons
   guides to Christian life   248.862
Mercedarians   255.45
   church history   271.45
Merit (Christian doctrine)   234
Messiahs
   Christianity   232.1
   Judaism   296.336
   role and function   206.1
   see Manual at 200.92 and
     201–209, 292–299
Messianic Judaism   289.9
   see also Christian
     denominations
Messianic prophecies
   Christianity   232.12
   Judaism   296.336
Messianism   202.3
   Judaism   296.336
Methodist Church   287
   church government   262.07
     parishes   254.07
   church law   262.987
   doctrines   230.7
     catechisms and creeds   238.7

Methodist Church (continued)
   guides to Christian life   248.487
   missions   266.7
   moral theology   241.047
   public worship   264.07
   religious associations   267.187
   religious education   268.87
   seminaries   230.073 7
   theology   230.7
Methodist Church (U.S.)   287.631
   see also Methodist Church
Methodist Church of Great
   Britain   287.536
Methodist Episcopal Church   287.632
   see also Methodist Church
Methodist Episcopal Church,
   South   287.633
   see also Methodist Church
Methodist New Connexion   287.53
   see also Methodist Church
Methodist Protestant Church   287.7
   see also Methodist Church
Methodist sacred music
   public worship
     religion   264.070 2
Methodists
   biography   287.092
Mevleviyeh   297.482
Mezuzot   296.461
Micah (Biblical book)   224.93
Micmac Indians
   religion   299.783 43
Middle-aged persons
   guides to Christian life   248.84
   guides to Jewish life   296.708 44
   guides to religious life   204.408 44
   religion   200.844
     Christianity   270.084 4
Middle Ages
   church history   270.3
Middot   296.123 5
Midrash   296.14
Mikva'ot (Tractate)   296.123 6
Mikveh   296.75
Militarism
   ethics
     religion   205.624 2
     see also War — ethics —
       religion
   social theology   201.727 3
     see also War — social
       theology
Military religious orders   255.791
   church history   271.791

Millennium	
Christianity	236.9
Minarets	297.351
Minims (Religious order)	255.49
church history	271.49
Ministerial authority	262.8
Ministers (Christian clergy)	270.092
ecclesiology	262.14
see also Clergy — Christian	
Minor Clerks Regular	255.56
church history	271.56
Minor Prophets (Bible)	224.9
Minor tractates (Talmud)	296.123 7
Miracles	202.117
Christianity	231.73
of Jesus Christ	232.955
Gospels	226.7
of Mary	232.917
spiritual gift	234.13
Judaism	296.311 6
philosophy of religion	212
Mi'rāj	297.633
Mishnah	296.123
Mishneh Torah	296.181 2
Missals	264.36
Anglican	264.030 36
texts	264.03
Roman Catholic	264.020 36
texts	264.023
Missionaries	207.209 2
Christian	266.009 2
occupational ethics	241.641
see Manual at 230–280	
occupational ethics	
religion	205.641
Missionaries of Charity	255.97
church history	271.97
Missionary stories	
Christianity	266
Missions (Religion)	207.2
Christianity	266
Islam	297.74
Mithraism	299.15
Mitzvot	
Jewish ethics	296.36
Jewish law	296.18
Modern art	
religious significance	203.7
Christianity	246.4
Modernism	
church history	273.9
Modesty	
moral theology	205.699
see also Virtues — religion	

Mo'ed (Order)	296.123 2
Babylonian Talmud	296.125 2
Mishnah	296.123 2
Palestinian Talmud	296.124 2
Mo'ed Katan	296.123 2
Babylonian Talmud	296.125 2
Mishnah	296.123 2
Palestinian Talmud	296.124 2
Moḥammed, Prophet	297.63
Molinism	273.7
persecution of	272.5
Monarchs	
objects of worship	202.13
Monasteries	206.57
Buddhism	294.365 7
Christianity	255
church history	271
religious significance of	
buildings	246.97
Monasticism	206.57
Buddhism	294.365 7
Christianity	255
church history	271
personal religion	248.894
Monks	206.57
Buddhist	294.365 7
Christian	255
biography	271.009 2
see Manual at 230–280	
ecclesiology	262.24
guides to Christian life	248.894 2
Monophysite churches	281.6
see also Eastern churches	
Monotheism	211.34
Christianity	231
comparative religion	202.11
Islam	297.211
Judaism	296.311
philosophy of religion	211.34
Monotheistic religions	201.4
Moral Rearmament	267.16
Moral renewal (Christianity)	248.25
Moral theology	205
Buddhism	294.35
Christianity	241
see Manual at 241 vs. 261.8	
Hinduism	294.548
Islam	297.5
Sufi	297.45
Judaism	296.36
Morality	
religion	205
see also Moral theology	

Moravian Church 284.6
  see also Christian
    denominations
Moravians (Religious group)
  biography 284.609 2
Mormon Church 289.3
  church government 262.093
    parishes 254.093
  church law 262.989 3
  doctrines 230.93
    catechisms and creeds 238.93
  general councils 262.593
  guides to Christian life 248.489 3
  missions 266.93
  moral theology 241.049 3
  priesthood 262.149 3
  public worship 264.093
  religious associations 267.189 3
  religious education 268.893
  seminaries 230.073 93
  temples 246.958 93
  theology 230.93
Mormons
  biography 289.309 2
Morning prayer 264.15
  Anglican 264.030 15
  texts 264.033
Mortal sin 241.31
Mosaic law (Bible) 222.1
Moses
  Biblical leader 222.109 2
  Islam 297.246
Mosques 297.351
  organization 297.65
Motazilites 297.834
Mothers
  Bible 220.830 687 43
  Christian devotional
    literature 242.643 1
  guides to Christian life 248.843 1
Motion pictures
  ethics
    religion 205.65
      see also Recreation —
        ethics — religion
Motivation
  religion 201.615 38

Mourning
  religion
    Christianity
      devotional literature 242.4
      religious guidance 248.866
      rites 265.85
    devotional literature 204.32
    Islam
      rites 297.385
    Judaism
      rites 296.445
        liturgy 296.454 5
      religious guidance 204.42
      rites 203.88
Muftis (Muslim officials) 297.140 92
Muḥammad, Prophet 297.63
Murder
  social theology 201.764
Murjiites (Islamic sect) 297.837
Mūsá
  Islam 297.246
Music
  Bible 220.878
  ethics
    religion 205.65
      see also Recreation —
        ethics — religion
  religion 203.7
    attitude toward secular
      music 201.678
    Buddhism 294.343 7
    Christianity 246.75
      attitude toward secular
        music 261.578
    Hinduism 294.537
    Jainism 294.437
    Judaism 296.462
    Native American religions 299.713 7
    public worship 203.8
      Christianity 264.2
      Judaism 296.462
      see also Public worship
Muslim ibn al-Ḥajjāj
  al-Qushayrī
    Hadith 297.124 3
Muslim saints (Sufi) 297.409 2
Muslim women
  guides to religious life 297.570 82
Muslims 297.092
  biography 297.092
    specific sects 297.8
  see Manual at 297.092
Mutazilites 297.834
Mystical body of Christ 262.77

Mystical Judaism	296.833
Mysticism	204.22
Buddhism	294.344 22
Christianity	248.22
comparative religion	204.22
Hinduism	294.542 2
Islam	297.4
Judaism	296.712
Mythological interpretation	
Bible	220.68
Mythologists	201.309 2
Mythology	
African religions	299.611 3
Arapaho Indians	299.783 54
Atsina Indians	299.783 54
Australian religion	299.921 5
Aztecs	299.784 520 13
Buddhism	294.333
Celtic religion	299.161 13
Chinese religions	299.511 13
Christianity	230
classical religion	292.13
Egyptian religion	299.311 3
Germanic religion	293.13
Greek religion	292.13
Haitian religion	299.689 729 401 3
Hawaiian religion	299.924 2
Hinduism	294.513
Masai (African people)	
religion	299.685
Middle Eastern religions	201.309 394
Native American religions	299.711 3
North American	299.711 3
South American	299.811 3
Navajo Indians	299.782 601 3
Norse religion	293.13
Pima Indians	299.784 552 901 3
Polynesian religion	299.924
Pueblo Indians	299.784 013
religion	201.3
sources	208
Roman religion	292.13
Scandinavian religion	293.13
Semitic religions	299.2
Shinto	299.561 13
see Manual at 398.2 vs. 201.3,	
230, 270, 292–299	

N

Nahum (Biblical book)	224.94
Names of God	
Islam	297.211 2
Judaism	296.311 2

Naming ceremonies	
Judaism	296.443
Nan-hua ching	299.514 82
Nanak, Guru	294.609 2
Naqshabandiyah	297.48
Narration	
Bible	220.66
Narrative theology	230.046
Nasāʾī, Aḥmad ibn Shuʿayb	
Hadith	297.124 5
Nashim	296.123 3
Babylonian Talmud	296.125 3
Mishnah	296.123 3
Palestinian Talmud	296.124 3
Nation of Islam	297.87
National Baptist Convention	
of America	286.134
see also Baptists	
National Baptist Convention	
of the United States of	
America	286.133
see also Baptists	
National conferences of	
bishops	262.12
National Council of the	
Churches of Christ in the	
United States of America	277.308 206
Nationalism	
social theology	201.72
Buddhism	294.337 2
Christianity	261.7
Hinduism	294.517 2
Islam	297.272
Judaism	296.382
Native American Church of	
North America	299.7
Native American religions	299.7
North America	299.7
South America	299.8
Nativity of Jesus Christ	232.92
Natural history and religion	201.650 8
Natural law	
ethical systems	
Christianity	241.2
Natural religion	210
Natural resources	
ethics	
religion	205.68
Buddhism	294.356 8
Christianity	241.68
Hinduism	294.548 68
Islam	297.568
Judaism	296.368

Natural resources (continued)
  social theology 201.77
    Christianity 261.88
Natural theology 210
Nature
  Christian doctrine 231.7
  religious worship 202.12
  respect for
    ethics
      religion 205.691
        Buddhism 294.356 91
        Christianity 241.691
        Hinduism 294.548 691
        Islam 297.569 1
        Judaism 296.369 1
Natures of Jesus Christ 232.8
Navajo Indians
  religion 299.782 6
Nazir 296.123 3
  Babylonian Talmud 296.125 3
  Mishnah 296.123 3
  Palestinian Talmud 296.124 3
Nebiim 224
Nedarim 296.123 3
  Babylonian Talmud 296.125 3
  Mishnah 296.123 3
  Palestinian Talmud 296.124 3
Nega'im 296.123 6
Negative theology
  Christianity 231
  philosophy of religion 211
Negro Methodist churches 287.8
  see also Methodist Church
Nehemiah (Biblical book) 222.8
Neopaganism 299.94
Neoplatonism
  Christian polemics 239.4
Nestorian churches 281.8
  see also Eastern churches
Nevi'im 224
Nevi'im aharonim 224
Nevi'im rishonim 222
New Age movement 299.93
  Christian polemics 239.93
  occultism
    Christian viewpoint 261.513
  religion 299.93
    see Manual at 299.93
New Age religions 299.93
  see Manual at 299.93
New American Bible 220.520 5
New Century Bible 220.520 8
New English Bible 220.520 6
New International version (Bible) 220.520 81

New Jerusalem Bible 220.520 7
New Jerusalem Church 289.4
New Jerusalemites
  biography 289.409 2
New King James Bible 220.520 8
New Living Translation (Bible) 220.520 83
New religions 200.903 4
  see Manual at 201–209 and
    292–299
New religious movements 200.903 4
  see Manual at 201–209 and
    292–299
New Revised Standard version
  Bible 220.520 43
New Testament 225
  exegesis 225.6
New Testament pseudepigrapha 229.92
New Testament theology 230.041 5
New Thought 299.93
  Christian 289.98
    see also Christian
      denominations
New Year
  Jewish 296.431 5
    liturgy 296.453 15
Nezikin 296.123 4
  Babylonian Talmud 296.125 4
  Mishnah 296.123 4
  Palestinian Talmud 296.124 4
Nicene Creed 238.142
Nichiren Shoshu 294.392 8
Niddah (Tractate) 296.123 6
  Babylonian Talmud 296.125 6
  Mishnah 296.123 6
  Palestinian Talmud 296.124 6
Niddah practice 296.742
Night journey of Muḥammad 297.633
Ninth of Av 296.439
Nirvana
  Buddhism 294.342 3
  Hinduism 294.523
Noah (Biblical person)
  Bible stories 222.110 950 5
Noah's ark
  Bible stories 222.110 950 5
Non-Trinitarian concepts
  Christianity
    God 231.044
    Jesus 232.9
Nonconformists (British churches) 280.4
  see also Protestantism
None (Divine office) 264.15
  see also Liturgy of the hours
Nontheistic religions 201.4

Nonviolence	
ethics	
religion	205.697
Buddhism	294.356 97
Christianity	241.697
Hinduism	294.548 697
Islam	297.569 7
Judaism	296.369 7
Norse religion	293
Northern Baptists	286.131
see also Baptists	
Novenas	264.7
Novitiate (Monastic life)	248.894 25
women	248.894 35
Nuclear warfare	
ethics	
religion	205.624 22
Christianity	241.624 22
social theology	201.727 5
Christianity	261.873 2
Judaism	296.382 7
Nuer (African people)	
religion	299.685
Numbers (Biblical book)	222.14
Numerical interpretation	
Bible	220.68
Koran	297.122 68
Nuns	206.57
Buddhist	294.365 7
Christian	255.9
biography	271.900 2
see Manual at 230–280	
ecclesiology	262.24
guides to Christian life	248.894 3
Nursing orders (Christianity)	255.07
church history	271.07
women	255.907
church history	271.907

O

Obadiah (Biblical book)	224.91
Obedience (Christian doctrine)	234.6
Obituary sermons	
Christianity	252.9
Oblates	255.76
church history	271.76
women	255.97
church history	271.97
Obscenity	
ethics	
religion	205.667
Christianity	241.667
Judaism	296.366 7

Occasional sermons	204.3
Christianity	252.6
Occultism	
religious practice	203
Christian polemics	239.9
see Manual at 130 vs. 200	
Occultism and religion	201.613
Christianity	261.513
Islam	297.261
Judaism	296.371
Occupational ethics	
religion	205.64
Christianity	241.64
Islam	297.564
Judaism	296.364
see also Ethical problems —	
religion	
Occupational groups	
religion	200.88
Christianity	270.88
guides to life	248.88
Odes of Solomon	229.912
Offenders	
pastoral care	
Christianity	259.5
Offerings (Religion)	203.4
Christianity	248.6
Judaism	296.492
Offertory	264.36
Office hours (Religion)	264.15
Anglican	264.030 15
Roman Catholic	264.020 15
texts	264.024
Oglala Indians	
religion	299.785 2
Oholot	296.123 6
Ojibwa Indians	
religion	299.783 33
Old Catholic churches	284.8
church government	262.048
parishes	254.048
church law	262.984 8
doctrines	230.48
catechisms and creeds	238.48
guides to Christian life	248.484 8
missions	266.48
moral theology	241.044 8
public worship	264.048
religious education	268.848
theology	230.48
Old Catholics	
biography	284.8
Old School Baptists	286.4
see also Baptists	

Old Testament | 221
  exegesis | 221.6
  see Manual at 221
Old Testament Apocrypha | 229
Old Testament pseudepigrapha | 229.91
Old Testament theology
  Christianity | 230.041 1
Older persons
  religion | 200.846
    Christianity | 270.084 6
      devotional literature | 242.65
      guides to life | 248.85
      pastoral care of | 259.3
    guides to life | 204.408 46
    Judaism | 296.084 6
      guides to life | 296.708 46
Olivetans | 255.13
  church history | 271.13
  women | 255.97
    church history | 271.97
Omens
  religion | 203.2
Omnipotence of God | 212.7
  see also Attributes of God
Omniscience of God | 212.7
  see also Attributes of God
Opus Dei (Society) | 267.182
Oracles
  religion | 203.2
Oral traditions (Religion) | 208.3
  Bible | 220.663
  Buddhism | 294.383
  Hinduism | 294.593
  Islam | 297.1
  Judaism | 296.1
Ordinary of the mass | 264.36
Ordination of clergy | 206.1
  Christianity | 262.14
    ecclesiology | 262.14
    sacrament | 234.164
      public worship | 265.4
    theology | 234.164
  Judaism | 296.61
Ordination of gays | 206.108 664
  Christianity | 262.140 866 4
Ordination of lesbians | 206.108 664 3
  Christianity | 262.140 866 43
Ordination of women | 206.108 2
  Christianity | 262.14
  Judaism | 296.610 82
Ordos
  Roman Catholic liturgy | 264.021

Organizations
  religious | 206.5
    see also Religious
      organizations
Oriental churches | 281.5
  see also Eastern churches
Origin of life
  religion | 202.4
    Christianity | 231.765
    philosophy of religion | 213
Origin of universe
  religion | 202.4
    Christianity | 231.765
    philosophy of religion | 213
Original sin | 233.14
Orlah | 296.123 1
  Mishnah | 296.123 1
  Palestinian Talmud | 296.124 1
Ornamental glass
  church architecture
    religious significance | 246.952 8
Orphans
  Bible | 220.830 523 086 945
Orthodox Christmas | 263.915
  devotional literature | 242.335
  sermons | 252.615
Orthodox Eastern Church | 281.9
  see also Eastern Orthodox
    Church
Orthodox Judaism | 296.832
Osee (Biblical book) | 224.6
Oxford Movement (Religious
  movement) | 283.420 903 4

P

P document (Biblical criticism) | 222.106 6
Pacifism
  ethics
    religion | 205.624 2
    Christianity | 241.624 2
    see also Peace —
      ethics — religion
  social theology | 201.727 3
    see also Peace — social
      theology
Paganism | 292
  Christian polemics | 239.3
Palestine
  Biblical geography and
    history | 220.9
Palestinian Talmud | 296.124

Palm Sunday	263.925	Passiontide	263.92
devotional literature	242.35	devotional literature	242.34
sermons	252.625	sermons	252.62
Panentheism	211.2	Passover	296.437
Pantheism	211.2	liturgy	296.453 7
Pantheistic religions	201.4	Passover Haggadah	296.453 71
Papacy	262.13	Pastoral care	206.1
Papal administration	262.136	Christianity	253
Papal bulls and decrees	262.91	Pastoral counseling	206.1
Papal infallibility	262.131	Christianity	253.5
Papal schism, 1378–1417	282.090 23	Judaism	296.61
Papal systems (Ecclesiology)	262.3	Pastoral Epistles	227.83
Parables in the Gospels	226.8	Pastoral psychology	206.1
Paradise	202.3	Christianity	253.52
Christianity	236.24	Pastoral theology	206.1
Islam	297.23	Christianity	253
Parah	296.123 6	Islam	297.61
Paralipomena (Biblical books)	222.6	Judaism	296.61
Parapsychology and religion	201.613	Pastors	270.092
Christianity	261.513	ecclesiology	262.14
Islam	297.261	*see also* Clergy — Christian	
Judaism	296.371	Patience	
see Manual at 130 vs. 200		moral theology	205.699
Parenting		*see also* Virtues — religion	
personal religion	204.41	Patriarchate	262.13
Christianity	248.845	Patriarchs	200.92
Judaism	296.74	Biblical	222.110 922
Parents		biography	200.92
Christian devotional		Christian	270.092
literature	242.645	biography	270.092
guides to religious life	204.41	specific denominations	280
Christianity	248.845	*see Manual at* 230–280	
Judaism	296.74	ecclesiology	262.13
pastoral theology		*see also* Clergy — Christian	
Christianity	259.085	Patristics (Christianity)	270
Parish missions	266.022	Pauline epistles	227
Parishes	250	exegesis	227.06
administration	254	Pawnee Indians	
ecclesiology	262.22	religious rites	299.789 330 38
see Manual at 260 vs.		Peace	
251–254, 259		ethics	
Parseeism	295	religion	205.624 2
Parties		Buddhism	294.356 242
indoor amusements		Christianity	241.624 2
religion	201.679 32	Hinduism	294.548 624 2
Pascha (Orthodox Easter)	263.93	Islam	297.562 42
see also Easter		Judaism	296.362 42
Passion of Jesus Christ	232.96	social theology	201.727 3
Passion plays		Buddhism	294.337 273
religious significance	246.723	Christianity	261.873
Passionists	255.62	Hinduism	294.517 273
church history	271.62	Islam	297.27
		Judaism	296.382 7

Pe'ah	296.123 1
Mishnah	296.123 1
Palestinian Talmud	296.124 1
Pelagianism	273.5
Penance	203.4
Christianity	234.166
public worship	265.6
theology	234.166
Pentateuch	222.1
Pentecost	263.94
devotional literature	242.38
Jewish	296.438
liturgy	296.453 8
sermons	252.64
Pentecostal churches	289.94
see also Christian	
denominations	
Pentecostalism	270.82
independent denominations	289.94
Protestantism	280.4
Pentecostals	
biography	289.940 92
People of God (Church)	262.7
Persecutions (Christian	
church history)	272
Person of Jesus Christ	232.8
Personal religion	204
Buddhism	294.344
Christianity	240
Hinduism	294.54
Islam	297.57
Sufi	297.4
Judaism	296.7
Personifications (Religion)	202.14
Persons	
objects of worship	202.13
Pesach	296.437
liturgy	296.453 7
Pesaḥim	296.123 2
Babylonian Talmud	296.125 2
Mishnah	296.123 2
Palestinian Talmud	296.124 2
Peter (Biblical books)	227.92
Pews	247.1
Peyotism	299.7
Phallicism	202.12
Pharisees	296.812
Philemon (Biblical book)	227.86
Philippians (Biblical book)	227.6
Philippine Independent Church	284.8
see also Old Catholic churches	
Philosophical theology	210
Christianity	230.01

Philosophy and religion	201.61
Christianity	261.51
Islam	297.261
Judaism	296.371
see Manual at 200 vs. 100	
Philosophy of religion	210
Phoenicians	
religion	299.26
Phylacteries	296.461 2
Physical sciences	
religion	201.650 02
Physics and religion	201.653
Christianity	261.55
philosophy of religion	215.3
Piarists	255.58
church history	271.58
Pidyon haben	296.442 3
liturgy	296.454 23
Pietism	273.7
Pilgrimage to Mecca	297.352
Pilgrimages	203.51
Christianity	263.041
Islam	297.35
Judaism	296.481
Pillars of Islam	297.31
Pima Indians	
religion	299.784 552 9
Pious societies	
Christianity	267
Pirke Avot	296.123 47
Pitakas	294.382
Piyyutim	296.452
Plants	
Bible	220.858
Pluralism (Religion)	201.5
Buddhism	294.335
Christianity	261.2
Hinduism	294.515
Islam	297.28
Judaism	296.39
Plymouth Brethren	289.9
see also Christian	
denominations	
Poetic books (Old Testament)	223
pseudepigrapha	229.912
Polemics	
Christianity	239
comparative religion	202
Islam	297.29
Judaism	296.35

Political ethics
  religion | 205.62
    Buddhism | 294.356 2
    Christianity | 241.62
    Hinduism | 294.548 62
    Islam | 297.562
    Judaism | 296.362
Political theology | 201.72
  Christianity | 261.7
Politics
  Bible | 220.832
Politics and religion
  social theology | 201.72
    Buddhism | 294.337 2
    Christianity | 261.7
    Hinduism | 294.517 2
    Islam | 297.272
      see Manual at 297.26–.27
    Judaism | 296.382
  see Manual at 322.1 vs. 201.72,
    261.7, 292–299
Pollution
  social theology | 201.77
    Christianity | 261.88
Polyglot Bibles | 220.51
Polynesian religion | 299.924
Polytheism | 211.32
  comparative religion | 202.11
  philosophy of religion | 211.32
Polytheistic religions | 201.4
Pontificale Romanum | 264.025
Poor Clares | 255.973
  church history | 271.973
Poor people
  social theology | 201.762 5
    Buddhism | 294.337 625
    Christianity | 261.832 5
    Hinduism | 294.517 625
    Islam | 297.27
    Judaism | 296.38
Popes | 282.092
  biography | 282.092
  ecclesiology | 262.13
Popol vuh | 299.784 23
Popular practices (Islam) | 297.39
Population control
  social theology | 201.7
    Christianity | 261.836
    Judaism | 296.38
Pornography
  ethics
    religion | 205.667
      Christianity | 241.667
      Judaism | 296.366 7

Postmodern theology | 230.046
Postpartum care
  social theology | 201.762 198 6
Poverty
  religious practice | 204.47
    Buddhism | 294.344 47
    Christianity | 248.47
    Hinduism | 294.544 7
  social theology | 201.762 5
    Buddhism | 294.337 625
    Christianity | 261.832 5
    Hinduism | 294.517 625
    Islam | 297.27
    Judaism | 296.38
Praise of God | 204.3
  Christianity | 248.3
Prayer | 204.3
  Buddhism | 294.344 3
  Christianity | 248.32
  Hinduism | 294.543
  Islam | 297.382
    Sufi | 297.438 2
  Judaism | 296.45
  public worship | 203.8
    Buddhism | 294.343 8
    Christianity | 264.1
    Hinduism | 294.538
    Judaism | 296.45
Prayer books | 204.33
  Buddhism | 294.344 33
  Christianity | 242.8
    public worship | 264.13
  Hinduism | 294.543 3
  Islam | 297.382 4
    Sufi | 297.438 24
  Judaism | 296.45
Prayer desks
  church furniture | 247.1
Prayer Meeting Revival
  (1857–1858) | 269.097 309 034
Prayer meetings
  Christianity
    public worship | 264.7
Prayer of Manasseh (Bible) | 229.6
Prayer shawls | 296.461
Prayers (Private devotions) | 204.33
  Buddhism | 294.344 33
  Christianity | 242
  Hinduism | 294.543 3
  Islam | 297.382 4
    Sufi | 297.438 24
  Judaism | 296.45

Prayers (Public worship)	203.8
Buddhism	294.343 8
Christianity	264.13
Hinduism	294.538
Islam	297.382 4
Sufi	297.438 24
Judaism	296.45
Pre-Islamic prophets	297.246
Preaching	206.1
Christianity	251
Islam	297.37
Judaism	296.47
Preaching orders (Christianity)	255.04
church history	271.04
Predestination	202.2
Christianity	234.9
Islam	297.227
Predictions	
religion	203.2
eschatological	202.3
Prehistoric religions	201.42
Prejudice	
Bible	220.830 338 5
ethics	
religion	205.675
see also Discrimination —	
ethics — religion	
religion	200.8
Christianity	270.08
Premarital counseling	
Christian pastoral counseling	259.13
Premonstratensians	255.19
church history	271.19
Presbyterian Church	285
church government	262.05
parishes	254.05
church law	262.985
doctrines	230.5
catechism and creeds	238.5
general councils	262.55
guides to Christian life	248.485
missions	266.5
moral theology	241.045
public worship	264.05
religious associations	267.185
religious education	268.85
seminaries	230.073 5
theology	230.5
Presbyterian Church (U.S.A.)	285.137
see also Presbyterian Church	
Presbyterian Church in the	
United States	285.133
see also Presbyterian Church	

Presbyterian Church in the	
United States of America	285.132
see also Presbyterian Church	
Presbyterian Church of Wales	285.235
see also Presbyterian Church	
Presbyterian sacred music	
public worship	
religion	264.050 2
Presbyterianism	285
Presbyterians	
biography	285.092
Presbyteries	
Christian ecclesiology	262.4
Presence of God	202.117
Christianity	231.7
Judaism	296.311 4
Presentation of Jesus Christ	232.928
Presentation religious orders	255.977
church history	271.977
Pride	
moral theology	205.698
see also Vices — religion	
Priesthood	206.1
Christianity	262.1
pastoral theology	253
Jewish	296.495
Priesthood of believers	234
Priesthood of Jesus Christ	232.8
Priests	200.92
biography	200.92
Buddhist	294.309 2
role and function	294.361
Christian	270.092
biography	270.092
specific denominations	280
see Manual at 230–280	
ecclesiology	262.14
pastoral theology	253
see also Clergy — Christian	
Jewish	296.495
role and function	206.1
see Manual at 200.92 and	
201–209, 292–299	
Prime (Divine office)	264.15
see also Liturgy of the hours	
Primitive Baptists	286.4
see also Baptists	
Primitive Methodist Church	287.4
see also Methodist Church	
Primitive religions	201.42
Priories	
church history	271
religious significance of	
buildings	246.97

Prison chaplaincy	206.1
Christianity	259.5
Judaism	296.610 869 2
Private revelations	204.2
Christianity	248.29
Pro-choice movement	
social theology	201.763 46
Christianity	261.836
Judaism	296.38
Pro-life movement	
social theology	201.763 46
Christianity	261.836
Judaism	296.38
Probation after death	236.4
Process theology	230.046
Processions	
religious rites	203.8
Christianity	265.9
Procrastination	
religion	205.698
see also Vices — religion	
Profanity	
ethics	
religion	205.695
see also Blasphemy	
Profession of faith	
Islam	297.34
Professional ethics	
religion	205.64
Christianity	241.64
Islam	297.564
Judaism	296.364
see also Ethical problems —	
religion	
Progressive National Baptist	
Convention	286.135
see also Baptists	
Promiscuity	
ethics	
religion	205.66
see also Sexual	
relations —	
ethics — religion	
Proofs of God's existence	212.1
Christianity	231.042
Islam	297.211
Proper of the mass	264.36

Prophecies	
religion	203.2
Biblical	220.15
eschatological	202.3
Christianity	236
Islam	297.23
Judaism	296.33
Koranic	297.122 1
messianic	
Christianity	232.12
Judaism	296.336
Prophecy (Concept)	202.117
Christianity	231.745
spiritual gift	234.13
in Bible	220.15
Islam	297.211 5
Judaism	296.311 55
Prophetic books (Old Testament)	224
Prophetic books (Pseudepigrapha)	229.913
Prophetic message	
Bible	220.15
Prophetic office of Jesus Christ	232.8
Prophets	200.92
biography	200.92
Islam	297.246
role and function	206.1
see Manual at 200.92 *and*	
201–209, 292–299	
Prophets (Biblical books)	224
Proselytizing	207.2
Christianity	266
Judaism	296.69
Protestant art	
religious significance	246.4
Protestant churches	280.4
see also Protestantism	
Protestant Methodists	287.53
see also Methodist Church	
Protestantism	280.4
church law	262.980 4
conversion to	248.244
doctrines	230.044
guides to Christian life	248.480 4
missions	266
moral theology	241.040 4
public worship	264
religious associations	267.180 4
religious education	268.804
seminaries	230.071 1
theologians	230.044 092
theology	230.044
Protestants	
biography	280.409 2
Proverbs (Biblical book)	223.7

Providence of God 214.8
  Christianity 231.5
  comparative religion 202.117
  Judaism 296.311 4
  philosophy of religion 214.8
Prudence
  moral theology 205.699
  see also Virtues — religion
Psalms 223.2
  exegesis 223.206
Psalters 264.15
  Anglican 264.030 15
    texts 264.038
  Roman Catholic 264.020 15
    texts 264.028
Pseudepigrapha 229.9
Pseudo gospels 229.8
Psychology and religion 201.615
  Christianity 261.515
  Islam 297.261
  Judaism 296.371
Psychology of religion 200.19
Public life of Jesus Christ 232.95
Public relations
  local churches 254.4
  religion 200
Public worship 203.8
  Buddhism 294.343 8
  Christianity 264
  Hinduism 294.538
  Islam 297.38
  Judaism 296.45
  see also Worship
Pueblo Indians
  religion 299.784
Punishment
  social theology 201.764
  Christianity 261.833 6
Puppetry
  Christian religious use 246.725
  religious education 268.67
Puranas 294.592 5
Pure Land Buddhism 294.392 6
Purgatory
  Christianity 236.5
Purim 296.436
  liturgy 296.453 6
Puritanism 285.9
  doctrines 230.59
  moral theology 241.045 9
  persecution of others 272.8
Puritans 285.9
  biography 285.909 2

Q

Q hypothesis (Gospels) 226.066
Qādarīyah (Islamic sect) 297.835
Qādirīyah (Sufi order) 297.48
Qiblah 297.382
Qirā'āt 297.122 404 5
Qohelet 223.8
Qoran 297.122
Quakers 289.6
  biography 289.609 2
  see also Society of Friends
Quiché Indians
  religion 299.784 23
Quietism 273.7
  persecution of 272.5
Qumran community 296.815
  Dead Sea Scrolls 296.155
Quran 297.122

R

Rabbinical literature 296.1
Rabbinical seminaries 296.071 1
Rabbis 296.092
  biography 296.092
    specific denominations 296.8
  professional ethics 296.364 1
  role and function 296.61
  training 296.071 1
Race relations
  religion 200.89
  Christianity 270.089
Racism
  ethics
    religion 205.675
    see also Discrimination —
      ethics — religion
  religion 200.89
  Christianity 270.089
Radha Soami Satsang 294
Radio
  religion 201.7
  Christianity 261.52
    evangelism 269.26
    preaching 251.07
    use by local Christian
      church 253.78
      administration 254.3
Radio evangelism 269.26
Raja yoga
  Hinduism 294.543 6
Rajneesh, Bhagwan Shree 299.93

Ramadan 297.362
Ramakrishna movement 294.555
Ramayana 294.592 2
Rape (Crime)
  social theology 201.764
Rapture (Christian doctrine) 236.9
Ras Tafari movement 299.676
Rastafari movement 299.676
Rastafarians
  biography 299.676 092
Rationalism
  Christian polemics 239.7
  philosophy of religion 211.4
Reason (Theology)
  Christianity 231.042
Rebekah (Biblical matriarch) 222.110 92
Reception of baptized Christians
  Catholic Church 264.020 99
Recitation
  Koran 297.122 404 5
Reconciliation (Christian
  doctrine) 234.5
Reconstructionist Judaism 296.834 4
  liturgy 296.450 48
Recovery from addiction
  devotional literature 204.32
    Christianity 242.4
  pastoral theology 206.1
    Christianity 259.429
  religious guidance 204.42
    Christianity 248.862 9
  social theology 201.762 29
    Christianity 261.832 29
  see Manual at 616.86 vs. 158.1,
    204.42, 248.8629, 292–299,
    362.29
Recreation
  church work 253.7
  ethics
    religion 205.65
      Christianity 241.65
      Islam 297.565
      Judaism 296.365
Recreation and religion 201.679
Redaction criticism
  sacred books 208.2
    Bible 220.66
    Talmud 296.120 66
Redemption 202.2
  Christian doctrine 234.3
    Christology 232.3
  Islam 297.22
  Judaism 296.32

Redemptorists 255.64
  church history 271.64
Reform Judaism 296.834 1
  liturgy 296.450 46
Reform movements
  religion 209
Reformation 270.6
Reformed Christians 284.2
  American 285.7
    biography 285.709 2
  biography 284.209 2
  European 284.2
    biography 284.209 2
Reformed Church 284.2
  church government 262.042
    parishes 254.042
  church law 262.984 2
  doctrines 230.42
    catechisms and creeds 238.42
  guides to Christian life 248.484 2
  missions 266.42
  moral theology 241.044 2
  public worship 264.042
  religious associations 267.184 2
  religious education 268.842
  seminaries 230.073 42
  theology 230.42
Reformed Church (American
  Reformed) 285.7
  church government 262.057
    parishes 254.057
  church law 262.985 7
  doctrines 230.57
    catechisms and creeds 238.57
  guides to Christian life 248.485 7
  missions 266.57
  moral theology 241.045 7
  public worship 264.057
  religious associations 267.185 7
  religious education 268.857
  seminaries 230.073 57
  theology 230.57
Reformed Church in America 285.732
  see also Reformed Church
    (American Reformed)
Reformed Church in the
  United States 285.733
  see also Reformed Church
    (American Reformed)
Reformed Episcopal Church 283.3
  see also Anglican Communion
Reformed Hinduism 294.556

Reformed Presbyterian
    churches   285.136
  see also Presbyterian Church
Refugees
  social theology   201.762 87
    Christianity   261.832 8
Regeneration (Christian doctrine)   234.4
Regular Baptists   286.1
  biography   286.109 2
  see also Baptists
Reincarnation
  religion   202.37
    Buddhism   294.342 37
    Hinduism   294.523 7
Relics
  Christianity   235.2
  Passion of Jesus Christ   232.966
Religion   200
  see Manual at 130 vs. 200;
    also at 200 vs. 100;
    also at 201–209 and
    292–299
Religion and culture   201.7
  Christianity   261
  Islam   297.27
  Judaism   296.38
Religion and politics
  social theology   201.72
    see also Politics and
      religion —
      social theology
Religion and science   201.65
  see also Science and religion
Religion and secular
    disciplines   201.6
  Buddhism   294.336
  Christianity   261.5
    see Manual at 261.5
  Hinduism   294.516
  Islam   297.26
    see Manual at 297.26–.27
  Judaism   296.37
  philosophy of religion   215
Religion and state
  social theology   201.72
    see also Politics and
      religion —
      social theology
Religion historians   200.92
Religions   200
  see Manual at 201–209 and
  292–299

Religious (Members of
    Christian orders)   255
  biography   271.009 2
    see Manual at 230–280
  church history   271
  ecclesiology   262.24
  guides to Christian life   248.894
Religious arts
  religious significance   203.7
    see also Arts — religious
      significance
Religious authority   206.5
  Christianity   262.8
  Judaism   296.67
Religious broadcasting
  Christianity   269.26
Religious buildings
  religious significance   203.5
    Christianity   246.9
    Judaism   296.46
Religious dance
  religious significance   203.7
    Christianity   246.7
    see also Arts — religious
      significance
Religious dietary limitations   204.46
  Hinduism   294.544 6
  Islam   297.576
  Judaism   296.73
Religious education   207.5
  Buddhism   294.375
  Christianity   268
  Hinduism   294.575
  Islam   297.77
  Judaism   296.68
  see Manual at 207.5, 268 vs.
    200.71, 230.071, 292–299
Religious ethics   205
  Buddhism   294.35
  Christianity   241
  Hinduism   294.548
  Islam   297.5
    Sufi   297.45
  Judaism   296.36
Religious experience   204.2
  Buddhism   294.344 2
  Christianity   248.2
  Hinduism   294.542
  Islam   297.57
    Sufi   297.4
  Judaism   296.71
Religious fanaticism   201.72

Religious freedom
  social theology — 201.723
    Christianity — 261.72
    see also Politics and
        religion — social
        theology
Religious holidays — 203.6
  see also Holy days
Religious language — 210.14
  Christianity — 230.014
Religious law — 208.4
  Buddhism — 294.384
  Christianity — 262.9
  Hinduism — 294.594
  Islam — 297.14
  Judaism — 296.18
Religious leaders — 200.92
  biography — 200.92
  Buddhist — 294.309 2
    biography — 294.309 2
      specific sects — 294.39
    role and function — 294.361
  Christian — 270.092
    biography — 270.092
      specific denominations — 280
      see Manual at 230–280
    ecclesiology — 262.1
    occupational ethics — 241.641
    pastoral theology — 253
    personal religion — 248.892
    training — 230.071 1
  Hindu — 294.509 2
    biography — 294.509 2
      specific sects — 294.55
    role and function — 294.561
  Islamic — 297.092
    biography — 297.092
      specific sects — 297.8
    role and function — 297.61
    see Manual at 297.092
  Jewish — 296.092
    biography — 296.092
      specific denominations — 296.8
    professional ethics — 296.364 1
    role and function — 296.61
    training — 296.071 1
  occupational ethics
    religion — 205.641
  role and function — 206.1
  see Manual at 200.92 and
    201–209, 292–299

Religious life — 204.4
  Buddhism — 294.344 4
  Christianity — 248.4
  Hinduism — 294.544
  Islam — 297.57
  Sufi — 297.44
  Judaism — 296.7
  see also Monasticism
Religious medals
  religious significance — 203.7
    see also Symbolism —
      religious significance
Religious mythology — 201.3
  see also Mythology
Religious observances — 203
  Christianity — 263
  Judaism — 296.4
  private — 204.46
    Christianity — 248.46
    Judaism — 296.7
    Sikhism — 294.644 6
  Sikhism — 294.63
Religious orders — 206.57
  Buddhism — 294.365 7
  Christianity — 255
    church history — 271
    ecclesiology — 262.24
    organization — 255
Religious organizations — 206.5
  Christianity — 260
    associations for religious
      work — 267
    denominations — 280
    local church — 250
      specific local churches — 280
    religious orders — 255
    see Manual at 260 vs.
      251–254, 259
  congregations — 206.5
  Islam — 297.65
  Judaism — 296.67
  see Manual at 322.1 vs.
    201.72, 261.7, 292–299
Religious pageants
  religious significance — 203.7
    Christianity — 246.72
Religious plays
  religious significance — 203.7
    Christianity — 246.72
      religious education — 268.67
Religious pluralism — 201.5
  see also Pluralism (Religion)
Religious rites — 203.8
  see also Rites — religion

Religious services	203.8
see also Rites — religion	
Religious studies	200.71
see Manual at 207.5, 268 vs.	
200.71, 230.071, 292–299	
Religious symbolism	203.7
see also Symbolism —	
religious significance	
Religious therapy	
religion	203.1
see also Spiritual healing —	
religion	
Religious tolerance	
moral theology	205.699
see also Virtues — religion	
social theology	201.723
Christianity	261.72
see also Politics and	
religion — social	
theology	
Reliquaries	
Christianity	247
Remarriage	
ethics	
religion	205.63
Christianity	241.63
Judaism	296.363
Judaism	296.444
social theology	201.7
Christianity	261.835 84
Remonstrant churches	284.9
see also Christian	
denominations	
Remonstrants	
biography	284.9
Renaissance art	
religious significance	246.4
Reorganized Church of Jesus	
Christ of Latter Day Saints	289.333
see also Mormon Church	
Repentance	202.2
Christianity	234.5
Islam	297.22
Judaism	296.32
Reproduction	
ethics	
religion	205.66
Buddhism	294.356 6
Christianity	241.66
Hinduism	294.548 66
Islam	297.566
Judaism	296.366
Reproductive technology	
humans	
ethics	
religion	205.66
see also Reproduction —	
ethics — religion	
Requiem mass	264.36
Reredoses	247.1
Rescue missions (Church work)	266
Responsa (Jewish law)	296.185
Responsive readings	
public worship	203.8
Christianity	264.4
Judaism	296.45
Restoration movement	
(Christianity)	286.6
Resurrection	202.3
Christianity	236.8
Islam	297.23
Judaism	296.33
Resurrection of Jesus Christ	232.5
life	232.97
Retired persons	
religion	200.869 6
Christianity	270.086 96
pastoral theology	253.086 96
Retreats (Religion)	
Christianity	269.6
men	269.642
women	269.643
Return to Orthodox Judaism	296.715
Revelation (Biblical book)	228
Revelation of God	212.6
Bible	220.13
Christianity	231.74
comparative religion	202.117
Islam	297.211 5
Koran	297.122 1
Judaism	296.311 5
philosophy of religion	212.6
Revised English Bible	220.520 6
Revised Standard version	
Bible	220.520 42
Revised versions of Bible	220.520 4
Revival meetings	269.24
Revolution	
ethics	
religion	205.621
Christianity	241.621
Judaism	296.362 1

Revolution (continued)
social theology 201.72
  Buddhism 294.337 2
  Christianity 261.7
  Hinduism 294.517 2
  Islam 297.272
  Judaism 296.382
Rheims-Douay Bible 220.520 2
Rhythmic arts
religious significance 203.7
  Christianity 246.7
  see also Arts — religious
    significance
Right and wrong
religion 205
Right to die
ethics
  religion 205.697
    Buddhism 294.356 97
    Christianity 241.697
    Hinduism 294.548 697
    Judaism 296.369 7
Right to life
ethics
  religion 205.697
  see also Human life —
    respect for — ethics —
    religion
Right to life (Prenatal)
ethics
  religion 205.697 6
  see also Abortion —
    ethics — religion
social theology 201.763 46
  Christianity 261.836
  Judaism 296.38
Right-to-life movement
social theology 201.763 46
  Christianity 261.836
  Judaism 296.38
Righteousness (Christian doctrine) 234
Rigveda 294.592 12
Rinzai 294.392 7
Rishonim 296.180 92
Rites
religion 203.8
  African religions 299.613 8
  Buddhism 294.343 8
  Christianity 264
  comparative religion 203.8
  Hinduism 294.538
  Islam 297.38
  Judaism 296.45
  Native American religions 299.713 8

Ritual bath
  Judaism 296.75
Ritual purity 204.46
  Islam 297.38
  Judaism
    family purity 296.742
Ritual slaughter (Dietary laws) 204.46
  Islam 297.576
  Judaism 296.73
Rituale Romanum 264.025
Rituals 203.8
  Roman Catholic liturgy 264.025
  see also Rites — religion
Rñin-ma-pa (Sect) 294.392 3
Rock (Music)
  attitude of Christianity
    toward 261.578
Roman Catholic Church 282
  canon law 262.9
  church government 262.02
    parishes 254.02
  conversion to 248.242
  doctrines 230.2
    catechisms and creeds 238.2
  general councils 262.52
  guides to Christian life 248.482
  Inquisition 272.2
  liturgy 264.02
  missions 266.2
  moral theology 241.042
  papacy 262.13
  persecution under Queen
    Elizabeth 272.7
  public worship 264.02
  religious associations 267.182
  religious education 268.82
  religious orders 255
    church history 271
    women 255.9
      church history 271.9
  seminaries 230.073 2
  social teaching 261.808 828 2
  theologians 230.209 2
  theology 230.2
  see Manual at 270,
    230.11–.14 vs. 230.15–.2,
    281.5–.9, 282
Roman Catholic sacred music
public worship
  religion 264.020 2
Roman Catholic schisms 284.8
  see also Old Catholic churches
Roman Catholics 282.092
Roman religion 292.07

Romanesque art
  religious significance   246.2
Romans (Ancient people)
  religion   292.07
Romans (Biblical book)   227.1
Rood screens   247.1
Rosary   242.74
Rosh Hashanah   296.431 5
  liturgy   296.453 15
Rosh Hashanah (Tractate)   296.123 2
  Babylonian Talmud   296.125 2
  Mishnah   296.123 2
  Palestinian Talmud   296.124 2
Royal office of Jesus Christ   232.8
Rural churches   250.917 34
  administration   254.24
  pastoral theology   253.091 734
Russian Orthodox Church   281.947
  see also Eastern Orthodox
    Church
Ruth (Biblical book)   222.35

S

Sabbath   296.41
  Christianity   263.1
  Judaism   296.41
Sabbatianism   296.82
Sabbatical Year (Judaism)   296.439 1
Sabellianism   273.3
Sacramental furniture   247.1
Sacramentals   264.9
Sacramentaries
  Roman Catholic   264.020 36
    texts   264.023
Sacraments   234.16
  public worship   265
    Anglican   264.030 8
      texts   264.035
    Roman Catholic   264.020 8
      texts   264.025
  theology   234.16
Sacred books   208.2
  Buddhism   294.382
  Christianity   220
    Latter-Day Saints   289.32
  Hinduism   294.592
  Islam   297.122
  Judaism   296.1
    Bible   221
    see Manual at 221
  Taoism   299.514 82
  see Manual at 130 vs. 200

Sacred Heart religious orders   255.93
  church history   271.93
Sacred music
  public worship   203.8
    see also Public worship
  religious significance   203.7
    see also Music — religion
Sacred places   203.5
  Buddhist   294.343 5
  Christianity   263.042
  Hindu   294.535
  Islam   297.35
  Jain   294.435
  Judaism   296.48
  public worship   203.8
  Sikh   294.635
Sacrifice of Jesus Christ   232.4
Sacrifices (Religion)   203.4
  Judaism   296.492
Ṣadaqah   297.54
Sadducees   296.813
Ṣaḥābah   297.648
Saint Joseph religious orders   255.976
  church history   271.976
Saints   200.92
  biography   200.92
  Christian   270.092
    biography   270.092
      specific denominations   280
      see Manual at 230–280
    doctrines   235.2
  Islam
    Sufis   297.409 2
  objects of worship   202.13
  role and function   206.1
  see Manual at 200.92 and
    201–209, 292–299
Saints' days   263.98
  devotional literature   242.37
  sermons   252.67
Saivism   294.551 3
Ṣalāt   297.382 2
Salesians   255.79
Salvation   202.2
  Christianity   234
  Islam   297.22
  Judaism   296.32
  see also Humans — religion
Salvation Army   287.96
  see also Christian
    denominations
Samaritan language
  Biblical texts   220.45
Samaritans (Judaism)   296.817

Samaveda	294.592 13
Same-sex marriage	
religion	204.41
Samhitas	294.592 1
Samoyed	
religion	299.44
Samuel (Biblical books)	222.4
Sanctification (Christian doctrine)	234.8
Sanctifying grace	234.1
Sanctus	264.36
Sanghas	
Buddhism	294.365 7
Sanhedrin	296.67
Sanhedrin (Tractate)	296.123 4
Babylonian Talmud	296.125 4
Mishnah	296.123 4
Palestinian Talmud	296.124 4
Sanskrit language	
Vedas	294.592 104 1
Santeria	299.674
Santos	
religious significance	246.53
Sarah (Biblical matriarch)	222.110 92
Saravastivada Buddhism	294.391
Satan	
Christianity	235.47
Islam	297.216
Judaism	296.316
Satanism	
religion	299
Satisfaction (Christian rite)	265.63
Saul, King of Israel	
Biblical leader	222.430 92
Sauraism	294.551 7
Sautrantika Buddhism	294.391
Ṣawm	297.53
Ṣawm Ramaḍān	297.362
Scandinavian religion	293
Schism between Eastern and Western Church	270.38
Schisms	
Christianity	262.8
church history	273
Science and religion	201.65
Buddhism	294.336 5
Christianity	261.55
Hinduism	294.516 5
Islam	297.265
Judaism	296.375
philosophy of religion	215
Scientists	
Islamic polemics	297.298
Scientology	299.936

Screens	
church furniture	247.1
Scribes	
Judaism	296.461 509 2
Scripture readings	
public worship	
Christianity	264.34
Scriptures (Religion)	208.2
see also Sacred books	
Second Coming of Christ	236.9
Sects (Religion)	209
Buddhism	294.39
sources	294.385
Christianity	280
see also Christian denominations	
Hinduism	294.55
sources	294.595
Islam	297.8
Jainism	294.49
Judaism	296.8
sources	296.15
Shinto	299.561 9
sources	208.5
see Manual at 201–209 and 292–299	
Secular humanism	211.6
Christian polemics	239.7
Secular institutes	
Christianity	255.095
church history	271.095
women	255.909 5
church history	271.909 5
Secularism	211.6
Seder service	296.453 71
Sees	
Christian ecclesiology	262.3
Self-control	
moral theology	205.699
see also Virtues — religion	
Self-reliance	
moral theology	205.699
see also Virtues — religion	
Seminarians	
Christianity	230.071 1
Seminaries	200.711
Christianity	230.071 1
Judaism	296.071 1
Semites	
religion	299.2
Semitic languages	
Biblical texts	220.4
Semitic peoples	
religion	299.2

Separated persons
  guides to religious life   204.41
    Christianity   248.846
Separation (Domestic relations)
  ethics
    religion   205.63
      Christianity   241.63
      Judaism   296.363
    Judaism   296.444 4
    social theology   201.7
      Christianity   261.835 89
Sephardic liturgy   296.450 42
Septuagint   221.48
Sequence   264.36
Sermon on the Mount   226.9
  Christian moral theology   241.53
Sermon outlines   251.02
Sermon preparation   206.1
  Christianity   251.01
  see also Preaching
Sermons   204.3
  Christianity   252
  Islam   297.37
  Jewish   296.47
Servites   255.47
  church history   271.47
Seven last words on cross   232.963 5
Seveners (Islamic sect)   297.822
Seventh-Day Adventist Church   286.732
  see also Adventists
Seventh-Day Baptists   286.3
  see also Baptists
Sex
  religious worship   202.12
  theological anthropology   202.2
    Christianity   233.5
    see also Humans — religion
Sext   264.15
  see also Liturgy of the hours
Sexual ethics
  religion   205.66
    see also Sexual relations —
      ethics — religion
Sexual orientation
  social theology   200.866

Sexual relations
  Bible   220.830 67
  ethics
    religion   205.66
      Buddhism   294.356 6
      Christianity   241.66
      Hinduism   294.548 66
      Islam   297.566
      Judaism   296.366
        laws of family purity   296.742
    social theology   201.7
      Christianity   261.835 7
Sexually abused children
  social theology   201.762 76
    Christianity   261.832 72
Shabbat   296.41
Shabbat (Tractate)   296.123 2
  Babylonian Talmud   296.125 2
  Mishnah   296.123 2
  Palestinian Talmud   296.124 2
Shabuoth   296.438
  liturgy   296.453 8
Shafiites (Islamic sect)   297.812
Shahāda   297.34
Shaiṭān   297.216
Shaivism   294.551 3
Shakers   289.8
  biography   289.809 2
  see also Christian
    denominations
Shaktaism   294.551 4
Shamanism   201.44
Shamans   200.92
  biography   200.92
  role and function   206.1
  see Manual at 200.92 and
    201–209, 292–299
Shanmukaism   294.551 6
Sharia
  religious law   297.14
Shavuot   296.438
  liturgy   296.453 8
Shehitah   296.73
Shekalim   296.123 2
  Mishnah   296.123 2
  Palestinian Talmud   296.124 2
Shemini Atzeret   296.433
Shemittah   296.439 1
Shevi'it   296.123 1
  Mishnah   296.123 1
  Palestinian Talmud   296.124 1

Shevu'ot — 296.123 4
  Babylonian Talmud — 296.125 4
  Mishnah — 296.123 4
  Palestinian Talmud — 296.124 4
Shia Islam — 297.82
  doctrines — 297.204 2
  Hadith — 297.124 8
  relations with Sunni Islam — 297.804 2
  worship — 297.302
Shiites — 297.82
Shin (Sect) — 294.392 6
Shinto — 299.561
Shinto temples and shrines — 299.561 35
Shintoism — 299.561
Shintoists
  biography — 299.561 092
Shivaism — 294.551 3
Shoghi, Effendi
  works by — 297.938 6
Shrines — 203.5
  Buddhist — 294.343 5
  Christianity — 263.042
  Hindu — 294.535
  Islamic — 297.35
  Jain — 294.435
  Shinto — 299.561 35
  Sikh — 294.635
Shroud of Turin — 232.966
Shulḥan 'arukh — 296.182
Sibyls
  religion — 206.1
Sick persons
  devotional literature — 204.32
    Christianity — 242.4
  guides to religious life — 204.42
    Christianity — 248.861
    Judaism — 296.708 77
  pastoral care — 206.1
    Christianity — 259.41
    Judaism — 296.610 877
  religious rites — 203.8
    Christianity — 265.82
  social theology — 201.762 1
    Christianity — 261.832 1
Siddurim — 296.45
Sikh gurus — 294.609 2
  biography — 294.609 2
  role and function — 294.663
Sikh temples and shrines — 294.635
Sikhism — 294.6
  Islamic polemics — 297.294
Sikhism and Islam — 294.615
  Islamic view — 297.284 6
  Sikh view — 294.615

Sikhs
  biography — 294.609 2
Simḥat Torah — 296.433 9
  liturgy — 296.453 39
Sin — 202.2
  Buddhism — 294.342 2
  Christianity — 241.3
    original sin — 233.14
  Hinduism — 294.522
  Islam — 297.22
  Judaism — 296.32
  moral theology — 205
    Buddhism — 294.35
    Christianity — 241.3
    Hinduism — 294.548
    Islam — 297.5
    Judaism — 296.36
Single-parent family
  social theology — 201.7
    Christianity — 261.835 856
Single parents
  religion — 204.41
Sirach (Bible) — 229.4
Sisters (Women religious) — 255.9
  biography — 271.900 2
    see Manual at 230–280
  ecclesiology — 262.24
  guides to Christian life — 248.894 3
Sisters of Bon Secours — 255.94
  church history — 271.94
Sisters of Charity — 255.91
  church history — 271.91
Sisters of Mercy — 255.92
  church history — 271.92
Skepticism
  philosophy of religion — 211.7
Sky
  religious worship — 202.12
Slavery
  ethics
    religion — 205.675
    see also Discrimination —
      ethics — religion
Sloth
  religion — 205.698
  see also Vices — religion
Small groups
  pastoral work
    Christianity — 253.7
Smith, Joseph, 1805–1844 — 289.309 2
Social classes
  religion — 200.862
    Christianity — 270.086 2

Social equality
  religion   200.8
    Christianity   270.08
    Judaism   296.08
Social groups
  religion   200.8
    Christianity   270.08
    Judaism   296.08
Social problems
  social theology   201.76
    Bahai Faith   297.931 76
    Buddhism   294.337 6
    Christianity   261.83
    Hinduism   294.517 6
    Islam   297.27
    Judaism   296.38
Social relations
  ethics
    religion   205.67
Social teaching of the Church   261
Social theology   201.7
  African religions   299.611 7
  Buddhism   294.337
  Christianity   261
    see Manual at 241 vs. 261.8
  Hinduism   294.517
  Islam   297.27
  Judaism   296.38
Socially disadvantaged
  persons
    religion   200.869 4
Society of Friends   289.6
  church government   262.096
    parishes   254.096
  church law   262.989 6
  doctrines   230.96
    catechisms and creeds   238.96
  general councils   262.596
  guides to Christian life   248.489 6
  missions   266.96
  moral theology   241.049 6
  persecution of   272.8
  public worship   264.096
  religious associations   267.189 6
  religious education   268.896
  seminaries   230.073 96
  theology   230.96
Society of Jesus   255.53
  church history   271.53
Socinianism   289.1

Socioeconomic problems
  social theology   201.76
    Buddhism   294.337 6
    Christianity   261.8
    Hinduism   294.517 6
    Islam   297.27
      see Manual at 297.26–.27
    Judaism   296.38
Sociology and religion
  Christianity   261.5
  Islam   297.27
  Judaism   296.38
Sodalities   267
Soferim   296.461 509 2
Soferim (Talmudic)   296.120 092
Sōka Gakkai   294.392 8
Solitude
  religious practice   204.47
    Christianity   248.47
Solomon, King of Israel
  Biblical leader   222.530 92
Somaschi   255.54
  church history   271.54
Son of God (Christian
    doctrines)   231.2
Song of Solomon   223.9
Song of Songs   223.9
Song of the Three Children
    (Bible)   229.6
Sophonias (Biblical book)   224.96
Sorcerers (Religious leaders)   200.92
  biography   200.92
  role and function   206.1
  see Manual at 200.92 and
    201–209, 292–299
Sotah   296.123 3
  Babylonian Talmud   296.125 3
  Mishnah   296.123 3
  Palestinian Talmud   296.124 3
Soteriology   202.2
  Christianity   234
  Islam   297.22
  Judaism   296.32
  see also Humans — religion
Soto   294.392 7
Soul
  religion   202.2
    Christianity   233.5
    Islam   297.225
    Judaism   296.32
  philosophy of religion   218
  see also Humans — religion
Southern Baptist Convention   286.132
  see also Baptists

Sovereignty of God	212.7
Christianity	231.7
comparative religion	202.112
Islam	297.211 2
Judaism	296.311 2
philosophy of religion	212.7
Speaking in tongues	234.132
Spiritual beings	202.1
Christianity	235
Spiritual direction	206.1
Christianity	253.53
Spiritual exercises	204.3
Christianity	248.3
Spiritual gifts	
Christian doctrines	234.13
Spiritual healing	
religion	203.1
African religions	299.613 1
Christianity	234.131
miracles	231.73
miracles	202.117
Native American religions	299.713 1
see Manual at 615.852 vs.	
203.1, 234.131, 292–299	
Spiritual life	204.4
Buddhism	294.344 4
Christianity	248.4
Hinduism	294.544
Islam	297.57
Judaism	296.7
Spiritual renewal	203
Christianity	269
Islam	297.3
Spiritual retreat centers	206.5
Christianity	269.6
Spiritual warfare	235.4
Spiritualism	
comparative religion	202.1
Spirituality	204
Buddhism	294.344
Christianity	248
Hinduism	294.54
Islam	297.57
Judaism	296.7
Sports	
ethics	
religion	205.65
see also Recreation —	
ethics — religion	

Spouses of clergy	
Christianity	253.22
biography	270.092
specific denominations	280
see Manual at 230–280	
pastoral theology	253.22
St. Thomas Christians	281.5
see also Eastern churches	
Stations of the Cross	232.96
Roman Catholic liturgy	264.027 4
Stewardship (Christian practice)	248.6
Stigmata	248.29
Substance abuse	
devotional literature	204.32
Christianity	242.4
pastoral theology	206.1
Christianity	259.429
religious guidance	204.42
Christianity	248.862 9
social theology	201.762 29
Christianity	261.832 29
see Manual at 616.86 vs. 158.1,	
204.42, 248.8629, 292–299,	
362.29	
Subud	299.933
Suburban churches	250.917 33
administration	254.23
pastoral theology	253.091 733
Suburban ministry	253.091 733
administration	254.23
Suffering	
consolatory devotions	204.32
Christianity	242.4
Judaism	296.72
religious guidance	204.42
Buddhism	294.344 42
Christianity	248.86
Judaism	296.7
theodicy	202.118
see also Theodicy	
theological anthropology	202.2
see also Humans — religion	
Suffrages (Liturgy)	264.13
Sufi orders	297.48
Sufis	297.409 2
Sufism	297.4
Suicide	
ethics	
religion	205.697
Buddhism	294.356 97
Christianity	241.697
Hinduism	294.548 697
Judaism	296.369 7

Suicide (continued)
pastoral care | 206.1
  Christianity | 259.428
social theology | 201.762 28
  Christianity | 261.832 28
Sukkah | 296.123 2
 Babylonian Talmud | 296.125 2
 Mishnah | 296.123 2
 Palestinian Talmud | 296.124 2
Sukkot | 296.433
 liturgy | 296.453 3
Sulpicians | 255.75
 church history | 271.75
Sun
 religious worship | 202.12
Sunday
 Christian observance | 263.3
Sunday school | 268
 Jewish | 296.680 83
Sunday school buildings
 administration | 268.2
Sunni Islam | 297.81
 doctrines | 297.204 1
 relations with Shia Islam | 297.804 2
 worship | 297.301
Sunyata | 294.342
Supernatural beings
 religious | 202.11
  see also Gods and goddesses
Suras (Koran) | 297.122 9
Surrogate motherhood
 ethics
  religion | 205.66
  see also Reproduction —
    ethics — religion
Susanna (Deuterocanonical
 book) | 229.6
Sūtrapiṭaka | 294.382 3
Suttapiṭaka | 294.382 3
Suttee
 Hindu practice | 294.538 8
Svetambara (Jainism) | 294.492
Swazi (National group)
 religion | 299.688 87
Swedenborg, Emanuel | 289.409 2
Swedenborgianism | 289.4
 see also Christian
  denominations
Swedenborgians
 biography | 289.409 2

Symbolism
 Bible | 220.64
 religious significance | 203.7
  Buddhism | 294.343 7
  Christianity | 246.55
  Hinduism | 294.537
  Islam | 297.3
  Judaism | 296.46
  Talmud | 296.120 64
Synagogue dedication | 296.446
 liturgy | 296.454 6
Synagogues | 296.65
 history of specific
  congregations | 296.09
 organization | 296.65
 religious symbolism of
  buildings | 296.46
Synod of Bishops | 262.136
Synod of Evangelical
 Lutheran Churches | 284.132 3
 see also Lutheran church
Synods
 Christian ecclesiology | 262.4
Synoptic Gospels | 226
Synoptic problem (Gospels) | 226.066
Syriac language
 Biblical texts | 220.43
Syrian Orthodox Church | 281.63
 see also Eastern churches
Syrians (Religious order) | 255.18
 church history | 271.18
Syro-Malabar Christians | 281.5
 see also Eastern churches

T

Ta'anit (Tractate) | 296.123 2
 Babylonian Talmud | 296.125 2
 Mishnah | 296.123 2
 Palestinian Talmud | 296.124 2
Tabernacles
 Christian church furniture | 247.1
 Judaism | 296.49
Tai peoples
 religion | 299.591
Tajwīd | 297.122 404 5
Talismans
 Islamic popular practices | 297.39
 religious significance | 203.7
  see also Symbolism —
    religious significance
Tallit | 296.461
Talmud | 296.12
Talmud Bavli | 296.125

Talmud Yerushalmi	296.124	Tefillin	296.461 2
Talmudic literature	296.12	Teleology	
Tamid	296.123 5	philosophy of religion	210
Mishnah	296.123 5	Television	
Palestinian Talmud	296.124 5	ethics	
Tanakh	221	religion	205.65
see Manual at 221		*see also* Recreation —	
Tannaim	296.120 092	ethics — religion	
Tantras		religion	201.7
Buddhist	294.385	Christianity	261.52
Hindu	294.595	evangelism	269.26
Tantric Buddhism	294.392 5	preaching	251.07
Tantric Hinduism	294.551 4	use by local Christian	
Tao te ching	299.514 82	church	253.78
Taoism		administration	254.3
religion	299.514	Television evangelism	269.26
Taoists		Temperance	
religion	299.514 092	moral theology	205.68
Targums	221.42	Buddhism	294.356 8
Tawhid	297.211 3	Christianity	241.4
Teachers		Hinduism	294.548 68
religious educators	207.509 2	Islam	297.568
Christian	268.092	Judaism	296.368
biography	268.092	Templars	255.791 3
see Manual at 230–280		church history	271.791 3
role and function	268.3	Temple of Jerusalem	296.491
Jewish	296.680 92	Temples	203.5
biography	296.680 92	Buddhist	294.343 5
role and function	296.68	Hindu	294.535
Teaching (Spiritual gift)	234.13	Jain	294.435
Teaching methods		Jewish	296.65
religious education	207.5	*see also* Synagogues	
Christianity	268.6	Jewish temple in Jerusalem	296.491
Teaching office of the church	262.8	Mormon	246.958 93
Teaching orders (Christianity)	255.03	Shinto	299.561 35
church history	271.03	Sikh	294.635
women	255.903	Temporal power of pope	262.132
church history	271.903	Temptation	
Teachings of Jesus Christ	232.954	moral theology	205
Technology and religion	201.66	Christianity	241.3
Christianity	261.56	Temptation of Jesus Christ	232.95
Islam	297.266	Temurah	296.123 5
Judaism	296.376	Babylonian Talmud	296.125 5
philosophy of religion	215	Mishnah	296.123 5
Teenage boys		Ten Commandments	222.16
guides to religious life		moral theology	
Christianity	248.832	Christianity	241.52
Teenage girls		Judaism	296.36
guides to religious life		Ten Sikh gurus	294.609 2
Christianity	248.833	biography	294.609 2
Teenagers		role and function	294.663
religion	200.835	Tenth of Muḥarram	297.36
see also Adolescents —		Terce	264.15
religion		*see also* Liturgy of the hours	

Terminal care
  pastoral theology — 206.1
    Christianity — 259.417 5
  social theology — 201.762 175
    Christianity — 261.832 175
Terumot — 296.123 1
  Mishnah — 296.123 1
  Palestinian Talmud — 296.124 1
Test-tube babies
  ethics
    religion — 205.66
    see also Reproduction —
      ethics — religion
Testaments
  pseudepigrapha — 229.914
Teton Indians
  religion — 299.785 2
Teutonic Knights — 255.791 4
  church history — 271.791 4
Tevul Yom — 296.123 6
Textual criticism
  sacred books — 208.2
    Bible — 220.404 6
    Koran — 297.122 4
    Talmud — 296.120 4
Theater
  religious significance — 203.7
    Christianity — 246.72
      religious education — 268.67
    see also Arts — religious
      significance
Theatines — 255.51
  church history — 271.51
Theism — 211.3
  Christianity — 231
  comparative religion — 202.11
  Islam — 297.211
  Judaism — 296.311
  philosophy of religion — 211.3
Theistic religions — 201.4
Theocracy
  religion — 201.721
    Christianity — 261.73
Theodicy — 202.118
  Christianity — 231.8
  comparative religion — 202.118
  Islam — 297.211 8
  Judaism — 296.311 8
  philosophy of religion — 214
Theologians — 202.092
  Christian — 230.092
    protestant — 230.044 092
    Roman Catholic — 230.209 2
  see Manual at 230–280

Theological anthropology — 202.2
  see also Humans — religion
Theological seminaries
  Christianity — 230.071 1
Theology — 202
  Buddhism — 294.342
  Christianity — 230
  Hinduism — 294.52
  Islam — 297.2
    Sufi — 297.41
  Judaism — 296.3
Theophanies
  Christianity — 231.74
Theosophists
  biography — 299.934 092
Theosophy — 299.934
Theravada Buddhism — 294.391
Thessalonians (Biblical books) — 227.81
Third Order Regular of St.
  Francis — 255.38
  church history — 271.38
  women — 255.973
    church history — 271.973
Third orders
  religious orders — 255.094
    church history — 271.094
  women — 255.909 4
    church history — 271.909 4
Thirteen Articles of Faith
  (Judaism) — 296.3
Three wise men (Christian
  doctrines) — 232.923
Tibetan Buddhism — 294.392 3
Tijānīyah — 297.48
Times
  religious observance — 203.6
    Christianity — 263
    Islam — 297.36
    Judaism — 296.43
Timothy (Biblical books) — 227.83
Tipiṭaka — 294.382
Tirmidhī, Muḥammad ibn ʿĪsá
  Hadith — 297.124 4
Tishah b'Av — 296.439
  liturgy — 296.453 9
Tithes
  Christian practice — 248.6
  local church fund raising — 254.8
Titus (Biblical book) — 227.85
Tobacco
  ethics
    religion — 205.687
    see also Ethical
      problems — religion

Tobias (Deuterocanonical book) 229.22
Tobit (Deuterocanonical book) 229.22
Today's English Bible 220.520 82
Tohorot (Order or tractate) 296.123 6
  Babylonian Talmud 296.125 6
  Mishnah 296.123 6
  Palestinian Talmud 296.124 6
Toleration
  moral theology 205.699
    see also Virtues — religion
  social theology 201.723
    Christianity 261.72
    Judaism 296.382
    see also Politics and
      religion — social
      theology
Torah (Bible) 222.1
Torah scrolls 296.461 5
Tosefta 296.126 2
Totem poles
  religious significance 299.713 7
Totemism 202.11
Tradition (Theology)
  Christianity 231.042
Transcendence of God 212.7
  see also Attributes of God
Transfiguration of Jesus Christ 232.956
Transubstantiation 234.163
Trappists 255.125
  biography 271.125 02
  church history 271.125
Trees
  religious worship 202.12
Trial of Jesus Christ 232.962
Trials (Law)
  Bible 220.834 707
Tribulation (Christian doctrine) 236.9
Tribunals
  papal administration 262.136
Trinitarians (Religious order) 255.42
  church history 271.42
Trinity 231.044
Trinity Sunday 263.94
  devotional literature 242.38
  sermons 252.64
Tripiṭaka 294.382
Twelve patriarchs
  pseudepigrapha 229.914
Twelve prophets (Bible) 224.9
Twelve step programs
  devotional literature 204.32
    Christianity 242.4
  pastoral theology 206.1
    Christianity 259.429

Twelve step programs (continued)
  religious guidance 204.42
    Christianity 248.862 9
    see Manual at 616.86 vs.
      158.1, 204.42, 248.8629,
      292–299, 362.29
  social theology 201.762 29
    Christianity 261.832 29
Twelvers (Islamic sect) 297.821
Tyndale Bible 220.520 1
Typology
  Biblical interpretation 220.64
  Christian doctrines 232.1
  Talmudic interpretation 296.120 64

U

Ukẓin 296.123 6
Ulama
  role and function 297.61
Ulema
  role and function 297.61
Ultra-Orthodox Jews 296.832
Umbanda 299.672
Ummah
  religion 297.272
Unification Church 289.96
  see also Christian
    denominations
Unitarian and Universalist
  churches 289.1
  church government 262.091
    parishes 254.091
  doctrines 230.91
  guides to Christian life 248.489 1
  missions 266.91
  moral theology 241.049 1
  public worship 264.091
  religious associations 267.189 1
  religious education 268.891
  seminaries 230.073 91
  theology 230.91
Unitarian churches 289.133
  see also Unitarian and
    Universalist churches
Unitarian Universalist
  Association 289.132
  see also Unitarian and
    Universalist churches
Unitarianism 289.1
Unitarians
  biography 289.109 2

United Brethren in Christ 289.9
  see also Christian
  denominations
United Church of Canada 287.92
  see also Christian
  denominations
United Church of Christ 285.834
  see also Congregationalism
United Church of Religious
  Science 299.93
United Conference of
  Methodist Churches 287.532
  see also Methodist Church
United Evangelical Lutheran
  Church 284.131 3
  see also Lutheran church
United Lutheran Church in
  America 284.133 5
  see also Lutheran church
United Methodist Church
  (Great Britain) 287.53
  see also Methodist Church
United Methodist Church (U.S.) 287.6
  see also Methodist Church
United Methodist Free Churches 287.53
  see also Methodist Church
United Pentecostal Church 289.94
  see also Christian
  denominations
United Presbyterian Church
  in the U.S.A. 285.131
  see also Presbyterian Church
United Presbyterian Church
  of North America 285.134
  see also Presbyterian Church
United Reformed Church in
  the United Kingdom 285.232
  see also Presbyterian Church
United Society of Believers
  in Christ's Second Appearing 289.8
  see also Christian
  denominations
United States
  religion 200.973
Uniting Church in Australia 287.93
  see also Christian
  denominations
Unity
  Christian church 262.72
Unity of God
  Islam 297.211 3
Unity School of Christianity 289.97
  see also Christian
  denominations

Universal House of Justice
  works by 297.938 7
Universal priesthood 234
Universalism 289.134
Universalist churches 289.134
  see also Unitarian and
    Universalist churches
Universalists
  biography 289.109 2
Untouchables
  religion 200.869 4
  Hinduism 294.508 694
Unwed parenthood
  ethics
    religion 205.63
    see also Family ethics —
      religion
  social theology 201.7
    Christianity 261.835 856
Upanishads 294.592 18
Urantia 299
Urban ministry 253.091 732
  church administration 254.22
Ursulines 255.974
  church history 271.974
Uru Indians
  religion 299.889
Ute Indians
  religion 299.784 576

V

Vaishnavism 294.551 2
Vaisnavism 294.551 2
Vālmīki. Ramayana 294.592 2
Vedas 294.592 1
Vedic religion 294.509 013
Vegetarianism
  ethics
    religion 205.693
      Buddhism 294.356 93
      Christianity 241.693
      Hinduism 294.548 693
      Judaism 296.369 3
Venial sin 241.31
Vespers 264.15
  Anglican 264.030 15
  texts 264.034
  see also Liturgy of the hours
Viaticum 265.7

Vices	
religion	205.698
Buddhism	294.356 98
Christianity	241.3
Hinduism	294.548
Islam	297.5
Judaism	296.369 8
Vijnana Buddhism	294.392
Vinayapiṭaka	294.382 2
Vincentians	255.77
church history	271.77
Violence	
ethics	
religion	205.697
Buddhism	294.356 97
Christianity	241.697
Hinduism	294.548 697
Islam	297.569 7
Judaism	296.369 7
Vipasyana	
Buddhism	294.344 35
Virgin birth of Jesus Christ	232.921
Virginity of Mary	232.913
Virtual reality	
religion	201.600 68
Virtues	
religion	205.699
Buddhism	294.356 99
Christianity	241.4
Hinduism	294.548
Islam	297.5
Judaism	296.369 9
Vishnuism	294.551 2
Visions	
religious experience	204.2
Christianity	248.29
Visitation Sisters	255.975
church history	271.975
Viticulture	
Bible	220.863 48
Vocation (Religious calling)	253.2
ecclesiology	262.1
guides to life	248.892
monastic and religious orders	255
men	255
guides to life	248.894 22
women	255.9
guides to life	248.894 32
Voice	
preaching	251.03
Voodoo	299.675
Voodooism	299.675

Votive offerings	203.7
Christianity	246.55
see also Symbolism —	
religious significance	
Vulgate Bible	220.47

W

Wahhabis (Islamic sect)	297.814
Wahhābīyah (Islamic sect)	297.814
Wakes	
Christian rites	265.85
Waldenses	
biography	284.4
Waldensian churches	284.4
see also Christian	
denominations	
Waldensianism	273.6
denomination	284.4
see also Christian	
denominations	
persecution of	272.3
War	
ethics	
religion	205.624 2
Buddhism	294.356 242
Christianity	241.624 2
Hinduism	294.548 624 2
Islam	297.562 42
Judaism	296.362 42
social theology	201.727 3
Buddhism	294.337 273
Christianity	261.873
Hinduism	294.517 273
Islam	297.27
Judaism	296.382 7
Wards (Mormon Church)	262.220 882 893
Water	
religious worship	202.12
Way of the Cross	232.96
Roman Catholic liturgy	264.027 4
Wealth	
ethics	
religion	205.68
Buddhism	294.356 8
Christianity	241.68
Hinduism	294.548 68
Islam	297.568
Judaism	296.368
Weather	
Bible	220.855 16
Weddings	
rites	203.85

Welsh Calvinistic Methodist
   Church   285.235
   see also Presbyterian Church
Wesak   294.343 6
Wesley, John   287.092
Wesleyan Conference   287.53
   see also Methodist Church
Wesleyan Methodist Church   287.1
   see also Methodist Church
Wesleyan Reform Union   287.534
   see also Methodist Church
Wesleyan Reformers   287.53
   see also Methodist Church
Westminster Confession of Faith   238.5
White, Ellen Gould Harmon   286.709 2
Whitsunday   263.94
   devotional literature   242.38
   sermons   252.64
Wicca
   religious practice   <u>299.94</u>
Wisconsin Evangelical
   Lutheran Synod   284.134
   see also Lutheran church
Wisdom literature (Bible)   223
   Apocrypha   229.3
   Old Testament   223
   pseudepigrapha   229.912
Wisdom of God   212.7
   Christianity   231.6
   comparative religion   202.112
   Islam   297.211 2
   Judaism   296.311 2
   philosophy of religion   212.7
Wisdom of Solomon (Bible)   229.3
Wise men (Christian doctrines)   232.923
Witchcraft
   Bible   220.813 343
   religious practice   203.3
      African religions   299.613 3
      modern revivals   299.94
      Native American religions   299.713 3
Witches (Occultists)
   persecution by Church   272.8
Witches (Religious leaders)   200.92
   biography   200.92
   modern revivals of old
      religions   299.94
   role and function   206.1
   see Manual at 200.92 and
      201–209, 292–299
Witness bearing   248.5

Wives
   Christian devotional
      literature   242.643 5
   guides to Christian life   248.843 5
Wives of clergymen
   Christianity   253.22
   see also Spouses of clergy —
      Christianity
Wizardry
   religious practice   203.3
      modern revivals   299.94
Wizards (Religious leaders)   200.92
   biography   200.92
   role and function   206.1
   see Manual at 200.92 and
      201–209, 292–299
Womanist theology   230.082
Women
   Bible   220.830 54
   Hadith   297.124 008 2
   religion   200.82
      Christianity   270.082
         devotional literature   242.643
         guides to Christian life   248.843
         preaching   251.008 2
         guides to life   204.408 2
      Islam   297.082
         guides to life   297.570 82
      Judaism   296.082
         guides to life   296.708 2
Women and religion   200.82
   see also Women — religion
Women clergy   200.92
   biography   200.92
   Christian   270.092
      biography   270.092
      see Manual at 230–280
      ecclesiology   262.1
      ordination   262.14
      pastoral theology   253.082
      see also Clergy — Christian
   Judaism   296.092
      see also Women rabbis
      ordination   206.108 2
      role and function   206.108 2
      see Manual at 200.92 and
         201–209, 292–299
Women of the Bible   <u>220.920 82</u>
Women rabbis   296.092
   biography   296.092
      specific denominations   296.8
   ordination   296.610 82
   role and function   296.610 82

Word of God	
Bible	220.13
Jesus Christ	232.2
Work	
ethics	
religion	205.64
see also Labor —	
ethics — religion	
religion	201.73
see also Labor — religion	
Workers	
religion	
Christianity	
guides to life	248.88
Working class	
religion	200.862 3
Christianity	270.086 24
World Community of al-Islam	
in the West	297.87
World politics and religion	
social theology	201.727
Christianity	261.7
Judaism	296.382 7
see also Politics and	
religion — social	
theology	
Worship	204.3
Buddhism	294.344 3
Christianity	248.3
Hinduism	294.543
Islam	297.3
Sufi	297.43
Judaism	296.45
see also Public worship	
Worship programs	203
Christianity	264
Writings (Bible)	223
Wycliffe Bible	220.520 1
Wycliffites	284.3

Y

Yad ha-ḥazaḳah	296.181 2
Yadayim	296.123 6
Yajurveda	294.592 14
Yantras	294.537
Yaqui Indians	
religion	299.784 542
Yearly Conference of People	
Called Methodists	287.53
see also Methodist Church	
Yeshivas	296.071 1
Yeshivot	296.071 1

Yevamot	296.123 3
Babylonian Talmud	296.125 3
Mishnah	296.123 3
Palestinian Talmud	296.124 3
Yezidis	
religion	299.159
Yi jing	
religion	299.512 82
YMCA (Association)	267.3
Yoga	
Buddhism	294.344 36
comparative religion	204.36
Hinduism	294.543 6
Yogacara Buddhism	294.392
Yom Kippur	296.432
liturgy	296.453 2
sermons	296.473 2
Yoma	296.123 2
Babylonian Talmud	296.125 2
Mishnah	296.123 2
Palestinian Talmud	296.124 2
Yoruba (African people)	
religion	299.683 33
Young, Brigham	289.309 2
Young adults	
religion	200.842
Christianity	270.084 2
devotional literature	242.64
guides to Christian life	248.84
pastoral care of	259.25
religious associations	267.6
religious education	268.434
guides to life	204.408 42
Young Men's Christian	
Associations	267.3
Young people	
guides to religious life	204.408 3
Christianity	248.82
Judaism	296.708 3
religion	200.83
Christianity	270.083
devotional literature	242.62
pastoral care of	259.2
religious education	268.432
Judaism	296.083
religious education	296.680 83
Young Women's Christian	
Associations	267.5
YWCA (Association)	267.5

Z

Zakat	297.54
Zavim	296.123 6

Zaydites (Islamic sect)	297.824
Zealots (Judaism)	296.81
Zechariah (Biblical book)	224.98
Zen Buddhism	294.392 7
Zephaniah (Biblical book)	224.96
Zera'im	296.123 1
Babylonian Talmud	296.125 1
Mishnah	296.123 1
Palestinian Talmud	296.124 1
Zevaḥim	296.123 5
Babylonian Talmud	296.125 5
Mishnah	296.123 5
Zionism and Judaism	
social theology	296.382
Zizith	296.461
Zohar	296.162
Zombiism	
African religions	299.675
Zoroaster	295.63
Zoroastrianism	295
Zoroastrians	
biography	295.092
Zulu (African people)	
religion	299.683 986

200 Religion Class, an updated reprint from the 22nd edition of the Dewey Decimal Classification, was designed by Lisa Hanifan of Lisa Hanifan/Graphic Design, Albany, New York. Composition was done in Times Roman and Arial under the supervision of Lisa Hanifan. The book was printed and bound by Edwards Brothers, Inc., Ann Arbor, Michigan.